PATIENT CHOICE

BN07633

PATIENT CHOICE

How patients choose and how providers respond

Anna Dixon
Ruth Robertson
John Appleby
Peter Burge
Nancy Devlin
Helen Magee

The King's Fund>

© The King's Fund 2010

First published 2010 by The King's Fund

Charity registration number: 1126980

ISBN: 978 1 85717 596 7

A catalogue record for this publication is available from the British Library

Available from:
The King's Fund
11-13 Cavendish Square
London W1G 0AN
Tel: 020 7307 2591
Fax: 020 7307 2801
Email: publications@kingsfund.org.uk
www.kingsfund.org.uk/publications

Edited by Kathryn O'Neill

Typeset by Grasshopper Design Company

Printed in the UK by Hobbs the Printers Limited

Contents

List of figures and tables

About the authors

Anna Dixon is Director of Policy at The King's Fund. She has conducted research and published widely on health care funding and policy. She has given lectures on a range of topics including UK health system reform and patient choice. She was previously a lecturer in European Health Policy at the London School of Economics and was awarded the Commonwealth Fund Harkness Fellowship in Health Care Policy in 2005–6.

Anna has also worked in the Strategy Unit at the Department of Health where she focused on a range of issues including choice, global health and public health.

Ruth Robertson is a Senior Researcher in the policy department of The King's Fund. Her research on the impact of health system reforms has included a two-year evaluation of practice-based commissioning. Previous work focused on ways to promote behaviour change among health practitioners, patients and healthy people.

Ruth previously worked at the Healthcare Commission, and holds an MSc in social policy and planning from the London School of Economics.

John Appleby is Chief Economist at The King's Fund. He is an honorary professor at the Department of Economics, City University.

The focus of his research and commentary work at The King's Fund is on current health policy matters, in particular the economic issues associated with the government's reform agenda for health care such as the introduction of competitive forces into the NHS, the use of targets to reduce waiting times, patient choice, Payment by Results and patient-reported outcome measures (PROMs). He has published widely on a range of health care finance and economic issues in books, academic journals, reports, magazines and newspapers. He co-authored a major study of NHS performance since 2002 with Sir Derek Wanless and colleagues, published by The King's Fund (2007), an analysis of the public's attitudes to the NHS, an analysis of future prospects for NHS funding written in partnership with the Institute for Fiscal Studies (The King's Fund 2009) and *Getting the Most Out of PROMs* (The King's Fund 2010).

John has also acted as an adviser to the UK government and parliament in various capacities, including carrying out a review for ministers of the future funding needs of Northern Ireland's health service, and, currently, serving as a task force member for the Marmot Commission on Health Inequalities. He is also a special adviser to the House of Commons Health Select Committee, a member of the National Quality Board's priorities sub-committee and a health economics expert for the Prime Minister's Commission on the Future of Nursing and Midwifery.

Peter Burge is Associate Director of Modelling at RAND Europe, an independent not-for-profit research institute whose mission is to help improve policy and decision-making through research and analysis. His main area of focus is the modelling of choice-making behaviour to gain insight in to the trade-offs that individuals make. Much of his research revolves around issues where policy interventions may seek to influence the choices of individuals by offering new alternatives that may not have existed before. Peter has been active in modelling the patients' responses to choice from its early inception in the London Patient Choice Project pilot, through the development of the policy relating to choice at the point of referral, and into its implementation as part of Choose and Book.

Nancy Devlin is the Director of Research at the Office of Health Economics (OHE), London, and a Senior Associate of The King's Fund. She is an honorary professor at the Centre of Health Economics, University of York, and at Cass Business School, City University, London. She is also an elected member of the executive of the EuroQol Group, the European-based international network of researchers that developed the EQ-5D.

Nancy is co-author of a leading UK textbook on health economics, *Economic Analysis in Health Care* (Morris *et al* 2007), and has published widely on health economics topics in economics, health services research and health policy journals. Her publications include papers on the National Institute for Health and Clinical Excellence's cost-effectiveness threshold, methods of analysing and reporting patient-reported outcomes measures (PROMs) data, National Health Service (NHS) patient choice policies, and the effects of government targets on waiting times. She is engaged in theoretical and empirical research on measuring and valuing patient benefit, is currently leading European research studies to develop new 'time trade-off' methods for valuing quality of life, and is leading a programme of research funded by the Department of Health to provide English values for the new EQ-5D-5L.

Prior to her appointment at the OHE, Nancy was Professor of Economics at City University, where she was Head of the Economics Department and Acting Dean of Social Sciences.

Helen Magee is a freelance qualitative researcher. She worked for eight years as a Senior Research Associate at Picker Institute Europe where she undertook a wide range of projects investigating the experiences of patients and health care professionals, and co-edited *The European Patient of the Future* with Angela Coulter (Open University Press 2003).

Helen has also produced and researched a number of health-related documentaries for Channel 4, BBC and ITV including an observational series in a large teaching hospital, a series based in an inner city health centre and a series on adolescent mental health. She has a degree in history from Cambridge University.

Acknowledgements

This is an independent research project commissioned and funded by the Policy Research Programme of the Department of Health. The views expressed are not necessarily those of the Department of Health. This project has been granted ethical approval by the National Research Ethics Service.

We worked in partnership with: RAND Europe, Picker Institute Europe and the Office of Health Economics.

The research team would like to dedicate this report to fellow researchers at the Picker Institute, Professor Janet Askham and Nick Richards, who sadly died during the research. Their contributions were greatly valued.

We would like to acknowledge support and contributions from the following colleagues:

- The King's Fund: Francesca Frosini, Ros West, Candace Imison, Catherine Foot, Sarah Henderson, Alex Henry and Matthew Watson

- The Picker Institute: Bridget Hopwood, Arwenna Davis, Dr Esther Howell

- RAND Europe: Chong Woo Kim, Charlene Rohr and Ellen Nolte

We would also like to thank the participating research sites and all those who gave up time to be interviewed and respond to the survey; and Rowena Jacobs, for her assistance in providing data on hospital characteristics from the York database. We would like to thank Professor Nick Mays at the London School of Hygiene & Tropical Medicine (LSHTM) and Alan Glanz and David Nuttall at the Department of Health for their advice throughout the research process. Finally, we would like to thank the anonymous reviewers and Mark Wightman for their helpful suggestions.

Executive summary

Introduction

Over the past decade, the government introduced a set of market-based reforms into the NHS with the aim of increasing efficiency, reducing inequities in access to care and increasing the responsiveness and quality of services. Their policies included the introduction of fixed-price reimbursement (Payment by Results), greater devolution of central control (foundation trusts), encouragement of a more pluralistic mix of public and private provision, and an emphasis on patient choice and competition.

Since January 2006, patients requiring a referral to a specialist have been entitled to a choice of four or five providers. Since April 2008 patients in England should have been able to choose treatment from any hospital listed in a national directory of services, which includes NHS acute trusts, foundation trusts and independent sector providers, so-called 'free choice' of provider. In 2009 the NHS Constitution made this a right for patients.

This report considers how free choice of provider is operating in practice and what impact patient choice is having on hospital providers. More specifically, the report aims to answer the following questions:

■ How do patients experience choice?

■ What factors are important to patients when choosing between providers in practice?

■ How do GPs support choice?

■ How are providers responding to choice?

The study was conducted in four local health economies in England between August 2008 and September 2009. They were all outside London and they represent a mix of urban and rural locations which differed in both their potential for competition and their progress with implementation.

We adopted a mixed method that combined interviews with patients, GPs and senior executives from hospital providers (including the private sector) with patient questionnaires (which asked patients how they exercised choice both in practice and in hypothetical situations).

Findings

Awareness, understanding and opinions on choice

The model of patient choice which underpins the policy requires that patients are aware of their ability to choose, want to choose and think choice is important. In our patient survey, 75 per cent of respondents said choice was either 'very important' or 'important' to them; older respondents, those with no qualifications, and those from a mixed and non-white background were more likely to value choice. The results show there is some intrinsic value in offering patients a choice of provider, and that GPs' perceptions that it is younger, more educated patients who want choice are misguided.

Around half (45 per cent) of the patients surveyed said that they knew before visiting their GP that they had the right to choose a hospital. Older patients and those looking after their family at home were more likely to know about choice, possibly because of their more regular contact with the health service, as were men and those holding a university degree. This went against GPs' perceptions that most patients were unaware of choice and that the young were more likely to be aware.

Although providers and GPs did not recognise choice as being important to their patients, on the whole they were either positive or ambivalent about the policy. Some had concerns that inequalities would result from richer and more educated patients choosing higher quality services and that the extra capacity required to facilitate choice would lead to inefficient use of resources. However, it was difficult to disentangle GPs' views on patient choice from their views on the often-criticised electronic appointment booking system (Choose and Book). Although a few GPs saw the benefits of Choose and Book in giving patients greater control and certainty, technical issues, inability to refer to a named consultant, increased consultation times, lack of directly bookable appointment slots, and inaccurate and inconsistent information in the directory of services were raised as issues. Despite recent improvements in the system, GPs remain reluctant to use it and some said they would stop altogether if the incentive they are paid for doing so stopped.

How is patient choice operating in practice?

Are patients offered a choice?

The policy assumes that patients are offered a range of options (including private sector providers), that that they use quality as the major factor when choosing a hospital and that they have relevant and appropriate information on quality to inform their decision. Although GPs maintained that they always offered their patients a choice, we found that just under half (49 per cent) of patients recalled being offered a choice.

Very few patients recalled being offered a private sector option (just 8 per cent of those offered a choice) and few were aware, before visiting the GP, that they had a right to this (19 per cent were aware of the option to be treated in the private sector). This might be due in part to patients' lack of awareness that some treatment centres are independently owned and run, as they often use NHS branding.

The design of Choose and Book allows patients to make a choice themselves and book an appointment at the chosen hospital via the web or through a telephone booking adviser. Most patients were offered a choice by their GP (60 per cent of those offered choice) although a significant number of patients were offered their choice by a telephone booking adviser (20 per cent) or in written correspondence (21 per cent).

There was some resistance, even among our sample of 'enthusiastic' GPs, to offering choice to every patient regardless of circumstances. GPs appeared to be more willing to let patients choose when the referral was fairly routine but were more directive when more specialist treatment is required.

Are patients exercising choice?

In our study, most patients chose their local provider (69 per cent of those offered choice), and providers and GPs described their patients as loyal to their local trust and reluctant to consider travelling further for treatment. When considering hypothetical situations, almost one in five respondents always chose the local provider regardless of their characteristics.

Despite the strong propensity to choose a local provider, when patients were presented with hypothetical situations, in 45 per cent of cases they chose a non-local provider; this suggests that a significant minority would be willing to change to a provider whose characteristics better suit their preferences. We found that in practice patients who are offered a choice are more likely to travel to a non-local provider than those who are not offered a choice, but the difference was small (29 per cent vs 21 per cent using unweighted data).

There may be many reasons why a patient (including one who is not offered a choice) attends a non-local provider – for example, they may need specialist care not available at the local hospital. Among those who were offered a choice, one of the main reasons for choosing a non-local hospital was a bad experience with the local hospital. This suggests that the biggest threat to a hospital's market share is providing poor-quality care to individual patients because they are less likely to return, more willing to go to a non-local provider and may not recommend the hospital to friends and family.

Concerns were raised in the literature about the possible negative impact of choice on equity as higher educated groups and middle classes were thought more likely to exercise choice. In this research, while there were no apparent inequities in terms of who was offered a choice (younger and highly educated patients were no more likely to be offered a choice than older or less educated patients), there were differences in the profile of those who attended a non-local provider. Older and more educated patients were more likely to choose a non-local provider. We were not able to assess the impact of language difficulties on exercising choice, but GPs working in areas of greater ethnic diversity felt that non-English speakers may not be getting equal opportunity to choose.

While mode of transport used for getting to hospital was not a significant factor in predicting whether patients were more likely to choose a non-local provider in practice (when data was weighted), those who normally do not travel by car were more likely to select their local trust irrespective of performance or other attributes under hypothetical conditions. This suggests that lower educated people living in cities and without access to a car may be less likely to choose a non-local provider. Some inequities might arise if these patients are not able to exercise choice in line with their preferences while others can choose to travel further to access a higher quality alternative provider.

GPs and providers believed that choice was relevant only in urban centres; in fact, patients living outside urban centres were more likely to be offered a choice and were more likely to choose to travel to a non-local provider. This may be because these small towns are unlikely to have their own hospital – leading patients (and GPs) to perceive there to be a genuine choice.

Why are patients choosing particular providers?

Our research found that patients value aspects of quality including the quality of care, cleanliness of the hospital, and standard of facilities. This was shown in responses about their recent referral in the patient survey, revealed preference analysis of the comparative characteristics of the hospitals patients chose compared to those nearby hospitals they could have chosen, and discrete choice experiment data on hypothetical choices. However, patients made little use of available information on the performance of hospitals; just

4 per cent consulted the NHS Choices website and 6 per cent looked at leaflets, both of which provide comparative information on hospital performance. Instead patients relied heavily on their own experience (41 per cent), that of friends and family (10 per cent) or the advice of their GP (36 per cent).

GPs we spoke to did not think patients were interested in information about comparative performance and distrusted it themselves. They said they used their knowledge from relationships with specific consultants, feedback from patients and their experience of systemic problems at particular hospitals to help them advise patients. Although this 'soft' intelligence may provide information to aid choices locally, it does not help patients who want to travel beyond the providers with which the GP is familiar.

Does patient choice create competition between providers?

Patient choice was intended to create competition between providers for NHS-funded patients and thereby increase efficiency and improve quality.

Interviews with providers revealed that there was some competition between providers, but the dynamics of competition differed depending on the local configuration of providers, their proximity to each other, the population they served, the type of services they provided and whether there were local agreements in place.

We were given many examples of how different providers (both NHS and private sector) were co-operating and collaborating. In some cases there were formal agreements to 'carve up' the market.

Most providers operated in a defined geographical market and their main competitors were neighbouring NHS hospitals. Generally, providers competed for patients directly only at the boundaries of their catchment areas, where another provider was equidistant. The main focus of competitive activity was securing GP referrals rather than directly competing for patients. Small and medium-sized trusts tended to compete *for* rather than *in* the market particularly where PCTs were actively tendering for community services and new outpatient services.

The independent sector was not perceived as much of a threat and rather than focusing on attracting patients via choice, they acted as a partner for the NHS, providing extra capacity to help the NHS meet waiting time targets. There were isolated examples where the NHS had actively sought to attract patients back from private providers, responding to competition by expanding their own facilities.

Providers saw GPs as a significant barrier to developing patient choice and establishing a competitive market for health care services. They perceived GPs' referral patterns to be fairly stable and giving little attention to quality. Practice-based commissioning and the development of community-based services run by GPs were also seen as a potential conflict of interest.

Providers were quite sceptical about the extent to which patients were acting as informed consumers. Any observed changes in referral patterns were largely seen to be a result of GP decisions rather than the preferences of individual patients. Consequently providers focused their promotional activities on GPs. Few providers were undertaking market research to understand what preferences influenced the choice of hospital for 'potential' patients but instead they were focusing on the experience of 'current' patients (that is, feedback and complaints) and the interests of GPs. Many providers were using this information to drive quality improvement.

The provider response to choice, competition and other factors

The model of choice as a driver for quality improvement assumes that providers receive clear signals from the choices patients make, analyse these and then use the analysis to improve the service provided. Our research suggests that choice did not act as a lever to improve quality in this way; providers were driven more by pressure from a range of other external factors such as the waiting time targets. However, providers believe this might change in the future, as choice becomes more established, more information becomes available and financial pressures limit growth in activity.

As part of their 'mission' to provide a good service to the local population, many providers we spoke to saw it as their job to be aware of what problems the hospital had (eg, high infection rates) and resolve them. They did not wait for 'signals' from patients' choices to highlight the weaknesses or problems with the services.

Choice however, did appear to provide a motivation for providers to maintain their reputation to ensure that patients returned or influenced others by speaking highly of their experience. Taken together with our finding that patients base their choices on personal experience or 'soft' knowledge, the emphasis placed on delivering a positive patient experience is not surprising.

Most providers focused on retaining patients rather than expanding into new markets or new areas and appeared unlikely to compete actively for patients in the future unless there was spare capacity or lower demand within the system. Other providers, however, suggested that the implications for income of even small shifts in elective activity could change their approach. However, none of the providers we interviewed were concerned about the financial impact of choice.

As financial pressures and reductions in waiting times decrease pressure on hospital capacity, and private sector providers are motivated to compete for NHS patients, there may be more competition for patients and the impact on providers of patient choice may increase.

Discussion

The research raises a number of key questions about the future of the patient choice policy and its potential impact on providers.

First, should the NHS continue to promote patient choice of hospital? Even if relatively few patients chose to attend a non-local provider, our evidence shows they valued having the ability to choose. We therefore conclude that given its intrinsic value, the NHS should continue to offer patients a choice of hospital.

Second, how is choice affecting providers? Choice appears to impact on quality indirectly, by creating a threat to providers that they might potentially lose patients. Our research shows that patients rely on their own or others' experience to inform their choice and that providers are aware of the need to deliver a high-quality experience to retain the loyalty of patients. Patient feedback is therefore likely to remain a significant driver of quality improvement. Because patients do not use objective measures of quality, it is hard for those with no experience to differentiate between services. More research is needed to understand what motivates individuals and organisations to improve quality.

Third, is patient choice working everywhere and for everyone? Although our research was conducted in only four areas of England, choice and competition were operating to some extent in all of the areas, despite differences between them. We found that providers were competing most actively for patients (or GP referrals) on the geographical fringes of their catchment areas and that patients outside of urban centres were more likely to be offered choice and to attend a non-local hospital. This challenges the belief (widely held among those we interviewed) that choice is relevant only in urban areas. Choice may have therefore increased competition in some areas.

There were no significant differences between different population groups (by age, gender, ethnicity or education) in whether patients were offered a choice, suggesting that the opportunity to choose is reasonably equitable at present. However, GPs' misconceptions about the type of patients who want choice could lead them to offer choice selectively in future and there may be value in communicating to GPs which patients value choice.

There were some inequities in who chose to travel to a non-local provider; there is a potential risk that less educated patients or those without access to transport could be disadvantaged in areas where a trust is failing to maintain quality standards and large numbers of people exercise choice to be seen or treated elsewhere. It underlines the need to ensure, through regulation, that all providers meet minimum standards to protect patients.

Fourth, is choice cost effective? Our research did not try to answer this question. However, we believe that in view of the large sums invested in choice – through incentive payments, the booking system and support – policy-makers should quantify the costs and benefits of choice more clearly to convince GPs and providers of its value.

Finally, has choice been implemented effectively? Both GPs and providers had complaints about the way in which Choose and Book operates. While some of the technical problems have been solved, concerns remain that functionality does not support referral practices. If Choose and Book is to be used more widely, continued improvements will be needed in the system and training in its functionality, especially if local incentives are dropped.

Patients place a high value on the quality of care and other related dimensions of quality and safety, including the quality of care, cleanliness of the hospital and the standard of facilities, but rarely use objective measures of performance to help them choose a hospital. Systems that provide information about the quality of hospital services may need to be designed to make it easier for patients to search and compare these measures. For example, more work is needed to establish a set of standardised variables for acute hospital care with which patients can over time become more familiar. In future, patient experience data at the level of service lines and patient-reported outcomes data will be available. These offer an opportunity to present more specific data of relevance to patients when making a choice in future. Recent investments to expand NHS Choices to include feedback will allow patients to access more 'soft' knowledge. NHS Choices – and other resources – could also be promoted to GPs, as they are the main agents of choice and they currently distrust performance data.

There remains some resistance among GPs to offering choice routinely to all patients regardless of circumstances. In future if there is more direct access to diagnostics and consultant advice, GPs may be referring fewer patients to hospital and may be more likely to be referring for treatment rather than diagnosis when they do so. This could change the nature of the referral consultation and make it more likely that GPs will be willing and able to engage patients in a decision about where to refer. A GP is currently only likely to encounter a few patients per week that need a referral, and for these patients it may be appropriate to extend the standard 10-minute GP consultation slot to allow a meaningful discussion of choice.

One way of encouraging GPs to offer choice is to present it as part of a wider agenda to engage patients in shared decisions about treatment and care. It would also be helpful to promote GPs' understanding of the value of choice to a wide range of patients. There may be limits to the extent to which the implementation of choice can be improved and, indeed, to GPs' willingness to offer choice systematically in all circumstances.

In conclusion, the policy of offering patients a choice of provider is valued by patients, and is operating to some extent within the NHS, but is not operating in exactly the way envisaged by policy. While the implementation of choice has not been perfect, it still represents a threat to providers that can keep them focused on what is important to patients.

Introduction

Policy background and theory

Over the last decade, health policy in the English NHS has developed in three overlapping phases, broadly along the lines described by Simon Stevens, former health adviser to Tony Blair (Stevens 2004). The first phase – categorised by Stevens as 'provider support' – recognised the historically low levels of funding for the NHS not only relative to other comparable countries but relative to the general wealth of the country. Derek Wanless's 2002 review of future funding for the NHS supported the notion that a necessary condition for improving the NHS was a need for more resources (Wanless 2002). NHS funding has since increased at an unprecedented rate.

However, Stevens argued that there was also a recognition that simply increasing funding (and the input resources extra funding could buy) was not enough, by itself, to achieve the goals for improving quality and efficiency as set out in, for example, The NHS Plan (Department of Health 2000). Hence, policies were developed to provide the second phase – what Stevens called 'hierarchical challenge'. This involved an expansion of the Department of Health's role through the setting of targets (backed by tough if not punitive sanctions) to improve, for example, waiting times; it also involved the mapping out of disease-based care pathways in the form of national service frameworks, and new national regulator bodies to monitor and promote the performance of local NHS organisations.

While 'targets and terror' (Hood and Bevan 2005), nationally developed service guidelines and regulatory mechanisms had their place – and indeed, achieved some success (Propper *et al* 2006; Harrison and Appleby 2009) – ultimately, according to Stevens, they had only limited power to effect significant improvements in the quality of care, patients' experience of care and the efficiency of the NHS. Moreover, pushed too far, central management of the system also had unwanted side effects, producing adverse professional reaction. Hence, the third policy phase – 'localist challenge' – which aimed to introduce more automatic incentives into the NHS in order to boost provider organisations' 'internal' motivations to improve their performance.

So, the third phase has laid emphasis on a number of key areas:

- new financial mechanisms such as the prospective, activity-based fixed price reimbursement system (Payment by Results);

- greater devolution and independence from central control (foundation trust status);

- encouragement for a more pluralistic mix of public and private provision of NHS care;

- an emphasis on competitive quasi-market forces between providers; and

- more formalised provision of choice of hospital for patients.

These policies, designed to introduce more competition into publicly funded (and provided) health care and to strengthen patient choice, had a number of objectives.

First, promoting patient choice was seen as an important way of promoting competition between providers, thus sharpening the incentives to be efficient. Together with fixed prices per episode of care, choice was designed to create incentives for providers to reduce their operating costs and become more technically efficient. It was also seen as a means of making more efficient use of capacity within the hospital sector, particularly where there were differential waiting times in different providers (or areas).

Second, it was argued that choice would lead to greater equity. Rich patients have the choice of opting out of the NHS altogether, if they view clinical quality, timeliness of treatment or other areas of performance to be unacceptable. By providing choices *within* the NHS, this potentially satisfies an equity goal by giving *all* patients some degree of 'ability to choose'. These views of patient choice are exemplified in the following quote:

> *Choice mechanisms enhance equity by exerting pressure on low-quality or incompetent providers. Competitive pressures and incentives drive up quality, efficiency and responsiveness in the public sector. Choice leads to higher standards. The overriding principle is clear. We should give poorer patients… the same range of choices the rich have always enjoyed. In a heterogeneous society, where there is enormous variation in needs and preferences, public services must be equipped to respond.*
>
> (Blair 2003, cited in Appleby *et al* 2003)

Another potential merit of choice, noted by Fotaki *et al* (2005), is that it might result in fewer wealthy people opting out of the NHS, increasing social solidarity for the NHS, and lowering the likelihood of the NHS becoming a safety net service for the poor.[1] The extent to which choice has the potential to be equity-reducing or equity-enhancing is discussed in more detail elsewhere (Dixon and Le Grand 2006).

Finally, patient choice was seen as an important way of encouraging providers to be more responsive to patients' preferences about how and where health care is delivered. Ideas about how consumer markets operate to drive quality improvements have been influenced heavily by the ideas of Hirschman (1970) and his concepts of 'exit, voice and loyalty'.

Hirschman suggested that when consumers exit from a low-quality provider, the provider notices the decrease in demand (and associated drop in income) and either responds by improving their quality in order to stay in the market, or goes out of business. He compares these signals with the impact of voice mechanisms whereby consumer dissatisfaction with the quality of service is expressed directly in the form of feedback or complaint. Finally, he recognises that producers may generate considerable loyalty, which means that even if quality falls, consumers may continue to purchase goods and services rather than go to an alternative producer.

These concepts have been used in recent years to support arguments that the power of exit is necessary (even if not exercised) to ensure that providers raise their game. Applied to fixed price markets in health care, where revenue depends on activity, it is argued that this will sharpen incentives to improve quality and outcomes.

---

[1] This argument is consistent with, in the theory of public choice, the wealthy having 'double peaked preferences' (ie, more than one utility maximum point) with respect to public spending (Boadway and Bruce 1984). The wealthy, weighing up the benefits to them of NHS services against the tax they pay, will either prefer a minimum level of NHS spending (where they themselves are using private sector services) or, beyond some threshold level of NHS spend, will prefer a much higher NHS budget (at which point they opt into the NHS, and demand high quality).

Therefore, strengthening patient choice aims to increase efficiency, reduce inequities in access to care, and increase the responsiveness and quality of services.

There are a number of different types of choice that patients could be involved in:

- choice of treatment (what)
- choice of individual health professional (who)
- choice of appointment time/date (when)
- choice of which provider (where).

In recent years, policy in England has focused on the latter two choices – where and when to be treated. These choices are not always mutually exclusive – for example, a particular treatment might only be available at one provider, or the choice of provider might be driven by a desire to see a particular consultant, and so on. There are also different decision points along a patient pathway where different choices might be faced. The choice of hospital provider is offered at the point of referral for specialist care, regardless of whether the patient will need further treatment or not. The referral may be for further investigations and diagnostic tests, specialist opinion or elective treatment.

Before the introduction of the internal market, GPs were in effect at liberty to refer to any NHS provider. As a means of saving money, health authorities (as purchasers) restricted the ability to refer out of area. GP fundholders who took on purchasing responsibilities were, however, free to refer to any provider without restriction.

Patient choice was (re-)introduced under the Labour government as a series of pilots launched in 2002, allowing patients on waiting lists to choose alternative hospitals with shorter waiting times (*see* Figure 2 on page 6). The choice pilots were aimed at maximising the use of NHS capacity in order to reduce waiting times. Patients were already on a waiting list and therefore the 'choice' available to them was to be treated more quickly at an alternative hospital. Choice was largely supply driven, and there was no penalty for the originating hospital; indeed, getting the patient off their waiting list was a plus.

From January 2006, patients requiring a referral to a specialist were to be offered a choice of four or five providers; thus, at the time of this research, choice at the point of referral had been operating for around three years. Since April 2008, patients in England being referred to a non-urgent hospital appointment by their GP can choose to be treated at any hospital listed in a national directory of services, including NHS acute trusts, foundation trusts and independent sector providers – so-called 'free choice' of provider. In 2009 the NHS Constitution made this a right for patients (Department of Health 2009b).

Research aims and approach

This report considers how free choice at the point of referral is operating in practice, and the impact it is having on hospital providers. More specifically, the report aims to answer the following questions.

- How do patients experience choice?
- What factors are important to patients when choosing between providers in practice?
- How do GPs support choice?
- How are providers responding to choice?

This study was conducted in four local health economies in England between August 2008 and September 2009 (Figure 1, below and opposite, sets out some basic details of each area and the providers selected). We adopted a mixed method that combined interviews with patients, GPs and senior executives from hospital providers (including the private sector) with patient questionnaires. This has enabled us to build up an in-depth understanding of how choice has been implemented at a local level, and to explore the impact of local factors on how choice is operating.

Figure 1 Overview of case study areas

Local health economy A

Area information: Largely urban area, situated on the edge of a large metropolitan area. Relatively young population, with larger than average numbers of children aged 16 years and under. Approximately 14 per cent of the population are from a black or minority ethnic group, and 20 per cent have a limiting long-term illness. There are pockets of deprivation.

Structure of general practice: There are 47 local GP practices in the main primary care trust (PCT). Six practices are managed by the PCT. Twenty GPs in the area are salaried. Most practices are small but there are 10 larger health centres.

PCT financial situation 2008/9	Surplus
Approx population served by PCT	230,000
PCT Care Quality Commission (CQC) rating 2008/9 (quality/financial)	Good/Good
% appointments booked through Choose and Book (C&B) 2007/8	78
Site selection criteria	High potential for choice High penetration of choice
% offered choice	70

Provider	A1 NHS	A2 ISTC
% of PCT A's 2004/5 outpatient referrals	81	N/A
Provider CQC rating 2008/9 (quality/financial)	Good/Good	N/A
Provider financial situation 2008/9	Continued surplus	N/A

Local health economy B

Area information: Situated in a large city. The population is slightly younger than average. Approximately 21 per cent of the population are from a black or minority ethnic group. There are pockets of deprivation.

Structure of general practice: The main PCT is responsible for 237 GPs, working in 82 practices.

PCT financial situation 2008/9	Surplus
Approx population served by PCT	440,000
PCT CQC rating 2008/9 (quality/financial)	Fair/Good
% appointments booked through C&B 2007/8	41
Site selection criteria	High potential for choice Low penetration of choice
% offered choice	51

Provider	B1 NHS FT	B2 NHS	B3 NHS FT	B4 Independent sector
% of PCT B's 2004/5 outpatient referrals	70	14	6	N/A
Provider CQC rating 2008/9 (quality/financial)	Fair/Excellent	Good/Good	Excellent/Excellent	N/A
Provider financial situation 2008/9	Continued surplus	Continued surplus	Continued surplus	N/A

ISTC: independent sector treatment centre
FT: foundation trust

The research benefits from having these multiple perspectives. Existing research mostly focuses on patients' views (through surveys) and, to a lesser extent, the views of GPs. This is the first study to combine these perspectives with the views of hospital providers. The methodology we used is explained in more detail in Appendix A (pages 159–75).

The theory of competition and its application to health care has been widely debated, but there is a general paucity of evidence about how patient choice is being implemented in

Figure 1 *continued*

Local health economy C

Area information: Situated in a mixed urban/rural area. The population has slightly more older people and fewer in younger age bands than the national average. There are pockets of deprivation.

Structure of general practice: There are 74 GP practices within the main PCT. Five are managed by the PCT.

PCT financial situation 2008/9	Surplus
Approx population served by PCT	440,000
PCT CQC rating 2008/9 (quality/financial)	Fair/Good
% appointments booked through C&B 2007/8	41
Site selection criteria	High potential for choice High penetration of choice
% offered choice	57

Provider	C1 Ind. sector	C2 NHS	C3 NHS	C4 NHS
% of PCT C's 2004/5 outpatient referrals	N/A	30	29	27
Provider CQC rating 2008/9 (quality/financial)	N/A	Fair/Good	Good/Good	Good/Good
Provider financial situation 2008/9	N/A	Continued surplus	Continued surplus	Surplus, previous year deficit

Local health economy D

Area information: Situated in a mainly rural, coastal area. Approximately 30 per cent of the population are above retiring age, and there are fewer young people than the national average. The region has a low birth rate and is 98 per cent ethnically indigenous.

Structure of general practice: There are 59 local general practices in the main PCT, and a range of other services are provided by 11 local community hospitals and health centres. Five practices are managed by the PCT.

PCT financial situation 2008/9	Balanced
Approx population served by PCT	400,000
PCT CQC rating 2008/9 (quality/financial)	Good/Good
% appointments booked through C&B 2007/8	68
Site selection criteria	Low potential for choice High penetration of choice
% offered choice	61

Provider	D1 NHS FT	D2 NHS FT	D3 NHS FT	D4 NHS FT	D5 ISTC
% of PCT D's 2004/5 outpatient referrals	46	19	16	8	N/A
Provider CQC rating 2008/9 (quality/financial)	Good/Good	Excellent/Excellent	Excellent/Excellent	Good/Excellent	N/A
Provider financial situation 2008/9	Deficit, previous year surplus	Continued surplus	Continued surplus	Continued surplus	N/A

Figure 2 Patient choice and system reform: policy timeline

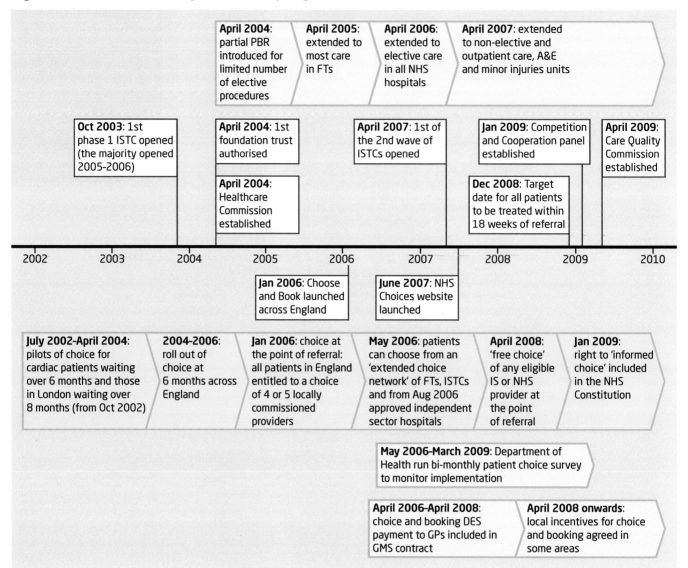

practice since the introduction of choice at the point of referral. In Section 1, we review some of these debates and summarise some of the empirical research published to date.

Our study explores how choice is working from the perspectives of patients, GPs and hospital providers. Section 2 presents data on the awareness, understanding and opinions of these different actors who are all directly involved in the implementation of choice. While it is interesting to examine whether choice is valued in its own right, we are primarily concerned with choice as a means to achieve improvements in the delivery of health services.

In analysing the implementation of choice, in Section 3 we examine the extent to which the reality of patient choice matches the model that underpins the policy assumptions behind it (*see* Figure 3 opposite). This identifies the various elements of the choice process which need to be in place to effect change in providers' behaviour and services. We explore issues such as whether patients are offered choice and given a range of options to choose from, whether quality is a major factor in the choices patients make, and what information and support patients receive when choosing a provider. We also examine the extent to which there are equal opportunities for patients to choose and, where possible, identify any systematic differences between groups in the factors influencing their choices.

Figure 3 A model of patient choice as a driver for quality improvement

Patient	GP	Provider
■ Aware of ability to choose ■ Wants to choose/thinks choice is important ■ Offered choice of all potential providers including NHS and independent sector ■ Quality is primary discriminator in choosing which provider to attend ■ Has access to relevant and appropriate information on quality and ability to interpret	■ Believes choice is important to patients ■ Offers choice to all patients ■ Involves patient in decision-making ■ Has access to information about the quality of providers and conveys this to patient ■ Has time and resources to support patients to make an informed choice	■ Competes for patients with other providers ■ Receives clear 'signals' as a result of patients' choices ■ Analyses and understands meaning of choices ■ Responds to loss of market share by improving services ■ Providers that don't respond lose money and may eventually fail and exit the market

In theory, choice is intended to create competition between providers. There are other sources of competition – for example, for commissioning contracts and GP referrals – which we expect to also have an impact on the extent to which providers are competing. In Section 4, we analyse the views of providers about the extent of competition in their markets and the area in which they operate. We are interested in the extent to which patient choice drives competition (as opposed to other drivers such as commissioning decisions or referral decisions by GPs).

The model of choice assumes that patient choice and competition influence providers and act as a driver for service improvements. However, there are clearly a range of factors (both external and internal) that influence providers' behaviour (*see* Figure 4, below). The extent to which choice drives service improvements and its relative influence alongside other factors is explored in Section 5.

Figure 4 Analytical framework showing relationship between choice, competition and provider behaviour

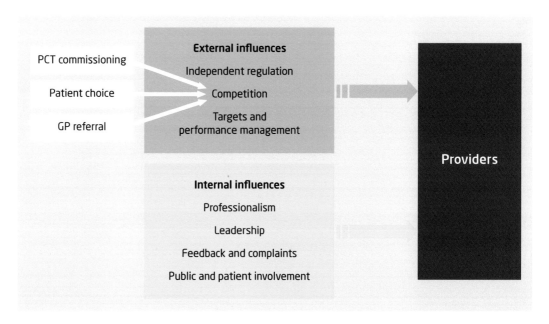

In Section 6, we explore how the local context affects the way choice operates in each of the case study areas. Here, we bring together the findings from each of the other sections to assess whether the differences in the potential for choice and penetration of choice (on which the sites were selected) has made a difference to how choice is operating and the impact on providers.

This research was conducted when the NHS was particularly focused on the requirement to meet the government's commitment that, by 2008, no patient would wait more than 18 weeks from GP referral to treatment (first made in the NHS Improvement Plan 2004 (Department of Health 2004). The NHS was also becoming increasingly aware that the wider economic recession and financial crisis was likely to have an impact on the level of funding available in future.

While there appears to be political commitment to patient choice in the NHS, there continues to be some public debate about the role of competition in the NHS. In the final section of the report, Section 7, we explore the views of those we interviewed about the future of choice and competition. We discuss the overall findings of the research and, highlight key implications for policy and practice. We consider whether patient choice can continue to be seen as a lever for improving quality and whether, in order to achieve the intended aims of the policy, the implementation of choice needs to be modified.

1 Theory and evidence of patient choice

In this section, we review various elements of economics and decision theory, which provide the basis for hypotheses concerning how patients choose and how providers respond. These theories have informed some of the policy objectives of patient choice and are used to inform our framework for evaluating how choice is operating in the NHS in England. We also provide a brief review of the empirical evidence on the role of patient choice in health care markets. We conclude by considering the implications for this research.

Economic theory, market failure and consumer choice

The standard neoclassical model of a perfect market involves well-informed, rational consumers acting in their own best interests by systematically choosing which goods and services to buy, and who to buy them from, in a way that maximises their well-being ('happiness' or 'utility'). In the theory of perfect competition, the supply side of this idealised market comprises a sufficiently large number of existing or potential providers, so that competition forces prices close to the marginal cost of production. The theory of contestable markets relaxes the requirement that there be large numbers of suppliers, noting that provided there are no barriers to entry, the threat of competition will produce efficient outcomes. The self-interested actions of individual consumers and firms lead to socially optimal quantities of goods being bought and sold.

Real world markets – including health care markets – depart from this idealised world in many ways. Indeed, most markets do not conform to the basic requirements of a perfectly competitive market as described above. The ways in which consumers and providers in health care markets behave differently from the 'idealised' market model, and the implications of this for the appropriate balance of private market and public sector in health care, is a particular focus of health economics. The question 'Is health care different?' has been a constant refrain since health economics first emerged as a sub-discipline of economics (for a review, *see* Hurley 2000).

Arrow (1963) was the first to systematically analyse the failures in health care markets and to consider their implications for social welfare. The box overleaf summarises the key characteristics of consumer and provider behaviour he identified, and notes the implications of these for patient choice. The central tenet of Arrow's analysis is that all of these special features of medical markets stem from *uncertainty*: about health care problems, and about treatments (Morris *et al* 2007).

All of the market failures observed in health care can also be found in other markets – but it is the *combination* of these features in health care markets (together with the grave consequences for consumers of making bad choices) that conspires to make these markets 'special'. Central to these market failures is asymmetry of information between consumers and providers in health care. In order to overcome the problems of information asymmetry (present in a number of markets), the principal may appoint an agent to make a decision on their behalf or to advise them.

Of particular relevance in the context of this current study is the application of principal–agent theory to the relationship between the patient and their GP, and the extent to which patients, invited to choose the provider of secondary care, will rely upon their GP (or another health care professional) for information and advice. The high stakes if a patient makes a 'bad' choice, the difficulty of gauging quality, and the often technical nature of the information being presented mean that patients may wish to rely on their doctor when making choices. It has also led to regulation of market entry concerning who may provide health care services in order to protect health care consumers, thus limiting the range of choices available, and limiting the impact of making a bad choice.

Market failures in health care: implications for patient choice

Patients do not behave in the same way as other consumers	Implications for patient choice
■ They cannot test the product before consuming it. Indeed, they often have difficulty gauging the quality of care even after experiencing it. Consumers of health care find it difficult to 'shop around' to get the best deal.	■ Health care markets cannot rely on the principle of 'Caveat Emptor' ('let the buyer beware') as consumers may not be able to identify low-quality providers.
■ It is difficult for patients to obtain information about what medical care is appropriate for their condition – medical knowledge is complex. As consumers, patients know considerably less than the seller, and place trust in their health care provider.	■ Consumers in health care markets have to be protected from making bad choices, eg, by regulating who can and cannot provide health care.
	■ Consumers delegate many of their decisions to the provider. The doctor acts as an 'agent' for the patient. There is an important element of trust in the patient's relationship with their provider.
■ There are interdependencies between consumers' actions: one person's consumption of a vaccine to reduce an infectious disease 'spills over' into benefits to others.	■ Choices made by some patients may have impacts (both positive and negative) on other patients.
Doctors do not behave in the same way as other firms	**Implications for patient choice**
■ Entry into the industry is limited by regulations.	■ Restricted number of providers to choose from.
■ Overt competition is not common as in other markets.	■ Consumers may not be aware of the differences between providers, paucity of information in the market.
■ Advice given by doctors is supposed to be divorced from self-interest: treatment is claimed to be dictated by clinical need, not by profit.	■ Doctors act as both 'agent' and provider of health care; possibility that self-interest might result in supplier-induced demand.
■ Providers with goals other than profit maximisation dominate provision.	■ Motivation of providers to compete for patients not clear.

Source: adapted from Morris *et al* 2007

In a simple view of markets, the greater the array of options available to consumers to choose between, and the more information provided on each, the better off consumers will be. However, this simple view turns out to depend on some important preconditions (*see* box below).

Preconditions for economic model of consumer choice and the reality of complex decision-making

Preconditions for economic model of consumer choice	Consumer choice in health care
■ 'Consumer search' – the process of obtaining information and weighing it up – is not costly or time-consuming.	■ Costs of 'search' may be high, particularly in markets where product differentiation means many characteristics to compare across many alternatives. Consumers may become overloaded by too many options or too much information.
■ Consumers choose rationally.	■ Consumers use heuristics or shortcuts to make decisions.
■ It is relatively easy for consumers to differentiate between the available options.	■ Health care is a reputation good; consumers have difficulty judging the quality of a service, even after receiving it.
■ The information on each option is relevant to consumers' preferences.	■ Consumers are poor at judging the experienced utility of an outcome, overestimating gains and losses.
■ Consumers have stable, consistent preferences – including in the presence of risk and uncertainty.	■ Consumers' decisions are affected by how the choice is offered, how information is framed, and the context.

Economic models of consumer choice tend to assume that consumers will make rational decisions in pursuit of utility maximisation. From the early writing on utility by Bentham (1789) and Mill (1863) (who regarded utility as a potentially cardinal measuring rod of human pleasures and pains), through to Pareto (1906) and Hicks (1939) in the late 19th and early 20th century (where utility is considered ordinally: a consumer either prefers A to B, B to A, or is indifferent), economics theory initially focused on the utility associated with *certain* events or circumstances. Later theoretical developments – principally von Neumann and Morgenstern (1944) – focused on the way consumers would maximise utility when confronted with *uncertainty*.

Expected utility theory (EUT), the main conceptual framework, posits human choice as a process of considering the payoffs from each possible outcome, the probability of its occurring, and the degree of risk aversion. EUT is not a model of how consumers should behave when faced with choices, but rather provides a basis for predictions and hypothesis testing. In practice, EUT fails to provide a good description of how people make choices in many circumstances.

Random utility theory (RUT), proposed by Marschak (1960), takes incomplete information into account by providing a probabilistic model of consumer choice, with the probability deriving from variability in the individuals' preferences when faced with repeated choices from the same finite choice set. RUT has subsequently come to be most closely associated with McFadden (1975), who reconstituted it from a model of an individual facing repeated choices, to a model of choices made by a population of individuals (Batley 2007).

RUT is best known as the theoretic foundation for econometric modelling of data from discrete choice experiments (an approach used in this report and described in more detail in Appendix A). As it is used in modelling such choices, RUT addresses situations where the *analyst* has incomplete information on the influences on individual choice – rather than being a model of individual choice behaviour per se. Discrete choice experiments, drawing on RUT as their foundation, have been an important source of empirical evidence on the way consumers make choices in health care (*see* below).

For most goods and services bought in private markets, consumers can judge the quality of the good before buying it – or can judge the quality after purchasing it ('experience goods'). Consumer research suggests that the 'moment of truth' when the consumer experiences the product is important to reputation. If the product or service delivers entirely on the promise, consumers become advocates; if, on the other hand, it does not deliver, then consumers become militant.

But for some goods or services, consumers have difficulty judging the quality of a service, even after consuming or experiencing it. Health care services are often used as an example of this sort of problem. In these cases, consumers are heavily reliant on the reputation of the provider when making their choices. Under these circumstances, economics suggests that consumer searches among sellers will consist principally of a series of queries to relatives, friends and associates for recommendations.

Satterthwaite (1979) suggests that the market for GPs is a good example of a monopolistically competitive market – that is, there are many sellers, each selling a slightly differentiated product – which has these 'reputation good' characteristics. Hospital care and dentists are other possible examples – for most consumers, there are a reasonably large number of options to choose between, and each provider is slightly different from the others but not distinctively so.

Consumers in other markets are usually choosing between differentiated products. Marketing and brand identity are used to differentiate essentially similar products. A differentiated brand identity acts as a visual shorthand, which enables consumers to make informed choices in other markets. But in the NHS, the rules surrounding such basics as visual identity are so constraining that this largely does not apply. It is generally more difficult for consumers to differentiate between services than products, because the former are less tangible (de Chernatony and McDonald 2003).

There is evidence that, when faced with choices between competing service brands (as opposed to tangible product brands), consumers rely on any available clues to make 'informed' decisions (Zeithaml and Bitner 1996). In health care, this might lead consumers to rely on visible and tangible 'clues' such as cleanliness, rather than on MRSA, which cannot be 'seen'. When choosing a hospital, patients are largely faced with non-differentiated services, thus limiting the motivation to bypass the local provider.

Spatial models of competition are of particular relevance in health care markets. Hotelling's (1929) model of location and firm differentiation, and later extensions of it such as Salop (1979), emphasise the importance of the firm's choice of location in markets. The standard duopoly (two-firm) Hotelling model suggests that firms select their location, then their price, and will minimise differentiation (spatial distance) in order to maximise market share. Empirical evidence from health care markets (reviewed below) clearly points to the importance of geographic proximity being a key determinant of patient choice and in understanding provider's response to potential competition.

Hotelling-type models have been developed to explain the way in which hospitals compete on location and quality (*see*, for example, Calem and Rizzo 1995). Montefiori (2003), in a model of spatial competition between hospitals, notes that asymmetry of information in such markets means that patients' choice of hospital depends on their *perceptions* of quality. Of course, it is likely that patients' perceptions of quality may be different from the 'true' quality of hospitals.

Underpinning most models of consumer choice is an assumption that patients will engage in 'consumer search' in a way broadly similar to that in other markets. That is, consumers will actively seek and can assess comparative information on quality and other attributes; and will use this information to systematically select those providers that best match their preferences. But recent contributions to the study of consumer choices, in particular from the fields of behavioural economics and decision theory, which draw on insights from cognitive psychology, suggest it may not be quite that straightforward. Given the features of the health care market noted above, we might anticipate the behaviour of consumers to depart from neoclassical models of choice. There is also evidence to suggest that consumers in complex markets may not act rationally.

Consumer choice in complex markets

In contrast to economics, decision theory approaches to choice focus on explanations for actual choice behaviours. Deriving from the field of psychology, these approaches take as their starting point observations of common and systematic violations of EUT or other theories of consumer choice – including preference reversals, choice inconsistencies and various forms of 'bounded rationality' (*see* Simon 1978). Studies in this field point to choice being much more complex and fraught than is assumed in most economic models.

> *When faced with a choice among several alternatives, people often experience uncertainty and exhibit inconsistencies. That is, people are often not sure which alternatives they should select, nor do they always make the same choice under seemingly identical conditions.*
>
> (Tversky 2004)

It is important to note that this literature also provides clear support for the assertion that choice per se is a 'good thing'. Across many different sorts of choices and contexts, research has repeatedly shown that there is a link between providing a choice and a number of positive psychological indicators such as perceived control, intrinsic motivation, task performance, and life satisfaction.

The positive effects of choice have been noted even in situations where the choice itself is trivial or incidental. However, that body of evidence has some limitations. In particular, the number of options presented in experiments of this kind are typically quite small (between two and five). Iyengar and Lepper (2006) conclude that '…it would appear, then, that what prior research has actually shown is that choice among relatively limited alternatives is more beneficial than no choice at all' (p 301).

A growing body of research in decision theory suggests that people have difficulty managing more complex choices and that, beyond some point, more choice – more options, and more information – can result in 'choice overload', and a demotivating effect on decision-making. Key findings are that as the attractiveness of the available alternatives rises, individuals experience conflict, and as a result will either defer making a decision, search for new alternatives, choose the default option, or simply choose *not* to choose. Consumer research reinforces these messages: as the number of options and information on each go *up*, the number of options considered and the fraction of the total information which is considered goes *down*. Having unlimited options can also make people more dissatisfied with the choices they make – referred to by Schwartz (2000) as 'the tyranny of choice'.

One way in which people respond to complex decisions is to try to simplify them by using simple rules of thumb ('heuristics') to narrow down the options. An example of this is the use of elimination strategies: research shows that as the number of options increases, the percentage of participants using elimination strategies (in effect, ruling out some options on the basis of some characteristic or 'aspect' – Tversky 1972) markedly increases (Iyengar and Lepper 2006). While such strategies render decision-making more manageable, they may also lead to consumers making systematic errors.

Consumers in other markets are capable of making seemingly rational decisions about complex purchases as long as they are sufficiently comfortable with the variables between the products and services. Hence, without a background in engineering or IT, consumers are making decisions about which car or laptop to buy because they can assimilate information about things like fuel consumption, emissions, service intervals, available memory, RAM, and so on. However, to be able to do this there needs to have been a period of time where the product variables have become the common, hard currency. Continual revisions to the indicators by which quality of provider is judged, and changes in the way this information is measured and presented, are likely to confuse patients.

Some of the major conclusions from consumer psychology research are summarised in the box below.

Insights from consumer research

Consumers choose between available options depending on:

- their *goals*. The option that is selected will depend on whether the consumers' goal is to minimise the effort required to make the choice; maximise the accuracy of the decision; minimise the experience of negative emotion during the decision; maximise the ease of justifying the decision; or some combination of these

- the *complexity* of the decision task

- the *context*. The value of an option depends not only on its characteristics or attributes, but also on the attributes of other alternatives in the 'choice set'

- how they are asked

- how the choice set is displayed ('framed'). A key issue in framing is whether the outcomes are represented as gains or losses, with losses affecting decisions more than corresponding gains.

Source: Bettman *et al* (2006)

Decision theory distinguishes the *experienced utility* of an outcome – the actual experience of the outcome of a decision (similar to Bentham's concept of utility) – from *decision utility*: the weight assigned to that outcome at the point where decisions are made. If consumers are perfect at predicting how happy they will feel when experiencing the outcomes of their decisions, then experienced and decision utility will equate. In practice, human beings are not good at this sort of 'affective forecasting', tending to overestimate the happiness that will result from improved outcomes, and the reductions in happiness from unfavourable outcomes.

Because of this, understanding decision utility is key to understanding why people make choices in particular ways. Three conclusions from research are particularly important in the context of patient choice. First, the main 'carriers' of utility are *events*, not 'states'. That is, utility is assigned to changes – gains or losses – relative to some reference point, often the status quo. Second, losses 'loom larger' than corresponding gains. Third, framing effects are crucial: the same objective outcomes can be evaluated as gains or as losses, depending on the way the 'reference state' is described (Kahneman 2006).

Other theories of decision-making such as social learning theory (Bandura 1977, 1997) emphasise the importance of social relations. They suggest that patients are likely to be influenced by a range of other factors such as lay knowledge and beliefs, the views of others (especially family and friends), and marketing and advertising.

Finally, personality appears to play a significant role in how people deal with complex choices. The response to choice depends on where the individual's personality lies on the satisficer–maximiser spectrum. A maximiser always tries to find the very best option from a choice set, and may worry after the choice is made as to whether it was indeed the best. Satisficers may set high standards but are content with a good choice, and place less priority on making the *best* choice. Maximisers are more likely to avoid making a choice when the choice set is large, probably to avoid the anguish associated with not knowing whether their choice was optimal (Norwood *et al* 2009). Maximisers are less happy in life, possibly due to their obsession with making optimal choices (Schwartz 2005).

The issues that arise when patients face complex choices have also been noted in analyses of behavioural economics in a related area of choice – that of health care insurer. A considerable body of evidence exists on these choices. A recent review article notes:

> *Consumers are rarely well equipped to deal with markets offering large numbers of complex, expensive, hard-to-evaluate products – products that, as in the case of health insurance policies, may nonetheless be critical to their wellbeing. Consumers facing complex, high-stakes choices are prone to predictable errors. They are likely to lack the skill and time to make choices based on a careful assessment of the relative costs and quality of competing health plans, tending instead to choose on the basis of anecdotal information, such as their friends' experiences.*
>
> (Frank and Zeckhauser 2009)

Studies of the response of consumers to options and information in these markets suggest that a number of predictable problems are likely to arise from the complexity inherent in the choices presented to patients.

- 'Choice overload': as people face an increasingly large number of similar choices, their tendency to switch is unlikely to go up, and may go down.[2]

- 'Inertia due to numbers': people offered more alternatives are less likely to switch. The result is greater price variation in markets offering more choice (Frank and Lamiraud 2009).

- This in turn reinforces 'status quo bias': people's tendency to stick with previous or familiar choices, even when market circumstances had changed, or where their initial choice was imposed on them (Samuelson and Zeckhauser 1988).

---

[2] In the case of hospital treatment, many patients will never have gone to a hospital before. In these cases, choosing a hospital other than their local hospital involves patients bypassing the local hospital, rather than 'switching' from one to another.

The choice that NHS patients are invited to make at the point of referral from their GP is quite complex – most obviously, because it entails patients being presented with a potentially large number of alternatives, where the differences in the services being offered may be minimal. The complexity inherent in that choice is exacerbated by two further characteristics, peculiar to the NHS policy we are interested in, explained below.

Uncertainty over *what* is being chosen. Patients being referred from their GP to a consultant do not know with certainty that they will require hospital treatment. In effect, they are therefore making two choices simultaneously: a *certain* choice about where to be referred for diagnosis, *and* a choice about where to receive surgery, under *uncertainty* it will be required. The relevant attributes and measures of quality in each case – quality of clinical *diagnosis* and quality of *treatment*, may differ, and may not be readily observable by the patient. Indeed, patients may be referred for any number of reasons. Coulter *et al* (1989) described the different reasons a GP may have for making a referral: to establish the diagnosis; for treatment or an operation; for a specified test/investigation which the GP cannot order; for advice on management; for a specialist to take over management; for reassurance for the GP/second opinion; or for reassurance for the patient and/or their family.

A further element of complexity is added when one considers that the likelihood of being referred by a GP – and therefore which patients are being offered choice – is known to vary considerably between GPs. The explanation for these variations in GP referral rates remains unknown (BMA 2009). Further, surgical intervention rates also vary across the country, so the probability of being deemed to require treatment after referral also varies across providers, in ways that are, similarly, not well understood – and which it is impossible for patients to judge. Uncertainty regarding the appropriateness of treatment, both on the part of referrers and providers, further compounds the uncertainty facing patients.

Uncertainty over the *relevance* of the information provided. Patients selecting a provider at the point of referral may be contemplating the possibility of requiring surgery or some other invasive treatment. However, for many patients, the referral may simply be for an outpatient consultation. Patients state that they regard information relating to the clinical quality of the individual consultant as being most important (Burge *et al* 2006). But information is generally not available at that level of disaggregation, and patients are not certain whether they will be treated by the consultant or another member of their clinical team.

Patients therefore face uncertainty about the extent to which the 'average' quality of the hospital, signalled through official information on hospital performance, reflects underlying variations between clinical departments and individual clinicians. Indeed, this 'aggregation problem' is even more pronounced in reality, as the data (eg, on waiting times) shown for each hospital on the NHS Choices website is generally the average for that NHS trust, which comprises multiple hospitals. Attributing these trust-level indicators to each of its constituent hospitals conveys a spurious degree of precision.

These findings support the scepticism about patient choice expressed by Callahan (2008) who, discussing the role of 'consumer-directed health care' in the United States, argues that the fundamental question is 'whether thinking of the patient as a savvy consumer could ever make full sense in the face of complicated, emotionally charged illnesses and complex decision-making situations' (p 301).

'Quasi-markets' and the role of patient choice

The context within which patients choose, the choices available to them, and how they choose, are closely linked to the specific arrangements that exist for funding and providing health care in each country. There are a number of features that particularly affect patient choice.

- First, and most obviously, the prevalence of third-party funding (via insurance or taxation) means that price will often not be the key influence on consumer choice that it is in other markets. Indeed, patients in the NHS do not face any price signals when seeking hospital care.

- Second, regulation often restricts (either directly or indirectly) consumer choice. For example, professional regulation via the General Medical Council (GMC) prevents unregistered or unqualified doctors from practising. Similarly, registration requirements set by the Care Quality Commission (CQC) restrict entry to the health and social care market to organisations that have met minimum quality and safety standards. Such restrictions on supply are justified as a consequence of the informational asymmetry between health care consumers and suppliers noted in the box on page 10.

- Third, government involvement in the provision of care can restrict the diversity of providers from which consumers can choose. Where the government's role extends beyond funding health care to direct provision (via government-owned and operated health care clinics and hospitals), this has tended to be (rather than being *necessarily*) associated with a 'one size fits all' approach to health care delivery. It also limits the likelihood that providers will be allowed to fail given the political costs of doing so, thereby weakening the impact of choice.

- Fourth, the role of regional agencies in strategic planning may also affect choice by limiting the range of services on offer in a particular area. Clinical-based networks such as those for cancer care may also result in particular configurations of services and limited availability of specialist services in some areas.

Neither public financing nor public provision, together or alone, preclude choice being offered. Indeed, patients have always had some degree of choice in the NHS, pre-dating the current patient choice policies – and constraints on choice are not unique to non-market health care systems (Appleby *et al* 2003).

Policies to increase patient choice can be traced back to the 1980s, and the growing interest in finding ways to combine the pursuit of equity goals, via the collective financing of health care, with competition in supply. It is argued that a greater 'mix' in health care provision promotes competition between providers, mimicking the discipline imposed by market forces in private markets. The use of these 'quasi-market' approaches is evident in health care reforms across a wide range of countries (Le Grand and Bartlett 1993; Jacobs 1998).

In the early 1990s, heavily influenced by the ideas of managed competition put forward by Alain Enthoven (Enthoven and Kronick 1989), the Conservative government introduced the 'internal' market into the NHS (Department of Health 1989). Enthoven's ideas have not only been influential in the NHS, where they led to the introduction of the internal or quasi-market and the separation of purchasers and providers, but also in social health insurance systems, such as in the Netherlands, where the focus was on extending choice of public health insurers (Enthoven and van de Ven 2007). In these countries, there was already a diversity of supply and patient choice of provider – at least in theory (Thomson and Dixon 2006).

However, quasi-market reforms do not always involve or rely on more choices for patients to create incentives for providers. For example, New Zealand's 'purchaser–provider split' reforms in the mid-1990s introduced supply-side competition between public hospitals. But competition in that context entailed hospitals competing for contracts from the (then) budget holder, the Health Funding Authority (Devlin *et al* 2001). Patient choice was not a primary goal of these reforms, and patients did not get more choice as a result of them. Similarly, the 'GP fundholding' policy reform in the NHS in the 1990s entailed GPs acting as NHS budget holders and using their role as purchasers to encourage competition between providers. Notwithstanding the rhetoric surrounding this reform, it did not in itself create any change in the choices available to patients using NHS services (Le Grand 2009).

Around the same time, policies were developed in a number of Scandinavian countries to strengthen the role of choice of provider. Denmark and Sweden led the way, strengthening the right of patients who were waiting for care to access treatment in other county councils. These policies were influential in the development of patient choice policy in England since 2000.

Empirical evidence

In this section, we provide a brief overview of the empirical evidence relating to patient choices and provider responses.

Isolating the effect of patient choice on provider behaviour and performance is confounded by other factors in the health system and policies associated with patient choice – not least how health care is funded, and how health care providers are reimbursed. As noted above, patient choice tends to be coupled with hospital competition – but hospital competition is not always coupled with increased patient choice. Payer-driven competition and patient-driven competition are difficult to distinguish and have often been confused by policy-makers (Propper *et al* 2006). While a range of studies have linked the degree of competition or contestability in the market for hospital services to the technical efficiency of providers, the greater challenge is to identify within this the distinctive role that patient choice may play.

The evidence has been grouped under a number of key questions, which we consider in our evaluation of patient choice.

How do patients experience choice?

In an analysis of data from the *British Social Attitudes* survey, Appleby and Phillips (2009) found that about three-quarters of respondents thought that patients should have a say over which hospital to go to if they need treatment. Only 19 per cent felt that patients actually have a say. However, in an earlier review, Fotaki *et al* (2005) conclude that compared with other aspects of health care, having a choice of provider is *not* a top priority for NHS patients.

Other research has also found that patients are positive about the opportunity to have a choice giving them an opportunity to question the GP and highlight their preferences, particularly if they were dissatisfied with the previous experience of the provider (Barnett *et al* 2008). However, patients were equally clear, particularly when faced with a more serious decision, that they did not always value having to make a choice and would rather rely on the expertise of their GP. In order to be meaningful, choice needed to be supported with information.

In England, there have been a number of studies of pilot projects, including choice for cardiac patients (Le Maistre *et al* 2003), choice for patients waiting for elective surgery in London (Dawson *et al* 2004; Burge *et al* 2005; Coulter *et al* 2005; Ferlie *et al* 2005), and choice at the point of referral (Taylor *et al* 2004). These include information on the level of uptake by different groups of patients.

In London, where patients on waiting lists were offered quicker treatment at an alternative provider, 82 per cent of respondents were willing to consider going to an alternative hospital; only 18 per cent were not willing to consider this under any circumstances. Two-thirds of those offered an alternative hospital took this opportunity.

There was no evidence of inequalities in uptake by social class, educational attainment, income or ethnicity. However, those in paid employment were more likely to opt for an alternative than those who were not (Coulter *et al* 2005). It is important to note that when this scheme was implemented, patients were supported by a patient choice adviser and were provided with free transport. Other research has suggested that these factors were particularly important for patients who were more vulnerable or socially excluded (Barber and Gordon-Dseagu 2003). There was also no financial or other penalty for the hospital 'losing' the patients as per case reimbursement was not in place, although the hospital 'gaining' the patient was reimbursed and waiting times were long so the hospital that lost patients benefited from reduced waiting lists.

Further insights into the extent to which choice is equitable are provided by studies that employ a discrete choice experiment design (similar to that employed in this study and described in Appendix A). Burge *et al* (2004) show that patients who consistently chose their local hospital over other alternatives (regardless of quality) were more likely to be older, to have left formal education before the age of 16, and to have lower incomes. Further, patients in richer households put a greater negative value on the poor reputation of a hospital than those from lower-income households. The authors suggest that:

> ... *[when] patient choice is offered, and information on reputation is available, all other things being equal, richer patients will migrate to hospitals with better reputations in greater numbers than poorer patients.*
>
> (Burge *et al* 2004, p 193)

These issues were explored in greater detail in Burge *et al* (2006). The conclusions were similar: those without formal educational qualifications placed significantly less weight on increases in clinical quality above an 'average' level, compared to those with higher levels of education. Certain patient characteristics – having poor health, being reliant on bus transport – were associated with greater loyalty to the local hospital; whereas those with internet access and a poor perception of the local hospital were more likely to attend a non-local hospital.

What factors are important to patients when choosing between providers?

As we noted earlier, location is likely to be a key factor in choice of health care provider. However, a review of health system reforms published by the Audit Commission and Healthcare Commission (2008), *Is the Treatment Working?*, looked at trends in the Department of Health monitoring surveys and noted that location has become less important while aspects of quality have become increasingly important to patients when choosing hospitals. This may partly be accounted for by a change in the method used for eliciting preferences.

In the survey of patients offered a choice as part of the London Patient Choice Project pilot, more than 70 per cent of respondents rated the following as very important: high success rates for operation; high standard of cleanliness; good communication between hospitals and GP; reputation of surgeon; follow-up care close to home; and the hospital's reputation (Coulter *et al* 2005). Shorter waiting times were very important to 65 per cent of respondents, while only 37 per cent said 'being not too far from home' was very important.

There is a body of empirical evidence on patients' stated preferences – that is, when considering hypothetical choices between hospitals – for example, see Ryan *et al* 2000 and Burge *et al* (2004). In a study of patient choice in the NHS using a discrete choice experiment, Burge *et al* (2004) found that 30 per cent of respondents consistently chose their 'current' (local) NHS hospital over any alternative, regardless of the attractiveness of the alternative hospitals in terms of waiting time, travel time and quality. The perceived 'reputation' of the alternatives (framed in terms of being better, the same, or worse than the patient's reference point – their local hospital) was a key influence on choice. In Burge *et al* (2006), which looked at patients' stated preferences when offered a choice of provider at the point of referral, a smaller proportion (20 per cent) consistently chose their local hospital. This study also considered the role of GP advice, and found that while GP advice is important, its effect is asymmetric. A recommendation against a particular hospital is likely to have more impact on a patient's choice than a positive recommendation in favour of a given option.

A recent study by Lim and Edlin (2009) examined the choices made by older people with respect to the time and location of surgical treatment for cataracts. The strongest determinant of whether or not to accept treatment was whether a consultant performs the operation. In this case, the preference for a consultant might be taken as a proxy for the expertise and quality of clinical care. The majority of the sample selected the nearest treatment centre available. However, travel times and waiting times also exerted a significant effect on choices.

Evidence is also available from studies of *revealed* preferences – that is, where 'real' patient choices have been observed, in a number of countries (eg, Imerman *et al* 2006; Gauthier and Wane 2008). Geographic distance and quality are key variables explored in empirical studies of patient choice of hospitals (eg, Tay 2003; Varkevisser and van der Geest 2007; Fabri and Robone 2009; Varkevisser *et al* 2010). Many of these studies focus on the identification of factors that lead to 'bypassing behaviour' – where patients explicitly choose to bypass their local hospital in favour of another (eg, Leonard *et al* 2002; Escarce and Kapur 2009) or on the factors that explain the choice between private and public facilities (eg, Hanson *et al* 2004).

In summary, the evidence suggests that most patients will consider their local hospital as the leading candidate (the 'default'), but will bypass that hospital where the additional travel costs are outweighed by improvements in quality. Broadly defined, these might include reputational, objective or 'proxy' evidence on better clinical quality, and other attributes such as shorter waiting times.

How do GPs support choice?

The introduction of patient choice has also been associated with efforts to improve the measurement and publication of hospital performance data. The availability of this information aims to inform choice, to overcome asymmetries of information between patients and hospitals, and to drive up quality. However, much of the evidence suggests that patients continue to rely on GPs to advise them or make decisions on their behalf and make little use of this information directly.

The publication of this data appears to have other effects on providers, regardless of their use by consumers. A number of studies have examined the effect of 'consumer reports' or 'report cards' used in the United States for over a decade to provide information on the performance of hospitals and doctors. Marshall *et al* (2000) report that, notwithstanding consumers' apparent lack of interest and trust in the data, there was evidence that providers nevertheless do respond to the publication of performance data by attempting to improve performance. A more recent systematic review found similar results (Fung *et al* 2008). Hibbard *et al* (2003) conclude that provider responses to the publication of performance information – regardless of whether patients act on the information – arise because of concerns about public image and reputation, rather than market share. Overall, it appears that the publication of hospital performance data stimulates quality improvement by hospitals, but not necessarily via the mechanism of patient choice (Shekelle *et al* 2008). Most of the studies in these reviews, however, are from the United States, and to date there has been little empirical research to measure the effects of public reporting in the UK context.

Although more performance data is available, it appears that this is not used by GPs either. In a study based on focus groups with GPs about their attitudes to offering choice, GPs were found to use a combination of 'soft' knowledge about providers with 'hard' published data to advise patients. Generally, GPs were found to be sceptical about official information sources (Rosen *et al* 2007). While GPs recognised the value of patient choice advisers, they were worried about the cost of these and of support centres.

What is the response of providers to choice?

In a review of the theoretical and empirical evidence on choice in health care, Propper *et al* (2006, p 537) conclude that 'there is neither strong theoretical nor empirical support for competition', while noting that there are cases where competition has led to improved outcomes. Most of the literature that examines the relationship between hospital competition and quality comes from the United States and has been reviewed elsewhere (see Propper *et al* 2006 or Cooper *et al* 2009b).

Gowrisankaran (2008) reviews the evidence on the extent to which competition between hospitals for patient demand will increase quality. In the presence of third-party funding, the outcome is argued to depend on the way the third-party funder reimburses the provider. For example, the impact on quality will vary depending on whether the market is one where prices are fixed (such as under Medicare, and under Payment by Results in the NHS) or one where hospitals with higher quality can charge higher prices. Fotaki *et al* (2005), reviewing the impact of choice on efficiency, note that there are very few studies that specifically address the impact of choice on efficiency – and that the wider evidence examining the effect of competition on efficiency is less than conclusive.

Other reviews have reached different conclusions on the theoretical and empirical evidence on choice in health care. For example, Gaynor (2006) finds that the trend emerging from the more recent work on competition and quality is that under fixed-price competition, higher levels of competition generally lead to improvements in clinical performance, so long as the reimbursement price covers the marginal cost. Recent empirical work supports this (Cooper *et al* 2009a).

Earlier empirical studies of the 'first' internal market in the NHS (1991–1997), which examined the impact of competition on quality, found that under variable prices, higher competition was associated with higher mortality (Propper *et al* 2004; Propper *et al* 2008). The mechanism by which competition leads to improved quality is not clear, but recent research has found that competition can lead to improvements in hospital management, which in turn appear to be associated with higher quality (Bloom *et al* 2009).

Several empirical studies have examined the impact of patient choice on waiting times for treatment, using the 'pseudo experimental' conditions surrounding the introduction of patient choice initiatives within the NHS. Dawson *et al* (2007) and Siciliani and Martin (2007), using different methodologies and variables, all conclude that the introduction of patient choice was associated with a significant reduction in waiting times for NHS treatment. Siciliani and Martin (2007) do not measure patient choice directly, but rather use as a proxy, measures of the degree of competition such as the Hirschman–Herfindahl index.

In contrast, Dawson *et al* (2007) use a 'difference in difference' approach, which arguably identifies the effect of patient choice per se more specifically. Their findings include not only a significant link between choice and reduced waiting times, but also a convergence of waiting times across competing providers (in the case of the London Patient Choice Project, which was the focus of that study, within the London area). Cooper *et al* (2009b) analysed changes in waiting times between 1997 and 2007 (ie, before and after the introduction of patient choice). They found that variation in waiting times by socioeconomic groups had reduced during this period. However, as a number of reforms and initiatives were introduced during this period aimed at reducing waiting times, it is difficult to isolate the impact of choice on reducing the differential waiting times for different population groups.

A complication with interpreting improvements in quality arising from patient choice (such as shorter waiting times) as 'welfare improving' is that the same outcome may be achieved by providers either managing existing resources more (technically) efficiently or spending more money on elective surgery, or some combination of both. There is evidence that meeting targets for NHS waiting times was associated (in part) with increased spending on elective surgery. If shorter waiting times arising from patient choice or other initiatives have been achieved at least in part by diverting resources from other NHS activities, the benefits need to be weighed up alongside the opportunity costs (of unknown magnitude) in terms of health outcomes forgone elsewhere.

There are a number of pathways by which quality information may have an impact on providers and lead to improvement (Berwick *et al* 2003). Where patients drive improvements by using measures to make choices between providers, incentivising providers to improve quality so as to attract patients (and therefore income) has been called the 'selection pathway'. As outlined above, research on the publication of comparative performance information suggests this has an impact on providers through the 'reputation pathway' – that is, where the publication of quality measures comparing performance between individuals, teams and organisations drives change through a desire to protect or improve reputations relative to others. Finally, there is a 'change pathway', where quality measures act on the intrinsic professional motivation of clinicians and organisations to improve where they see potential for improvement. We are interested in the role that patient choice plays in motivating service improvements.

Discussion

In this section we describe, on the basis of the theoretical and empirical literature reviewed above, a number of issues that will be considered as we seek to answer our major research questions.

- How do patients experience choice?
- What factors are important to patients when choosing between providers in practice?
- How do GPs support choice?
- What is the response of providers to choice?

How do patients experience choice?

Decision theory would suggest that when presented with a greater number of hospitals to choose from, and more information on each, patients consider fewer of the alternatives and assess less of the available information. The shift from the five providers initially offered to patients to 'free choice' means that we might expect patients to be 'overloaded' by the number of options and information available.

There is some mixed evidence on the impact of choice on equity, as well as the extent to which different patients are offered choice and are able to exercise it, particularly in an environment where support is limited and transport costs are borne by the patients. We might expect that patients from poorer backgrounds and with lower education levels will be less likely to be offered choice and less able to exercise choice and travel to a more distant provider.

What factors are important to patients when choosing between providers in practice?

To the extent that hospital treatment is a 'reputation good', we might expect patients to rely more on reputational, qualitative evidence than on objective performance indicators.

Decision theory suggests that the assessment of quality will be affected by what patients take as their 'reference point' – that is, the quality of available alternatives may be influenced by whether these are viewed as gains or losses relative to the perceived quality of their 'default' (local) hospital. We might expect patients' views on the quality of their local hospital to be important in understanding the likelihood of their actively deciding to 'bypass' it in favour of another alternative.

There is some evidence to suggest that, as waiting times have become shorter, this issue is now less important to patients and other issues such as quality are becoming increasingly important. We might expect to find that patients are willing to travel further in order to access a higher-quality provider.

How do GPs support choice?

Decision theory suggests that the way in which information on the available options is presented to patients will, *in itself*, have a very important impact on the way in which patients choose. The decisions patients make are not neutral to the way information is reported to them and the way choices are conveyed. We would therefore expect the way in which the policy has been operationalised *in practice*, and how choice has been actually experienced by the patient, to have an impact on the choices they make. Further, how patients exercise choice may depend on what information is presented on the available options, and how it is presented.

In particular, given that the setting for choice is the GP referral, it will be important to understand the nature of the agency relationship between the GP and patient and how this influences the choice of provider at the point of referral. We would expect GPs' attitudes towards choice, and the extent to which GPs offer choice consistently, to affect how patients experience choice.

What is the response of providers to choice?

Theory would suggest that the choices patients make send a signal to providers that can provoke actions by hospitals – for example, to improve the quality of their services. So, in theory, and as with private markets, the aggregate actions of patients should lead to a continuous process of responses by providers as they react to losses in custom (and hence income) by investigating the reasons for such losses and responding appropriately. Providers may also respond in ways that improve quality or other aspects of care, or the patient experience, on an anticipatory basis – that is, providers do not have to experience actual losses in order to respond, but react to defend/maintain income believed to be potentially under threat from choices patients may make.

We would expect that where patient choice is in operation, providers would be monitoring referrals, and where patients were choosing other providers they would investigate the reasons and put in place service improvements in order to attract patients back. Where patients are not actually switching provider, we might expect to find providers anticipating patients' preferences and changing services in line with these preferences. However, an alternative response would be for providers to seek to avoid the pressure of competition brought about by the introduction of patient choice by reaching agreements or understandings not to compete (in other words, colluding).

In the following sections, we present our empirical findings, before, in the final section, returning to discuss some of the issues highlighted in a brief review of the theoretical and empirical literature.

2 Awareness, understanding and opinions of patient choice

Before presenting the empirical findings concerning how choice is operating, the extent to which it is driving competition, and the impact choice is having on providers, we begin by analysing the views of patients, GPs and hospital providers about the policy itself. The views and actions of those involved in the implementation of policy have been shown to be critical in whether a policy achieves its desired impact (Lipsky 1983). If those responsible for implementing patient choice (GPs) or responding to the incentives it creates (hospitals) do not understand the policy and its objectives, it is unlikely that it will have the desired effect. A lack of impact may not necessarily be due to the design of the policy but rather the way in which it is interpreted and implemented locally.

In addition, we were interested in the level of awareness and understanding among patients of the choices available to them. Patients are central to the policy, and their awareness of it and reaction to it are also likely to shape its operation. Recent policy developments to create a right to choose (HM Government 2009, Department of Health 2009b) suggest that in future, the onus will be on the patient to demand more choice.

In this section, we examine the understanding of the patient choice policy among hospitals and GPs, awareness of choice among patients, and the opinions and attitudes towards choice among all three groups.

How aware are patients of their ability to choose?

We asked patients whether they were aware of their ability to choose before they saw their GP. In particular, we asked if they were aware of the ability to choose a provider in the private sector, and how important they think having a choice of hospital is.

Among our survey respondents, slightly less than half (45 per cent) knew they had a choice of hospital before visiting their GP. This is consistent with data from the Department of Health monitoring survey, which shows that about half of patients are aware of choice (this has risen from 29 per cent in May/June 2006, *see* Figure 5 overleaf) (Department of Health 2009a). Less than 20 per cent of respondents who were referred to an NHS provider were aware that they could choose to have NHS treatment in a private sector hospital, compared with 41 per cent among those who were referred to an independent sector treatment centre (ISTC) (*see* Table 3 on page 28).

Table 1, overleaf, shows the results of bivariate analysis of the relationship between demographic characteristics and awareness of choice. Differences by employment status and by age were statistically significant. About half of those looking after their family or dependants at home and retired were aware of choice compared with two in five of those in paid work (41 per cent). Fifty-one per cent of older respondents (aged 66–80) were aware that choice was available before visiting their GP compared with just 31 per cent of those aged 16–35. There were no significant differences in awareness by gender, ethnicity or level of education.

Figure 5 Awareness of choice and offer of choice (May/June 2006 to March 2009)

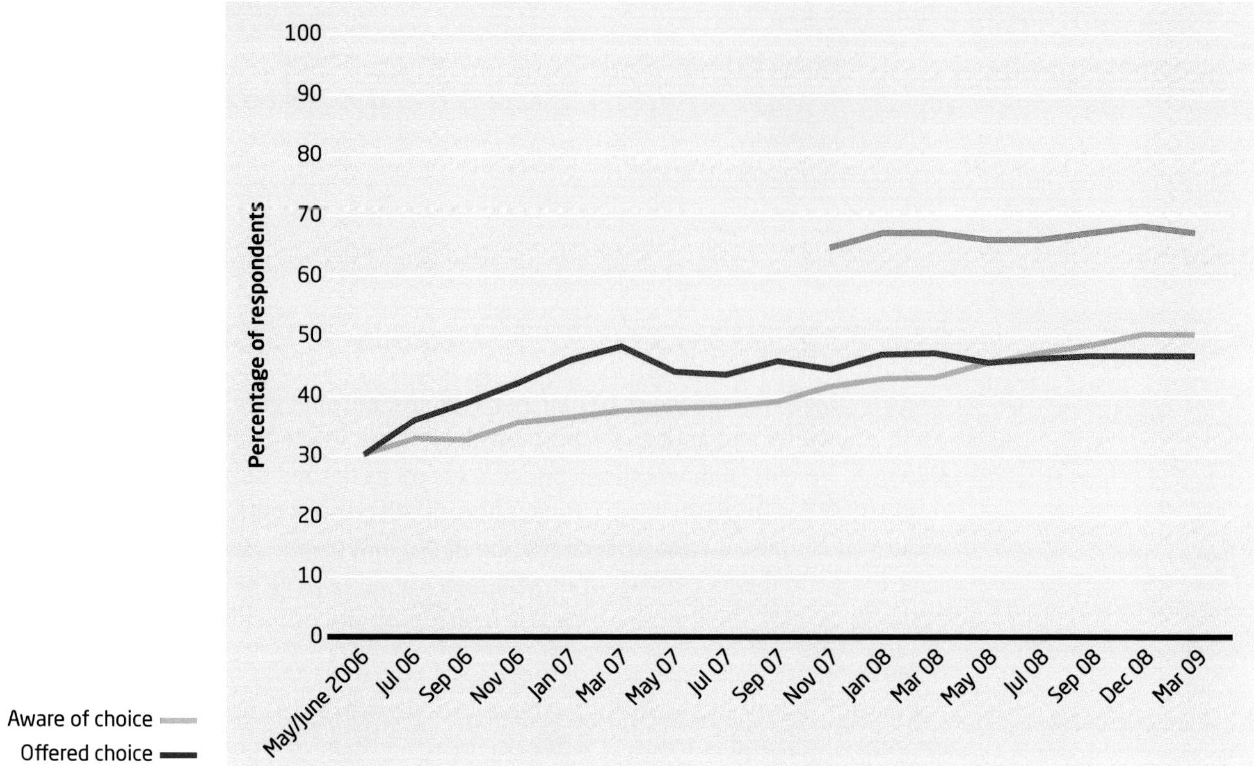

Aware of choice ▬
Offered choice ▬
Able to go ▬
where wanted

Source: Department of Health (2009a)

Table 1 Awareness of choice by patient characteristics

Before you visited the GP, did you know you now have a choice of hospital?		Percentage (number) patients answering yes	Percentage (number) answering no
Gender	Male	44 (407)	56 (520)
	Female	47 (574)	54 (660)
	Total	**45 (981)**	**55 (1,180)**
Ethnicity	White background	46 (901)	54 (1,039)
	Mixed and non-white background	40 (67)	60 (102)
	Total	**46 (968)**	**54 (1,141)**
Age group**	16–35	31 (70)	69 (156)
	36–50	44 (210)	56 (263)
	51–65	46 (323)	54 (381)
	66–80	51 (307)	49 (294)
	81 and over	45 (71)	55 (86)
	Total	**45 (981)**	**55 (1,180)**
Level of education	No formal qualifications	42 (285)	58 (392)
	GCSE/O level/A level or equivalent	45 (268)	55 (330)
	Professional qualification below degree level	49 (103)	51 (108)
	Degree level, equivalent or higher degree	50 (154)	50 (153)
	Other	50 (16)	50 (16)
	Total	**45 (826)**	**55 (999)**
Employment status**	In paid work	41 (304)	59 (436)
	Unemployed	40 (30)	61 (46)
	Retired from paid work	51 (416)	50 (408)
	Unable to work because of disability or ill health	42 (80)	59 (113)
	Looking after family, home or dependants	49 (43)	51 (45)
	In full-time education, including government training programmes	40 (8)	60 (12)
	Other	38 (13)	62 (21)
	Total	**45 (894)**	**55 (1,081)**

** Differences in awareness of choice significant at 1 per cent level using χ^2 test.

When awareness of choice was modelled using binary logistic regression to control for other factors (*see* Table 2 below), respondents' level of education became a significant predictor of awareness, with those holding a university degree more likely to be aware of choice than those with no formal qualifications. Older people, particularly those aged 66–80, were more likely to be aware of choice than younger respondents, and men more so than women. Respondents living in small towns, villages or rural areas were more likely to be aware of choice, and those living in PCT C were less likely to be aware of choice, although both of these location-related factors were no longer significant when the data was weighted to compensate for the over-sampling from the ISTCs in PCT A and D (*see* Appendix A). Respondents who attended ISTCs were more likely to be aware of their right to choose and to be treated in privately run hospitals than respondents who attended NHS-run trusts (*see* Table 3 overleaf).

We also asked patients whether they had heard or seen an advert for hospitals or about choice (*see* Table 4 overleaf). Nearly 30 per cent of patients had heard or seen an advert for private sector hospitals in their area compared with just one in 10 for NHS hospitals. More people reported seeing adverts for Choose and Book (18 per cent) than for NHS Choices (10 per cent), although it is the latter where patients can get information to support choice of hospital.

Table 2 Binary logistic regression model of awareness of choice before visiting the GP

Variable	(Comparison group) Response category	Odds ratio	Significance	Lower 95% CI	Upper 95% CI	Interpretation
Age group:	(16-35)					Those aged over 50, particularly those aged over 65 were significantly more likely to be aware of their right to choose than younger respondents aged 16-35.
	36-50	1.45	0.19	0.83	2.51	
	51-65*	1.87	0.02	1.10	3.17	
	66-80**	3.08	0.00	1.80	5.27	
	81+**	2.84	0.00	1.46	5.51	
Gender:	(Female)					Men were significantly more aware of their right to choose than women.
	Male*	1.33	0.03	1.04	1.72	
Urban/rural:	(City/large town/suburbs)					Those who lived in small towns, villages and rural settings were significantly more likely to be aware of their right to choose than those living in cities, large towns or suburbs.
	Small town**	1.51	0.01	1.11	2.06	
	Village/rural**	1.56	0.01	1.11	2.20	
Education:	(No formal qualifications)					Those with degree-level qualifications were significantly more likely to be aware of their right to choose than respondents with no formal qualifications.
	Below degree level	1.22	0.19	0.91	1.63	
	Degree level and higher**	1.91	0.00	1.33	2.75	
Resident PCT:	(Any other PCT)					Respondents who lived in PCT C were significantly less likely to be aware of their right to choose than those who lived in PCTs that were not case study areas for the research.
	PCT A	1.26	0.36	0.77	2.07	
	PCT B	0.98	0.94	0.57	1.68	
	PCT C**	0.53	0.00	0.36	0.79	
	PCT D	0.68	0.08	0.45	1.04	
Constant		0.08	0.00			

Note: Dependent variable: recall that choice was offered. Other variables included in the model were: age group; ethnicity (white and mixed/non-white); level of education; gender; EQ-VAS self-rated health status; PCT of residence; frequency of GP attendance; urban/rural. Employment status was not included in this regression due to colinearity with the age group variable. Analysis was conducted on unweighted data. Where there are significant differences in results from the weighted data, these have been highlighted in the text.

** significant at 1 per cent level

* significant at 5 per cent level

Table 3 Awareness of choice and private sector options for NHS and ISTC patients

		NHS respondents Percentage (number)		ISTC respondents Percentage (number)		Total	
Before you visited the GP did you know you now have a choice of hospital?*	Yes	45	(883)	53	(98)	45	(981)
	No	55	(1,094)	47	(86)	55	(1,180)
	Total	100	(1,977)	100	(184)		(2,161)
							(missing = 20)
Before you visited the GP did you know that you can now choose to have NHS treatment in a privately run hospital?**	Yes	17	(341)	41	(76)	19	(417)
	No	83	(1,641)	59	(108)	81	(1,749)
	Total	100	(1,982)	100	(184)		(2,166)
							(missing = 15)

** χ^2 test showed differences were significant at 1 per cent level.

* χ^2 test showed differences were significant at 5 per cent level.

Table 4 Patients' awareness of advertising related to choice

Have you ever heard or seen an advert for the following:	Percentage	Frequency (total valid responses)
The hospital you are attending	12	246 (n = 2039)
Other NHS hospitals in your area	11	211 (n = 1917)
Other private sector hospitals in your area	29	551 (n = 1921)
Patient choice	16	302 (n = 1895)
Choose and Book	18	341 (n = 1900)
NHS Choices website	10	188 (n = 1832)

When we spoke to some of the patients who had completed the questionnaire, we found that even if they were not formally offered choice, they were aware that they could have asked to go elsewhere if they had wanted to. Awareness of the ability to choose appeared to be greater among people who had frequent contact with the NHS, which supports the results of the quantitative analysis.

I've got a choice of hospitals if I want it. I'm pretty sure anyway if I said I'd wanted to go to another one he would have arranged it for me.

(Female patient, age 25, area B)

I still had the option of going to any hospital in the local area but clearly, at that time, my mind was frankly made up – I knew where I wanted to go.

(Female patient, age 78, area D)

Patients who were aware of their right to choose had generally either previously experienced a referral for which they were offered a choice, had seen information in GP waiting rooms and hospital literature about choice, or had read about it in the press.

I've seen it [adverts for patient choice] in the leaflets that they send in magazines that I get from the hospital and I read about it in there.

(Female patient, age 63, area B)

I tend to read the better type kind of newspaper so it's just one of these things you do know, you pick up on.

(Male patient, age 59, area C)

In contrast, the impression given by most of the GPs we interviewed was that patient awareness of the government's choice programme prior to a referral was very limited. Most practices appeared to make some attempt to raise awareness through posters and leaflets in the waiting room, although the value of these was questioned when there is often so much other information on display. But, in most cases, patients were considered to be generally ill informed about the choices available until GPs drew their attention to them at the point of referral.

> *They haven't got the foggiest idea.* (GP, area B)

> *When I mention it to people they're always surprised, they're not aware that they have a right to choose.*
> (GP, area C)

> *I mean, most patients, when you say 'right, at this point, we've now got to discuss choice...', they haven't a clue, haven't heard of it... don't really sort of fully understand what it's all about.*
> (GP, area A)

GPs thought that if there was awareness of choice, it tended to be among younger and more socially advantaged groups.

> *Well, it's probably helpful for the sort of* Guardian-*reading middle classes.*
> (GP, area B)

> *I think some of your sort of younger professionals may have explored it and may be more aware.*
> (GP, area B)

> *The people who are likely to sort of know anything about choice, they do tend to be the middle-class educated...* The Times *and* The Telegraph, Guardian-*type readers... and they're more likely to be internet users.*
> (GP, area A)

PCTs have been tasked with the implementation of patient choice, including raising awareness of choice locally and providing information to help patients choose (Department of Health 2009d). Activities by PCTs to promote awareness of choice among patients varied across our four case study areas.

PCT B had actively promoted awareness of patient choice to their population in a local campaign that included adverts on buses, on the radio and in leaflets and posters. They were about to start a new campaign based on a one-minute animated film to be shown in GP surgeries.

> *[PCT B] have been much more proactive, they've had advertisements on buses around choice and things like that... I don't think that the two local PCTs have done as much.*
> (NHS provider, area B)

Other PCTs have been less active in promoting choice to the general population, except via nationally produced material in GP surgeries.

Surprisingly, survey data shows that awareness levels were no higher where a public advertising campaign had taken place (PCT B); they were highest in PCT A, one of the areas with a less active approach to promoting awareness of their right to choose (*see* Table 5 overleaf).

Table 5 Awareness of choice and private sector option by PCT of residence*

	PCT A	PCT B	PCT C	PCT D
	Percentage (number) patients answering yes			
Before you visited your GP, did you know that you now have a choice of hospitals that you can go to for your first hospital appointment?	61 (90)	43 (59)	39 (133)	49 (121)
Before visiting the GP, did you know that you can choose to have NHS treatment in a private sector hospital?	25 (36)	18 (24)	15 (50)	20 (49)

* Results are the percentage of patients resident within each case study PCT. Patients resident outside of the PCT were excluded.

Even though the data shows that about half of patients were aware of choice before going to their GP, the perception of GPs was that most people are not aware of choice. Awareness appeared to be higher among groups of patients who are in more frequent contact with the NHS such as the elderly, again, in contrast to GPs' perceptions that younger patients were more likely to know about choice. More educated patients also appeared more likely to be aware of their right to choose, as were those attending ISTCs. Despite the fact that PCTs are responsible for promoting awareness of patient choice, only one of the four PCTs in our case study areas had invested in local public advertising campaigns. Somewhat surprisingly, awareness levels among patients were higher in an area where the PCT had been less active in promoting choice. However, this PCT was active in performance managing and promoting Choose and Book.

How important is choice to patients?

Patients' attitudes to choice were established by asking how important they thought it was to be offered a choice. Three-quarters of patients (75 per cent) said that being offered a choice was either important or very important to them. It is possible that patients who felt choice was important were more likely to return the questionnaire and, therefore, these figures may overestimate the importance of choice. When a sample of patients were interviewed about their responses, they were generally enthusiastic about their right to choose, but also expressed some reservations.

> *Yes. I think it's important to have the choice. Well, a lot of people think it's very important. I think it's fairly important but, really… If you're going to a GP, they're the ones who know the people. You've got to take advice.*
>
> (Female patient, age 55, area D)

> *I think it's nice to have [a choice]. If everything else was equal, then no, it doesn't matter about the choice. But unfortunately things aren't equal and therefore it's nice to have that choice if the circumstances allow it.*
>
> (Male patient, age 58, area A)

> *Is it important to you to be offered a choice of hospital? Did you want a choice? No… Well, as far as I'm concerned… I've paid my National Insurance contributions, there are hospitals that do jobs and if I need a job doing I'll go where they send me.*
>
> (Male patient, age 61, area A)

Differences in the importance given to choice by level of education, ethnicity, gender, employment status and type of hospital are significant (*see* Table 6 below). While 79 per cent of those with no qualifications said that choice was important or very important, only 67 per cent of those with degree-level or higher qualifications thought so. More women than men (79 per cent vs 70 per cent), more of those being seen at an ISTC than at an NHS provider (89 per cent vs 74 per cent) and more people from mixed or non-white backgrounds than white (85 per cent vs 74 per cent) thought that choice was either important or very important.

Table 6 The importance of being offered a choice of hospital by demographics, type of hospital attended and PCT of residence

How important to you is being offered a choice of hospital?		Important or very important (% (number))	Somewhat important (% (number))	Of little importance or unimportant (% (number))
All respondents		75 (1,623)	14 (293)	11 (246)
Age group	16-35	68 (154)	20 (45)	12 (27)
	36-50	73 (347)	14 (66)	12 (58)
	51-65	76 (535)	13 (94)	11 (78)
	66-80	79 (473)	11 (65)	11 (64)
	81 and over	73 (114)	15 (23)	12 (19)
Level of education**	No formal qualifications	79 (532)	10 (68)	12 (78)
	Qualifications below degree level	74 (602)	15 (123)	10 (84)
	Degree-level or higher qualifications	67 (209)	18 (57)	15 (45)
Ethnicity**	White background	74 (1,442)	15 (272)	12 (229)
	Mixed/non-white background	85 (144)	8 (13)	7 (12)
Gender**	Male	70 (645)	16 (145)	15 (138)
	Female	79 (978)	12 (148)	9 (108)
Employment status **	In paid work	71 (526)	16 (115)	13 (98)
	Unemployed	78 (59)	12 (9)	11 (8)
	Retired from paid work	76 (627)	13 (103)	12 (96)
	Unable to work because of disability or ill health	83 (160)	10 (20)	7 (13)
	Looking after family, home or dependants	79 (70)	15 (13)	7 (6)
	In full-time education, including government training programmes	55 (11)	40 (8)	5 (1)
	Other	71 (24)	18 (6)	12 (4)
Type of hospital**	NHS	74 (1,460)	14 (279)	12 (239)
	ISTC	89 (163)	8 (14)	4 (7)
PCT of residence	PCT A	84 (122)	11 (16)	6 (8)
	PCT B	75 (102)	12 (16)	13 (18)
	PCT C	72 (245)	16 (53)	13 (44)
	PCT D	72 (176)	17 (41)	11 (27)
	Other PCT	76 (978)	13 (167)	12 (149)

** Differences in awareness of choice significant at 1 per cent level using χ^2 test.

Note: PCT of residence figures show patients resident within each case study PCT. Responses from those residing outside of the case study PCTs are included in the 'other PCT' category.

Table 7 overleaf shows the results of a binary logistic regression that models the impact of demographic variables and past experience at the local hospital on how important respondents think it is that they have a choice (important vs less important). Here, older respondents (aged 51–80), women, those with no formal qualifications, mixed and non-white respondents, and those with a bad past experience of their local hospital were significantly more likely to rate having a choice as important or very important once other factors were controlled for, largely confirming the findings of the bivariate analysis.

Table 7 Binary logistic regression model of the importance of choice

Variable	(Comparison group) Response category	Odds ratio	Significance	Lower 95% CI	Upper 95% CI	Interpretation
Age group	(16-35)					Respondents aged 51-80
	36-50	1.46	0.07	0.98	2.18	were significantly more likely
	51-65**	1.87	0.00	1.26	2.78	than younger respondents
	66-80**	2.18	0.00	1.43	3.33	(16-35) to think choice is
	81+	1.66	0.08	0.95	2.92	important.
Gender	(Female)					Female respondents were
	Male**	0.53	0.00	0.42	0.67	significantly more likely to think choice is important than men.
Education	(No formal qualifications)					Respondents with no
	Below degree level	0.88	0.35	0.67	1.15	formal qualifications were
	Degree level and higher**	0.61	0.00	0.44	0.85	significantly more likely to think choice is important than those with university degrees.
Ethnicity	(White)					Respondents from a mixed or
	Mixed and non-white**	2.25	0.00	1.32	3.83	non-white background were significantly more likely to think choice is important than white respondents.
Past experience of local hospital	(Generally good)					Respondents who had a
	Generally bad**	2.65	0.01	1.22	5.77	generally bad experience of
	Mixed	1.26	0.11	0.95	1.67	their local hospital were
	No past experience	1.43	0.17	0.86	2.39	significantly more likely to think choice is important than those who had had a good experience.
Constant		2.34	0.00			

Note: Dependent variable: Indicating that choice is important ('important' or 'very important') rather than less important ('somewhat important', 'of little importance' or 'unimportant'). Other variables included in the model were: age group; ethnicity (white and mixed/non-white); level of education; gender; EQ-VAS self-rated health status; PCT of residence; past experience of local hospital; urban/rural.

Employment status was not included in the model due to co-linearity with age group.

** significant at 1 per cent level

When the regression analysis in Table 7 was weighted to compensate for the over-sampling of patients in ISTCs, it made no difference to the variables identified as significant in the model. However, Table 6 shows that ISTC respondents placed significantly more importance on being offered a choice than those attending NHS trusts.

The PCT with the highest awareness of choice was also the area where the highest proportion of patients said that choice was either very important or important (PCT A, 84 per cent). About three-quarters of patients in the other PCTs said they thought choice of hospital was important, similar to the average across all areas (*see* Table 6 on page 31). The differences were not statistically significant, and the importance put on choice by residents in PCT A does not appear to be connected to the implementation strategies used by that PCT, as when controlling for other factors, PCT of residence was not a significant predictor of importance (*see* Table 7 above).

The importance placed on choice by patients contrasted somewhat with the views of GPs, who were, on the whole, sceptical about whether patients really valued choice. Some GPs and providers felt that patients do not really want a choice but instead want a good local service, and want to delegate the decision to someone else. One GP termed this the 'paradox of choice'.

...and if you do surveys to look at whether people... want choice, the majority will say yes. If you put them in the position where a choice needs to be made, the majority actually want somebody to help them just get through the system.

(GP, area D)

If it was my public face I would say patient choice is a marvellous thing because it gives patients a choice. I think most patients don't want a choice you see... I think patients want to be advised of where the best place to go is with that service.

(NHS provider, area C)

Most people aren't interested in having a massive shopping list of different providers.

(GP, area D)

Actually, I think most patients will want to have access to the range of services as close to their home as possible, and every patient, all patients across the country should have the same standard that they achieve... So this shouldn't be a question of patients deciding, 'well, I'll go there because they do that'... They actually want to go to their own hospital.

(NHS provider, area C)

When asked about demand for choice, the overwhelming majority of GPs thought that it was very limited, even among those patients who were familiar with the choice programme. GPs' experience of offering patients a choice was that most wanted to be referred to their nearest local hospital; many failed to understand why they should have to consider other options, and in some cases even found the idea quite amusing.

If you ask about choice they'll look at you as if you're being stupid really. (GP, area B)

Actually, most people where we are, they look at you slightly taken aback when you say... would you like to choose your hospital? They'll say, 'well, no actually, I'll go to [hospital C3 NHS] please because it's our local hospital'.

(GP, area C)

So I tell them that they can choose any hospital in [large metropolitan area] if they want to... and I even joke with them sometimes that if you wanted to, you could go anywhere in the UK... and the patients find that quite funny... The vast majority of the time the answer just comes back as, 'oh, I'll go to [hospital name] or [hospital name] because we've got two local hospitals'.

(GP, area A)

One GP thought that some of his patients not only found the concept of choice confusing, but also questioned the motives behind the programme.

Sometimes they actually question the reasons we are doing it... That you know this is about somebody else's agenda... It's about trying to get me off to other places rather than where I really want to go.

(GP, area A)

In contrast, a GP in a more affluent area thought that his patients had responded enthusiastically to choice.

> *They love it... Once you say, look, this is the referral system and you turn the screen around to them... and say, they... are offering us [hospital D3 NHS FT], ... [another hospital name]... [hospital D2 NHS FT], we know [hospital D2 NHS FT]'s invested heavily in outpatient services so that might come out on top... And once you print off the chitty, often they're not dumbfounded but pleasantly surprised by how painless it was really.*
>
> (GP, area D)

Although there were no significant differences either in awareness or in importance according to the type of area in which the patient lived (eg, rural or urban), GPs and hospital providers, particularly those operating in more rural areas, saw choice as something that is more appropriate in areas such as London or urban areas where there is a larger number of providers.

> *In rural areas where there isn't an awful lot of choice... I don't really see how it makes much difference.*
>
> (NHS provider, area B)

> *So I think the choice thing is, is a bit different. The areas where it sort of does work differently, having worked round London, are where you've got a lot of hospitals on pretty good communications routes, all with similar offerings.*
>
> (Foundation trust provider, area D)

The majority of patients think that choice is important or very important – ISTC patients more so than NHS patients. Regression analysis showed that older patients (51–80), those without qualifications, those from a mixed or non-white background, and women, were more likely to think that choice is important. Many of the GPs interviewed thought that demand for choice was limited, and some reported that patients were often bemused when told that they could choose between a range of providers. GPs felt that patients often preferred to take their advice or simply chose the nearest local hospital. They appear to believe that someone who chooses a local provider does not value the right to be able to choose as much as someone who exercises their choice by travelling to a non-local provider.

What do GPs and providers think about patient choice?

Despite their scepticism about the importance of choice to patients, the overwhelming majority of GPs interviewed supported the principle of giving patients a choice. Generally, interviewees in hospital providers were positive or ambivalent about patients having a choice of provider. There were a few enthusiasts who were very vocal about their support for the policy.

> *Well, I sort of am a bit of a believer actually, I have to say.*   (NHS provider, area C)

> *I definitely think that choice is here to stay, and a good thing.*
>
> (Independent sector provider, area B)

One of the directors we interviewed who was pro competition within the NHS expressed some frustration that the government had not let market forces run completely free.

I guess it's sort of taking consumerism to the extreme, if you like, in terms of health care, and that's a philosophy I don't have a problem with... But where consumerism really works, [the] Department of Health sometimes gets a bit uncomfortable.

(Foundation trust provider, area D)

On the whole, support was muted – it was not something people felt they could disagree with, but some certainly had reservations about its value and applicability.

I think instinctively you have to say that patient choice has got to be a good thing. I mean, the opposite to that is, it would be daft.

(Foundation trust provider, area D)

Few providers expressed strong negative views about choice. The few negative views that were expressed were about the ISTC's ability to 'cherry pick', and that choice was a 'political tool'.

Both GPs and hospital providers argued that choice was nothing new. Long before the current policy, GPs had engaged their patients in discussions about choice of provider and type of treatment.

I've always been amenable to, even before the days of choice... just to have a conversation about... what style of treatment and where you want to go.

(GP, area B)

I think a choice agenda always went on with your patients anyway.   (GP, area A)

Furthermore, where PCTs supported out-of-area referrals, this choice was not limited to local options. One GP commented that prior to the purchaser–provider split within the NHS, everyone had the right to choose treatment at any hospital in the country.

In actual fact, the patient choice in this area has always existed very effectively without the recent initiatives... The PCT has always been very amenable. If, for example, someone has moved into the area and had a knee replacement... at the [privately run knee clinic] or somewhere, to actually refer back to that particular consultant, even if it's out of area.

(GP, area C)

From being in the NHS for 20 years, people have always had a right to choose any hospital they wanted in the country... And it was only restricted 10 years ago or so with all the purchasers' splits, and then you could only be seen at your local one. So it's actually restoring what they used to have.

(GP, area D)

Several people we spoke to on the provider side also made the point that there had always been a choice, but that this had not been formalised in the way it was now.

Patients actually had a choice for many, many, many years – it's just that has not been promoted as such... So it would be assumed that the patient will go to where the GP wanted them to go, but actually, if that patient sitting in front of the GP said 'I don't want to go to X hospital...', the GP would have, before patient choice came on to the agenda, the GP would have, and could have, sent that patient to another hospital.

(Foundation trust provider, area D)

If you talk to some of the clinicians here who've been around donkeys' years, they'll say patient choice existed 30 years ago... This is nothing new in a way, because patients years ago always had the option, if they didn't like their local hospital, they could go to any hospital in the country.

(Foundation trust provider, area B)

In contrast, one provider felt that patients had not always had a choice within the NHS and it was about time they were given it.

I think, well I mean, I think the customer's always right, so I think patients have been denied choice since 1948… So, you know, accelerating and enhancing the ability to have choice, I think, is fantastic.

(NHS provider, area C)

Although several GPs stated that they already offered patients a choice, a few interviewees suggested that the development of a specific choice policy had focused minds and embedded the concept within the health system.

Whether it's made as big a difference at, sort of, clinical level is more debatable. But the whole idea of, actually, 'patients are part of the health care system and have a right to some choices about how they make decisions, etc', that has… clearly got into the DNA of… health management systems.

(GP, area B)

I think it's encouraged us all to think about choice… It's encouraged patients to be aware.

(GP, area B)

Some of those we interviewed were more interested in choice of treatment, and felt that by only focusing on choice of hospital, the policy was too limited.

I think there is also something about being able to offer, not just different hospitals… but different treatments.

(Foundation trust provider, area D)

I think there's more than one level of choice. I think there's choice about where to go… And I think there's also choice about treatment.

(Foundation trust provider, area D)

The independent sector providers we interviewed were generally very positive about the patient choice policy. Their concerns focused on the impact of the policy on their own business, and the administrative burden and running costs of the system. While choice was seen as a business opportunity, it was believed to be a somewhat limited one. They also acknowledged that offering NHS patients treatment in the private sector might undermine demand from self-paying patients.

The negative views expressed about choice focused on a concern that it may leave disadvantaged patients who are less able to exercise choice (such as those unable to speak English) with the worst providers, and that it wastes resources.

Some felt that choice would contribute to greater inequalities, with those less aware of choice or less able to travel to exercise choice being left with a poor service (or, indeed, no service if it became unsustainable).

Patients who can travel do, and your service becomes unsustainable. And what's left is a very deprived population, with poor health outcomes, who are quite often from BME [black and minority ethnic] communities, lots of non-English speakers… Very low-income or unemployed people who can't get to the other places as easily or don't understand the thing about choice. And you haven't got a service that's good enough... either can't keep running it or you can't, can't offer it to them.

(NHS provider, area B)

This market confuses patients, it destabilises resources and unfortunately it panders to those, that group of patients who actually can afford [to exercise choice] and not to that group of patients that can't afford... So, if you like, it's almost a means testing, if you've got the means you can have choice.

(NHS provider, area C)

Some felt that the flow of resources to successful hospitals would increase inequalities in service provision.

In the current situation, I think it doesn't work at all and actually it's counter-productive because what it leads to is the 'best' hospitals actually attracting the activity, attracting the income and being able to invest in those services further. And actually what you do is you widen the disparities between hospitals rather than close them.

(Foundation trust provider, area B)

Some interviewees raised concerns that the choice policy was inefficient in its use of resources, requiring there to be excess capacity in the system and resulting in the duplication of services.

One hospital director raised a particular problem: if a hospital increases capacity to meet new demand generated by choice...

[but then] another hospital... gets their act together, will the patients decide to go back to what would be their local hospital... and leave us high and dry with the investment that we've made?

(Foundation trust provider, area D)

Another felt that the choice policy conflicts with the economic imperative to reduce duplication of services and over-supply, and felt that a system that allows choice would be *'economically unsustainable'*. He went on to say that:

...while in theory it sounds great, you can't economically sustain four or five different competitive services on the basis of the tariff at the current time, because it would simply be such an over-supply of the market that people can't remain viable. And I think that's a big gap in terms of the Department of Health thinking.

(Foundation trust provider, area D)

A number of GPs felt that the cost of the programme was unjustified and little change would be effected.

I also think it's taken an awful lot of money to set up... and I think the money could have been better spent on a lot of other things... I personally do not feel that it has added anything to the quality of patient care... and I haven't come across a patient who has told me that the quality of their experience has been vastly improved because they had a choice in where they went.

(GP, area C)

I don't think there are any real benefits. There might be tuppence on the bus fare or the car park might be cheaper at one hospital or another, but I don't think there are any clinical benefits.

(GP, area C)

In general, the majority of those we spoke to among GPs and hospital providers were positive or ambivalent about choice. Many felt that patient choice had existed within the NHS prior to the recent policy focus, and therefore choice was really nothing new. A small number of interviewees felt that the policy had focused the minds of GPs and providers on what really matters to patients.

There were a few enthusiasts among providers who regarded choice, competition and consumerism as important within the NHS, but on the whole, support was muted. There were no extremely negative views expressed among providers, though GPs were generally more negative than providers. GPs' concerns were mostly around the implementation of Choose and Book (*see* below) rather than patient choice *per se*. The independent sector providers were, on the whole, positive about the business opportunity that patient choice presented, but again, were concerned about how the policy was being implemented and the costs associated with it. While the overall attitude among providers was generally positive, they, together with GPs, identified a number of concerns – particularly about the impact of the policy on inequalities in terms of access and resource use. These concerns need to be addressed if providers and GPs are to support the full implementation of patient choice in future.

Understanding the objectives of patient choice policy

Most senior managers we interviewed had an overall understanding of the theory that choice creates a threat to providers' market share, which, in turn, generates pressure to do things that attract and retain patients. Only a few explicitly talked about choice and competition, but most implicitly understood the possibility that patients can choose to go elsewhere.

In the way managers spoke about choice, the emphasis was on keeping patients loyal and on retention, as well as attracting new patients.

> *I think that's relatively simple, isn't it? We as providers are supposed to be sitting here thinking, 'How do we retain and attract patients?' And so start to design services that patients want to use.*
>
> (NHS provider, area B)

> *But I think we recognise that patients have got choices about where they choose to go, and we've got to deliver the best job we can in order to make sure they come to us.*
>
> (Foundation trust provider, area D)

One ISTC interviewee was clear that patients needed to be attracted to their service:

> *It's like running a hotel. You've got to offer them [patients] something to come here.*
>
> (Independent sector provider, area A)

Interviewees at one trust had a sophisticated understanding that patient choice works through creating pressures to understand the market, be aware of patient preferences and respond to them. They seemed to understand the ultimate objective of choice – that is, to increase responsiveness of services to patients. One interviewee talked about choice in terms of making relevant [to providers] what 'the patients are going to use to make their choice' (foundation trust provider, area D). Interestingly, this trust had a strong focus on customer care as part of its own mission.

Few interviewees talked directly about patient choice driving competition. One provider talked about choice creating pressure on those hospitals that are losing patients to improve the quality of their services in order to win those patients back:

> *I think the theoretical model is that the best providers attract more patients, and therefore, that provides an incentive for other trusts to improve their services to try and repatriate that back to them.*
>
> (Foundation trust provider, area B)

At one trust in a rural area, two of the executive team we spoke to linked patient choice directly to competition. The threat of losing market share or patients voting with their feet was clearly linked to patient choice in their minds and also seen to be a driver for quality improvement.

> *Well, I think patient choice works around competitiveness. I mean, I think at the end of the day, we all want to at least maintain, if not increase, our market share, and that's got to be all about patient choice. So I think patient choice just encourages competitiveness, which is no bad thing because actually the quality improves.*
>
> (Foundation trust provider, area D)

> *I suspect that the powers that be think that choice is a big stick and that because we are frightened that patients might vote with their feet, that we must do something about improving all the things we've talked about… But that agenda's only just starting.*
>
> (Foundation trust provider, area D)

A few GPs referred to the potential for choice to drive improvements in the quality of health care. One interviewee listed a number of ways in which choice could increase the quality of the service for the patient and improve job satisfaction for the clinician.

> *I think that being able to look at the service options, being able to look at the time, gives confidence and security and satisfaction to both parties… The referrals are actually our forward order book… in a commissioning sense, and I think that has the potential for being a commissioning tool.*
>
> (GP, area D)

While patient choice was seen as an important driver for quality improvement, it was made more powerful due to the link with Payment by Results (PbR). Attracting more patients brings with it income, and therefore, increased resources are available for investing in new or improved services. Clearly, this is only possible when the trust's operating costs are below tariff, but there seemed to be little awareness of this among the NHS hospitals we spoke to. However, there was a clear and immediate response in the private sector to any change in the tariff.

> *I think people really understand money… staff understand money, and they understand that a really good service attracts more patients and brings more income into the trust. This means that we can develop the service and increase the staffing level, improve the quality and do the things that they are really fanatical about, the things that they want to do. So I think that connection between patient choice and money and income is a really strong driver. In a sense, it comes back to some of the more altruistic things because it isn't about 'and then I'll get paid more'. It is all about 'then I can improve my service and make it much better'.*
>
> (NHS provider, area C)

> *The theory of it is that, as a patient, I can choose the hospital that I want to go to, that I've chosen because it might have the best [lowest] infection rates or I know the*

particular surgeon that I want to see, or whatever. So then, as money follows the patient through PbR, then that's theoretically how it's supposed to work, that the better hospitals then attract more money.

(NHS provider, area B)

While our interest was in the extent to which hospitals saw choice as a driver for quality improvement, we did not define this for interviewees. Although most understood the theory of choice – that is, that it should prompt a change in provider behaviour – only a few saw any link between choice and changes in the quality of clinical care. When talking about quality, respondents referred to dimensions such as access and waiting times, patient experience, processes of care (such as the ability to book appointments), and the environment in which care is delivered (eg, the hospital facilities).

Several providers perceived that the choice policy was to do with reducing waiting times and improving access and convenience for patients. This view that choice was about waiting time reductions was shared by one of the private sector providers. They saw choice as being about putting extra private sector capacity alongside reduced NHS capacity in order to keep waiting times down.

...so I think choice really aimed at trying to improve, initially, the waiting times by putting more capacity in the system. And I think it's done that, you know, I think it has dropped.

(Foundation trust provider, area B)

In one trust, the person responsible for the implementation of Choose and Book thought that the policy was primarily about giving patients a choice of appointment time and date.

Well, I think it is about patients if they wish to have a choice of hospital but actually it is more about offering them choice of date and time that fits in with their lifestyle. And I think that, certainly from my involvement, is something that patients want. It was about the patient, as I understand it, the theory really that the patient should be able to leave the surgery with the appointment known because that's very reassuring.

(NHS provider, area C)

Another provider was clear that the ambition had been greater than this.

I always think Choose and Book was developed to push up quality, not just about waiting times but about your reputation, about the sort of experience that patients had, and I believe that's what the concept of Choose and Book was – to increase quality.

(NHS provider, area C)

Overall, providers appeared to understand the theory behind the patient choice policy, though they were less clear about whether it was designed to improve access or clinical quality. The link between PbR and choice was clear in that the financial rewards and potential losses were an important motivator for providers. They seemed less clear about the extent to which patient choice was intended to lead to greater competition for patients, and a few sceptics felt that choice was nothing new.

The majority of providers we spoke to understood the theory behind choice policy driving quality improvements. However, there was less clarity about the nature of these quality improvements. Reducing waiting times was seen as one of the main objectives; but other providers had a broader view of quality, which encompassed the patient experience and the quality of services on offer.

Opinions of Choose and Book

While GPs acknowledged the patient's right to choose, this was tempered by a great many reservations about the way the current choice policy was working in practice. Most of these reservations centred on the Choose and Book system itself. GPs, in particular, conflated patient choice with Choose and Book, in part because it is through this system of booking that the policy of patient choice is 'enacted'.

Choose and Book allows GPs to book appointments online in their surgery, or patients to book over the telephone or online from home. PCTs currently provide financial incentives to GPs to use Choose and Book via Local Enhanced Services (LES), which replaced the national Directed Enhanced Services (DES) introduced by the Department of Health when Choose and Book was launched in 2006. Under these local schemes, practices generally receive a payment for each patient registered according to the percentage of Choose and Book referrals they achieve.

The financial incentive is clearly important to GPs. In one PCT, a decision to withdraw the incentive was taken during the course of the fieldwork because it was costing too much. This decision has since been reversed and the incentive re-instated, although the PCT is still considering other options. Another PCT has recently subsumed the incentive into their practice-based commissioning arrangements. Although interviewees in one case study area implied they would continue to use the system even if the incentive were withdrawn, nearly a third overall thought that they would reconsider their use of Choose and Book or abandon it altogether, mainly because of the increase in workload it was thought to create.

> Our PCT has continued with a local enhanced service for Choose and Book to support utilisation. That's been a helpful consideration… so if that was withdrawn, I would stop using Choose and Book.
>
> (GP, area A)

> If there were no financial incentives, we would ditch it like a hot brick.　(GP, area D)

> In [area C], the PCT has just said that there isn't going to be any payment for Choose and Book… and we, in common with almost all the other GPs, are stopping it… because of all the disadvantages to us… Most people are giving three cheers that they're going to give it up.
>
> (GP, area C)

The GPs and providers we interviewed identified benefits and problems with the Choose and Book system.

Problems

Although all the GPs interviewed worked in practices where most referrals now go through the Choose and Book system, some GPs were obviously using the system more willingly than others. GPs expressed concern about the additional time it took to offer choice and use the Choose and Book system. Estimates for the amount of time Choose and Book took up in consultations varied wildly between the GPs interviewed, but many complained about an additional burden.

> In the small amount of time it takes to load up, one briefly introduces the patient to what Choose and Book is… talk the patient through the drop down menus, they can see the indicative waiting times… and a brief negotiation with the patient, it all takes seconds really.
>
> (GP, area B)

If you have to refer that patient and have to create a Choose and Book letter… you have to explain their choices… then you have to explain the process… and it takes… at least 15 minutes.

(GP, area A)

Chasing up and sorting out booking errors had increased the overall workload of several practices and they had found it necessary to employ more staff. One GP felt that they are now doing a lot of work that providers did in the past.

They've [hospitals] slashed back on their booking side and outpatients and stuff like that… so it's been good for them… It's not necessarily been as good for us and our staff.

(GP, area A)

One independent sector provider identified the cost of the necessary IT infrastructure to allow them to book appointments directly on Choose and Book as a major barrier to entry.

There is this national register, which we're not on because it's restrictive from a cost point of view, and something like £80,000 for the software to get onto that.

(Independent sector provider, area B)

Providers and GPs commented on the difficulties of getting certain services, such as community hospital slots and physiotherapy clinics, on the system.

It's very difficult to get local flexibility… We've got various sort of physio clinics scattered around… and the practicalities of getting those on to Choose and Book are very difficult.

(GP, area C)

The interviews revealed that implementation has been a challenge for many providers in this study in the way they administer and organise clinics (for a wider discussion of these issues, *see* Dixon *et al* 2010). Many found challenges in operating the new electronic appointments system, which requires appointment slots to be uploaded and then allocated. Some interviewees complained about the lack of flexibility and problems managing demand within the system while delivering care within the 18-week target.

GPs also experienced problems resulting from the 18-week target. Consultants who fail to meet this target become unavailable to patients through the Choose and Book appointment system, even though some patients may prefer to wait longer to see that consultant.

If patients want to see a particular consultant, but actually that consultant's clinics aren't running quite to the target, then it's virtually impossible to get that patient seen… We have a local orthopaedic surgeon who is very well respected… His clinics are always difficult to book in to. They disappear off Choose and Book.

(GP, area C)

There were a number of complaints from both GPs and providers that the Choose and Book system generated inappropriate referrals, with patients being booked in for appointments at the wrong clinics. Providers criticised information on Choose and Book and in the directory of services for not being detailed enough to facilitate appropriate referral, and one interviewee felt that waiting time information within Choose and Book was inaccurate. GPs reported difficulties in locating particular services caused by the constant revisions and anomalies in the way they were described.

It does sometimes lead to poor-quality referrals from GPs… We have had patients turn up for inappropriate appointments because the GPs have not understood the directory of services properly and booked into it.

(Foundation trust provider, area B)

It's a nightmare trying to find the same clinics in different hospitals. They're called different things… So it's very hard to provide any choice because they don't appear on the same screen.

(GP, area D)

They make odd changes, like all paediatrics was changed to child and adolescents… so there was a six-month period when we couldn't find it.

(GP, area B)

Most providers do not allow GPs to refer directly to named consultants in the Choose and Book system. The resultant increase in consultant-to-consultant referrals experienced in one of the PCTs was proving costly. A common theme across the interviews was the idea that referral flows were heavily influenced by the relationship between individual GPs and hospital consultants. The fact that GPs could not generally refer to a named consultant when using Choose and Book may in part explain their reluctance to use the system. It can also stand in the way of longstanding relationships between GPs and hospital consultants, which in themselves may be beneficial for the patient.

I think GPs persuade patients to go purely because I think there's still a lot of the 'old boy network' stuff going on, where GPs and consultants play golf together. GPs have a massive influence on where patients go.

(Foundation trust provider, area B)

It's pretty much an old boys' network and the patient choice is non-named referrals, which is a massive issue for GPs and the doctors. They don't like it at all because you are referred to a 'patient choice' clinic, if you like, for orthopaedics – you don't know who you're going to get. Sure as hell you're going to get an orthopaedic surgeon who is damn good, but it's very much an old boys' network, particularly in this area, and you have certain consultants who GPs will refer to all the time… That's been taken away from them and they don't like it. They want to refer on to their friends.

(C1.3 Independent sector provider, area C)

This belief was echoed by many of the GP interviewees. While some seemed to be able to get around the restriction, others felt that their inability to refer to named consultants undermines their professionalism and reduces patient choice.

The ones [GPs] I talk to feel frustrated… Again, they're not meant to refer to the person they want to refer to, they still feel that a personal relationship between patient, GP and hospital consultant is important.

(Foundation trust provider, area D)

I could say to a patient, 'well, I think Mr X at this hospital is really good', but through Choose and Book they can't choose to go and see him and they end up seeing Mr Y, who I may feel is not as good.

(GP, area C)

GPs were frustrated by the system's slowness, occasional poor connectivity and the fact that it shuts down too early. But the general trend suggested that early technical problems were slowly being ironed out.

I log in in the morning and then it shuts down at 5.20pm… And then I have to reboot it back up again because obviously we work til, we're seeing patients, 6 or 6.30pm.

(GP, area A)

Some interviewees explained GPs' reluctance to offer choice in terms of their dislike of the Choose and Book system, saying the two were closely connected in GPs' minds.

It's fair to say that GPs are not being awfully positive about Choose and Book. I think, mainly because of the clunkiness of the actual Choose and Book software application, and that's kind of coloured their view… of patient choice. If patient choice means Choose and Book, then we don't like it. But notwithstanding that, I think they would see patient choice as probably a fairly reasonable thing for patients to exercise, albeit that a lot of that is influenced by the GPs themselves.

(Foundation trust provider, area D)

Benefits

A few GPs had always supported Choose and Book or had been converted to it as time went on. One GP thought that the system encouraged them to offer choice instead of relying on the same providers, and another thought that it made out-of-area referrals easier.

The whole idea of actually patients… have a right to some choices about how they make decisions, etc… that has… clearly got into the DNA of… health management systems.

(GP, area B)

I think, with the old system, possibly doctors weren't tempted to offer a choice… They would just often have a habit of who they would refer to and they would just go with that.

(GP, area A)

One provider who had been an early adopter of the system and made virtually all of their appointment slots available for direct booking (as opposed to indirect booking, where the patient has to telephone the hospital to make their appointment) was positive about the convenience it brought for patients, and found it a useful tool in helping them meet the 18-week waiting time target. Two trusts thought that having appointments available for direct booking had increased referrals, which was positive, although there was frustration that GPs were not booking all appointments through the system.

…99.9 per cent of our services that are offered to GPs… are directly bookable, so that means they can be booked in the GP surgery, which is fantastic. I mean that's fantastic, that's why we're very disappointed we don't have more referrals being booked through that way. I mean, I've done loads of communication events, we go to lots of practices, GP practices.

(Foundation trust provider, area B)

Another trust was positive about the streamlined booking process and the fact that it allowed patients to leave the GP surgery with an appointment in their hand.

But the bottom line is, patient leaving a GP surgery, potentially with an appointment in their hand, is gold standard. You can't beat that.

(Foundation trust provider, area D)

Some of the GPs we interviewed agreed, and spoke about the sense of satisfaction and security in being able to confirm an appointment there and then.

I think both the clinician and the patient, who I think are partners in this process… would both like to know when the appointment is going to be.

(GP, area D)

However, for other GP interviewees, one of the main benefits of the Choose and Book system was that it gave the patient more control and made the process more transparent.

I think the whole concept of putting the patient in charge of the process, so that they have to phone the number to ring and they're booking the appointment, is a very powerful step forward in the process, whereas previously it was a sort of secret conversation… 'Well, I'll write to him and he'll write to you… and at some stage in the future, if you're really, really lucky, you'll hear'.

(GP, area B)

I personally give them a choice of several and then they can make the final deliberation when they've got home with their diary… And most people are quite impressed… knowing that they're in charge of making the booking, it's quite popular.

(GP, area D)

Several GPs appreciated the ability to track patients' bookings via the Choose and Book work list.

It is quite useful to be able to go back and track a referral to see that a letter's been sent on time, that the patient's appointment has been agreed with the provider.

(GP, area D)

The implementation of Choose and Book has not been problem-free and has coloured both GPs' and hospital providers' views of choice. Interviews with both providers and GPs revealed a number of challenges as well as benefits. The most common problems included increased consultation times, technical problems, slots that are not directly bookable, inaccurate and inconsistent information in the directory of services, managing capacity within the 18-week target, and the inability to refer to named consultants. It was acknowledged that not all patients like the responsibility of making their own appointments.

However, early technical problems are being ironed out and the flip-side of patients having to make their own appointments is greater control and potentially increased engagement in their own treatment.

Summary

There appears to be some discrepancy between GPs' perceptions about patients' awareness and interest in choice and the views of patients we surveyed. In general, GPs felt that most patients were not aware of their ability to choose a hospital, when, in fact, about half are aware of their right to choose before they visit the GP. Interestingly, older patients are more aware of their right to choose, perhaps because they are in more frequent contact with the NHS and therefore either have prior experience of choice or are more likely to have seen information promoting choice. The extent to which PCTs actively promote choice varies considerably, with only one of our case study PCTs having made significant efforts in this regard.

GPs also felt that choice was only really of interest to the more educated middle classes, whereas, in fact, almost three in four patients we questioned said that choice was important. Significantly more of those with fewer qualifications rated choice as important compared with those with higher levels of qualifications. GPs, however, are sceptical that this value placed on choice translates into a real desire for choice when actually faced with a decision at the point of referral. In their experience, most people wanted to go to their local hospital or wished to take the GP's advice about where to go.

Opinions about patient choice varied, but on the whole, hospital providers were positive or ambivalent. There were few passionate advocates or dissenters among those we spoke to. This did not mean that they were unable to identify challenges and limitations arising from the policy. Indeed, several issues were identified, including the potential inefficiencies generated by choice and the potential to increase inequities, running the risk that poor people will be treated by lower-quality providers. Interviewees from the independent sector were also generally positive about the policy, but identified different issues and challenges. They were particularly concerned about its potential impact on their business and the self-pay market.

Among GPs and hospital providers, there was an understanding of the theory behind choice – that is, that it was designed to make providers more responsive to patients and drive quality. When talking about quality, they referred to access and waiting times, patient experience, processes of care, and the environment, rather than clinical effectiveness or outcomes.

The GPs interviewed generally held positive attitudes towards the concept of choice, and all worked in practices that were using Choose and Book for most of their referrals. It is interesting, therefore, that although there were enthusiasts among those we interviewed, many expressed reservations about the system through which the policy of choice is implemented. Key concerns were the time involved, additional workload, and difficulty of referring to named consultants. It was clear that without the financial incentive from the PCTs, many GPs would not continue to use the system. Frustrations with Choose and Book have, to some extent, coloured GPs' overall views of patient choice, though they remain supportive of the policy in principle. The requirement to offer choice to every patient is resented by some, although others felt it had focused minds.

In this section, we have examined the opinion and attitudes of patients, GPs and providers towards choice. In the next section, we look in more detail at how choice is operating in practice.

3 How is patient choice operating in practice?

Section 1 outlined a model of choice in which GPs offered patients a choice, guided them through the available options, and helped them to use information to compare providers and select the one of highest quality. Section 2 established that most providers and GPs support the concept of choice, and most patients think it is important. In this section, we analyse how choice is experienced by patients in practice and how the policy has been implemented by primary care trusts (PCTs), GPs and providers in the four local health economies (A–D) we have used as case studies.

First, we examine whether patients are always offered a choice by their GP and whether some patients are more likely to be offered choice than others. We then examine whether those patients who were offered a choice were using the opportunity to travel beyond their local provider; we consider which patients are more likely to do this and what support and information they are given to help them choose. Finally, we consider how patients choose between providers in practice – by outlining results from our patient survey and GP and provider interviews – and also in hypothetical situations – using results from the discrete choice experiment.

Are patients offered a choice?

Since January 2006, government policy has required GPs (or other referring health care professionals) to offer patients a choice of at least four providers and, since April 2008, this has been extended to any NHS or independent sector provider in England that offers the treatment they need and is approved to provide NHS care (see 'Policy timeline', Figure 2, p 6).

The Department of Health has been monitoring implementation of this policy with a bi-monthly survey of patients. In March 2009, it showed that 47 per cent of patients in England recalled being offered a choice – a figure that has remained largely unchanged since the beginning of 2007 (Department of Health 2009a).

Our survey also asked patients who had recently been referred for an outpatient appointment whether they recalled being offered a choice of hospital. The results from respondents who booked their appointments in January 2009 in our four case study areas were similar to the Department of Health's own figures, with 49 per cent saying they were offered a choice. Patients who knew they had the right to choose before visiting their GP were more likely to be offered a choice (63 per cent) than those who were unaware of this (37 per cent).

We also asked patients for more detail on how many choices they were offered and whether they were given the option of referral to a privately run hospital or treatment centre. Figure 6, overleaf, shows that, of those who were offered a choice, half (49 per cent) said they were given two hospitals to choose between, and a similar number (49 per cent) said they were given between three and five options. A very small number of respondents (just 2 per cent) recalled being given more than five hospitals to choose from.

Figure 6 The choices offered to patients

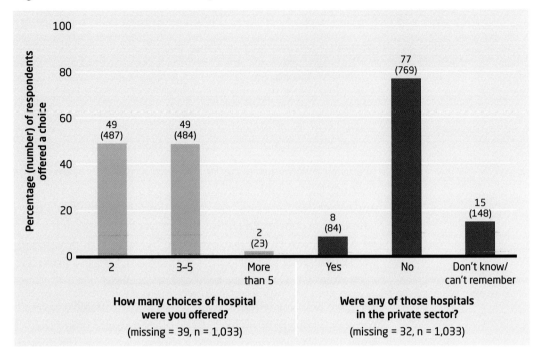

Although patients are entitled to choose treatment at privately run providers (as long as they are registered to provide NHS care), Figure 6 shows that 77 per cent of those offered a choice said they did not recall any of the hospitals being in the private sector.

Table 8 looks at responses from NHS patients who were referred to the two independent sector treatment centres (ISTCs) involved in the study and compares them with responses from patients who were referred to NHS trusts. It shows that patients referred to the ISTCs were more likely to recall being offered a choice than those referred to NHS providers (74 per cent vs 47 per cent) and were offered more options (61 per cent vs 50 per cent of those offered a choice recall having three or more options). Interestingly, 38 per cent of patients who chose to attend an ISTC did not think that any of the hospitals offered were in the private sector. This suggests that some patients are unaware that some of the options presented to them, in particular ISTCs, are privately run. However, this is unsurprising, as ISTCs are able to use the NHS brand.

Table 8 The choices offered to NHS and ISTC patients

		NHS Percentage (number)		ISTC Percentage (number)		Total Percentage (number)	
Were you offered a	Yes	47	(899)	74	(134)	49	(1,033)
choice of hospital?**	No	51	(985)	23	(43)	49	(1,028)
	Don't know	2	(46)	2	(4)	2	(50)
	Total	100	(1,884)	100	(177)	100	(2,111) (missing = 70)
How many choices	2	50	(437)	39	(50)	52	(556)
of hospital were	3–5	48	(412)	57	(72)	46	(498)
you offered*	More than 5	2	(18)	4	(5)	2	(23)
	Total	100	(867)	100	(127)	100	(994) (missing = 39)
Were any of those	Yes	3	(30)	44	(54)	8	(84)
hospitals from the	No	82	(722)	38	(47)	77	(769)
private sector?**	Don't know	14	(125)	19	(23)	15	(148)
	Total	100	(877)	100	(124)	100	(1,001) (missing = 32)

** χ^2 test shows differences significant at 1 per cent level.

* χ^2 test shows differences significant at 5 per cent level.

Another reason for the small number of patients who recalled being offered a referral to a private sector hospital may be the lack of awareness of and interest in private providers among GPs. GPs rarely mentioned private providers, possibly because they seldom discussed this option with their patients. In one study area, GPs thought there were no private options available.

Partly because of the good reputation of our district general hospital, we don't currently have private providers on the choice menu.

(GP, area C)

There are a number of different ways in which choice can be offered. Some of these reflect the way the Choose and Book system operates. After inputting some patient and clinical information into the system, GPs can show patients which hospitals are available for the specialty they require and, if the chosen provider has 'directly bookable' appointment slots, book their appointment on-screen in the GP surgery. If patients want time to think about their options, or a provider does not allow appointments to be booked directly online, the GP can print out a letter outlining the options, which gives the patient a reference number. The patient can then call a telephone booking line or book their appointment online using that reference number. In some cases, the patient may be required to phone the hospital directly to book an appointment, or wait for a call from the hospital. In areas with systems of referral management, GPs often pass referrals to a central point of contact. After verifying that a referral is needed, the patient is offered a choice of provider either by letter or telephone. Referral management initiatives work in different ways in different areas.

The patients we surveyed were asked who offered them a choice, and Figure 7, below, shows that in the majority of cases (60 per cent), it was their GP. Some patients (21 per cent) were offered a choice in a letter received after their GP consultation, and some by a telephone booking adviser (20 per cent). A small number were actually offered a choice by the GP's receptionist (3 per cent) or someone else in the GP surgery (1 per cent). Those who answered 'other' and wrote in their own response to this question were

Figure 7 Who offered you a choice of hospital?

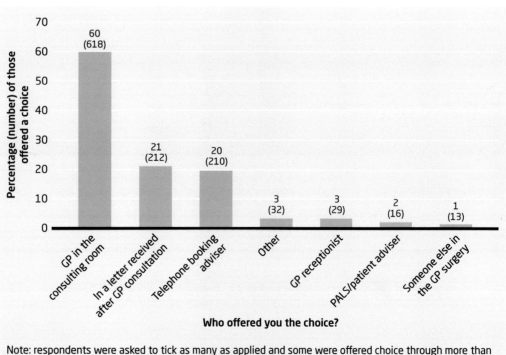

Who offered you the choice?

Note: respondents were asked to tick as many as applied and some were offered choice through more than one route. For this reason the percentages do not add up to 100. The number of respondents who ticked 'other' and the number who completed the free text response are different.

offered choice by: a hospital consultant (10 respondents); a nurse or other primary health care professional (9 respondents); ambulance crew (2 respondents); or online (18 respondents).

Patients were asked to tick as many options as applied when indicating who offered them a choice, and some were offered choice through more than one route. However, the results show that around half of patients were offered a choice outside the GP consultation; telephone booking line operators and other health care professionals also act as agents of choice for many patients.

Figure 8, below, shows how hospital appointments were booked for patients who were offered a choice and those not offered a choice. GPs only booked appointments for a quarter (26 per cent) of the patients who were offered a choice. These patients generally booked their own appointment over the telephone after the GP consultation (53 per cent); a far smaller number booked appointments online (6 per cent) or through the GP receptionist or another person in the GP surgery (7 per cent).

More than half of patients who were not offered a choice had their appointment booked by their GP (52 per cent). But a quarter booked their appointment after the GP consultation on the telephone (23 per cent), either through a telephone booking line or calling the hospital directly. In general, patients who were offered a choice booked their appointments after the consultation, whereas those who were not offered a choice were more likely to have the process handled by their GP. It may be that where the GP took control of the booking process, patients were less likely to recall being offered a formal choice of hospitals, even where some discussion of options may have taken place.

Figure 8 How the hospital appointment was booked

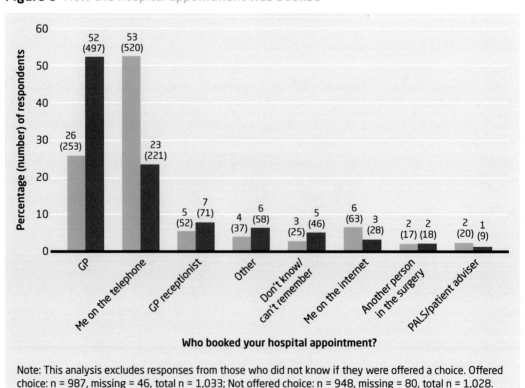

Who booked your hospital appointment?

Offered a choice ▢
Not offered a choice ▇

Note: This analysis excludes responses from those who did not know if they were offered a choice. Offered choice: n = 987, missing = 46, total n = 1,033; Not offered choice: n = 948, missing = 80, total n = 1,028.

GP and provider views

Although half of patients did not recall being offered a choice, all of the GPs who were interviewed said they offered patients a choice. This discrepancy can partly be explained by a bias in the sampling of GPs who were mainly high users of the Choose and Book system; they are therefore more likely to have offered patients a choice than the 'average' GP (*see* Appendix A, p 174). However, the discrepancy can also be partly explained by differences in GPs and patients' views on what constitutes offering a choice.

Many GPs described offering choice in a mechanistic (sometimes tokenistic) way that revealed the burden they felt has been put on them by government and their lack of interest in the process.

> *So I'll normally say… the government's asked us to give you a choice.* (GP, area B)

> *Our standard spiel we have in the practice is that… I am required to try and offer you five choices.*
>
> (GP, area A)

A number of GPs described framing choices in a way that may have led patients to feel they only had one option of where to be treated. If patients did state a preference for a particular hospital upfront, then it seemed unlikely that interviewees enter into any further discussion about choice, even if they or a member of the practice staff still went through the motions in order to satisfy the Choose and Book requirements.

> *Since Choose and Book I'll probably say to them, 'I would normally plan to send you to the [hospital B1 NHS FT] because it's across the road and they run a good service… Are you happy with that?' And they most probably say yes.*
>
> (GP, area B)

> *If I suggest look, this is your nearest hospital, although it doesn't have the shortest waiting time, what do you want to do, go there? And they say, 'Oh yes, that's fine'.*
>
> (GP, area B)

GPs and patients' views on what constitutes being offered a choice can differ. One example of this is a patient who responded to our survey that they had not been given a choice of hospital, but when interviewed, revealed that the GP had offered them a choice 'jokily'.

> *I went to my GP earlier this year and he said, jokily, 'You have choice', so I said, 'Well, on the doorstep then'.*
>
> (Female patient, age 76, area C)

In interviews with other patients when asked to describe the GP consultation where they were referred for treatment, a few who had said they were not offered a choice revealed that they simply knew where they wanted to go and had asked for a particular provider. This led them to state they had not been offered a choice in our questionnaire, although their GP may have felt they implicitly chose that particular provider.

> *[Did your GP offer you a choice of hospital?] No, I don't believe so, no. I probably said to him at the time that obviously somewhere local but I've got the feeling I said to him at the time either [hospital name], because my father lives near… or [hospital name] or something like that would be preferred, but I don't mind.*
>
> (Male patient, age 59, area D)

One GP described how offering patients a choice when they already know where they want to go can be confusing for the patient.

> *Obviously, now we have to offer a choice of five providers, which is generally fairly confusing to my patients when they've already, with me, opted to go for a specific provider... But we're told this is what we have to do, so I generate the thing with the five providers.*
>
> (GP, area A)

Providers were asked whether they thought GPs offered patients a choice, and they mainly described a situation similar to that outlined by GPs: that GPs do offer some patients a choice, but that they were often reluctant to do so, only offering an alternative to the local provider to patients who proactively requested it.

> *So I think they would do one of two things. If the patient says 'Where do you think I should go?' then the GPs will tell them. If the patient doesn't say that, then often they'll leave the patient to make the decision but explain what the options are...*
>
> (Foundation trust provider, area D)

> *I think patients who ask their GP about a choice are getting offered a choice in a way they didn't used to be. I think we still have a strong suspicion that, quite a lot of the time, what happens is, 'I need to refer you to an orthopaedic surgeon, the most local one is here, that'll do, won't it?' kind of discussion. But there clearly are cases where a more detailed conversation has gone on about where people want to go... But I think they're the minority rather than the majority at the moment.*
>
> (NHS provider, area B)

One independent sector hospital described 'anti-private sector' feelings among some local GPs, who they felt often did not offer their hospital as an option to patients.

> *Some are very anti sending any NHS patients to this hospital; others don't actually offer the patient a choice.*
>
> (Independent sector provider, area C)

When asked about how patients booked their hospital appointments, the majority of GPs (confirming our patient survey results) said that they left patients to book their own appointments by telephone. In some cases, this was because the GPs felt they did not have enough time to do it in the consultation. But it was also dictated by the fact that many local providers are still not offering directly bookable appointments online.

> *So in actual fact [hospital C3 NHS], for example, has now got a call centre that deals with Choose and Book referrals... So it's an extra stage in the process... It's very cumbersome because I would estimate that... the clinics and the hospitals that we use most frequently, probably only... 15 or 20 per cent of them are directly bookable.*
>
> (GP, area C)

However, both providers and GPs also acknowledged that not all patients want the responsibility of phoning up themselves. GPs also highlighted various difficulties when patients were elderly and frail, when phone lines were often engaged, or the online system failed.

> *It's been variable, it's a challenge [Choose and Book] and we've rolled it out to our specialties now. Some patients don't like to use it, of course, because they don't like phoning up, they want that to be done for them. And so we have to think about how we can deal with all patients. With some, of course, they love it, because it means they can choose a time on the phone with their diary in front of them, that's convenient to them and their arrangements, whether that might be family or otherwise. But some people don't like Choose and Book.*
>
> (NHS provider, area C)

People would say the big problem is the phone number, when they ring… and can't get through for days on end… And I think it's a shame that the online service is perhaps not more active… I've not met a single patient who has successfully booked their appointment online.

(GP, area B)

In PCT A, a triage system had been developed for services where there is now a primary care alternative, such as orthopaedics, diabetes, dermatology and urology. Patients were asked to call an assessment centre to find out if they were to be referred into secondary care and exercise choice at that point if necessary. In PCT D, patients ringing the National Telephone Appointment Line (NTAL) during office hours were automatically transferred to one of two call centres in different parts of the PCT, who were able to offer more local information to patients and were considered to provide a better service.

Both of these arrangements changed the way some referrals were processed locally and had some impact on when choice was offered to patients and the support they received. However, GPs outlined some concerns about these additional parts of the referral process, as they had received complaints from patients who were unable to get through.

We strongly advise people to ring before half six... otherwise, they get someone who... doesn't know local geography and we end up having to untangle that.

(GP, area D)

The other problem that can occur is when patients ring up outside of office hours, they get deferred to the national booking service, which is even less able to support the patient in making the choice that they wish to do.

(GP, area D)

It's nice that it's going through a central centre, but the downside is I have had patients complain that, one, they struggle to get through... and two, often what they thought they were going to get is often not available to them.

(GP, area A)

Our findings indicate the importance of telephone booking line operators as agents of choice, and that local and nationally run appointment booking services can differ in terms of the level of knowledge and advice they are able to provide for patients.

Differences between the case study areas

We would expect patients' experience of choice to differ depending on the PCT in which they live, as PCTs are responsible for implementing the policy and have taken different approaches to the task. Different forms of incentive payment, referral management programmes and advertising initiatives may affect the way patients experience choice. The number of patients offered a choice, and the choices they were offered, differed between our case study areas. To examine these differences, Figures 9 and 10, overleaf, present responses from patients who lived within the main case study PCT in each area (those who resided outside of the case study PCT were excluded from this analysis).

Figure 9 shows that respondents in PCT A were far more likely to recall being offered a choice than those resident in the other PCTs (71 per cent vs 41–45 per cent). Figure 11 shows that patients in PCT A recalled being given more hospitals to choose between than patients in the other PCTs (72 per cent were given more than two options, compared with between 26 and 49 per cent). One possible explanation for this is the structure of the GP incentive payment in this area, which specifically asked GPs to select at least five hospitals for patients to choose between. In other areas, the incentive payment did not specify how many choices should be offered, and was awarded based on the number of appointments booked through the system. The number of patients given just two hospitals to choose between was particularly high in PCT B (74 per cent) where the incentive payment was based on the number of appointments booked through the Choose and Book system rather than the number of choices offered.

With regard to questions about private sector hospitals, who offered patients a choice, and how their appointment was booked, responses were too few to analyse by PCT of residence.

Figure 9 Offer of choice by PCT of residence

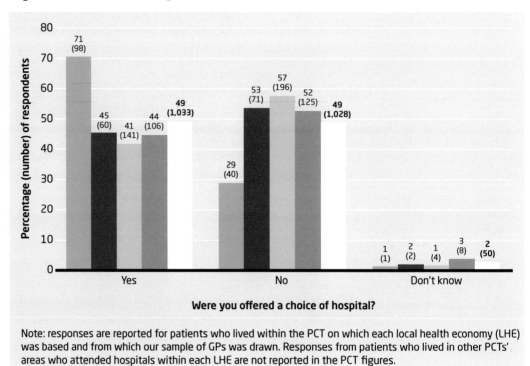

Note: responses are reported for patients who lived within the PCT on which each local health economy (LHE) was based and from which our sample of GPs was drawn. Responses from patients who lived in other PCTs' areas who attended hospitals within each LHE are not reported in the PCT figures.

Figure 10 Number of choices offered by PCT of residence

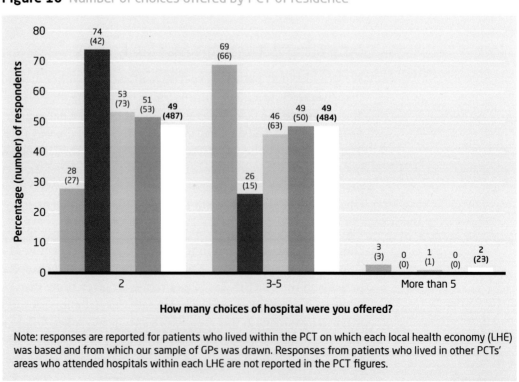

Note: responses are reported for patients who lived within the PCT on which each local health economy (LHE) was based and from which our sample of GPs was drawn. Responses from patients who lived in other PCTs' areas who attended hospitals within each LHE are not reported in the PCT figures.

The way choice operated in each of our case study areas and possible explanations for the differences, are discussed in more detail in Section 6. The next section of the report considers whether patients with particular characteristics (including where they lived) were more likely to have a choice over where they were referred when controlling for other factors.

While the majority of GPs we spoke to said they offered their patients a choice, only around half of patients recalled being offered a choice. Some of this discrepancy may be explained by recall bias. Patients surveyed some weeks after their initial GP consultation may have forgotten the choice discussion taking place. There also appears to be some difference in what GPs and patients consider constitutes a discussion about choice. There is some evidence from interviews with patients, GPs and providers that choice is often offered mechanistically or tokenistically, rather than as a meaningful discussion about the merits of different options. This is partly a consequence of the design of Choose and Book and the structure of the incentive payments system. Patients who were offered alternatives in what they felt to be a tokenistic way did not consider they had been given a real choice.

Patients attending ISTCs were more likely to recall being offered a choice than those attending NHS hospitals. Although patients were entitled to choose any eligible provider in England, most were presented with between two and five options, and very few said they were offered treatment in the private sector. This suggests that choice is not offered to all patients in the way envisaged by the policy.

However, patients' recall of choice may be influenced by the way in which choice was presented or structured, which may thus influence these results. It may be that patients who have to call a booking adviser to book their appointment, or who receive a formal letter outlining their choices, recall choice being offered because of the nature of the interaction. Those patients whose GP booked their appointment in the surgery may have been offered a choice but not recalled it as such, or not perceived the interaction to be a formal offer of choice.

Most patients were offered a choice by their GP; however, about 40 per cent of respondents were also offered a choice outside their GP consultation, either in a letter that outlined options or by a telephone booking adviser. This shows that, for many, much of the interaction around choosing a hospital and booking an appointment occurs outside of the GP consultation. It also shows that, in addition to GPs, there is an important role for other practice staff and telephone advisers in supporting the policy of patient choice.

The different ways in which choice was implemented locally may explain some of the differences between case study areas. Our analysis of case study areas (see also Section 6) showed that, in PCT A, the structure of the incentive payment given to GPs may be partly responsible for the high numbers of patients who were offered a choice. Although incentives can encourage GPs to offer choice where they might not have done otherwise, they do not influence whether patients exercise choice.

In the next section, we examine whether there are differences in which patients are offered a choice of hospital.

Who is offered a choice?

In Section 2 (pp 29–36), we described some of the concerns expressed by GPs and providers that choice was more relevant to certain population groups (younger, more educated and middle class) and people in certain areas (urban areas, particularly London). These concerns reflected similar fears expressed by commentators before the patient choice policy was implemented, that not all patients would have an equal opportunity to choose (Appleby *et al* 2003).

Many of the GPs we interviewed did not believe it was possible to ensure that all patients had an equal opportunity to exercise choice. Many thought that a significant proportion of their patients – particularly older patients – were happy to entrust the responsibility to them. The seriousness of the patient's condition could also affect their willingness to choose for themselves.

> *There are quite a high proportion of elderly in our area who basically just say, 'Doctor, you choose for me'.*
>
> (GP, area B)

> *I mean, on the whole, if someone's really got something wrong with them, they want to go where I think is the best place to go.*
>
> (GP, area C)

In cases where a patient's understanding was limited because of language difficulties, low levels of literacy or mental health problems, some GPs admitted that they tended to make certain assumptions on behalf of their patients.

> *I think inevitably there will be an issue... with some patients, it's hard enough coming to a diagnosis... because of communication issues... and having a conversation with people about choice is not one you'd go into with any great relish... But I suppose I'm heartened by the fact that actually those that I can have that sort of conversation with... that I know the vast majority of them all want to go to [hospital B1 NHS FT] anyway, and they're quite happy with that... which sounds terribly patronising and 'I know best and you go where I tell you', but... in all life it's trade-offs, isn't it?*
>
> (GP, area B)

> *I suppose the honest answer is that it will differ depending on certain factors and those factors might be age, ethnicity, etc... albeit that we would like to say that we do go through that same process, it's not always easy.*
>
> (GP, area A)

Several of the providers we spoke to also felt that choice was more applicable for the young, those from higher socioeconomic groups and those with higher levels of education. They described deprived populations as not being interested in choice of hospital.

> *Clearly, a lot of our areas are relatively deprived areas, and you wouldn't necessarily expect patients from that type of area to be looking at websites and making decisions in that way.*
>
> (NHS provider, area C)

> *Particularly in the population that we serve here, within [the south or west of the city], that patients are not actively using choice because probably they don't really know it's there... I just think it's not leafy middle-class England, where you know about all these things.*
>
> (NHS provider, area B)

There is evidence in terms of stuff through the membership and through complaints and so on and so forth, where the younger generations are starting to exercise choice more.

(Foundation trust provider, area D)

However, most providers felt that patients were not actively comparing hospitals whatever socioeconomic group they came from or whatever their level of education. One interviewee described savvy middle-class patients who researched treatment options on the internet but were not interested in researching providers and actively choosing between them.

They're a highly intelligent population, they're all on the internet, they all come into outpatient clutching their piece of paper around 'This is the treatment I want because I've researched it on the internet'. But I think even that population are not searching around to try and find comparative data, to say where should I choose to go, they're talking to their family doctor and saying 'Who do you know that would be good at doing this?'

(NHS provider, area C)

The two independent sector hospitals in the study felt that their NHS patients did not come from deprived populations, implying that either GPs were screening who they sent to independent sector providers, or patients from deprived populations were not selecting independent sector providers – which might be due to the location of those providers.

We don't get a lot of patients who are from the rougher end of the spectrum… Horrible way to put it, but people are going to come to what is nearest, convenient for the families or a bus route… Well, there isn't a bus route here so that puts off a lot.

(Independent sector provider, area C)

Here we tend to get more medium middle-class typical [name of suburb] punters who then go, of course, if they want to go to the private place, will go to the private place.

(Independent sector provider, area C)

Some GPs commented on choice being more applicable to patients living on the edge of metropolitan areas than those in more isolated rural locations with few hospitals nearby:

We're sitting on the edge of [large metropolitan area B], [another area], [area C], [a small town] and we can send people in five or six directions.

(GP, area C)

We have one district general hospital nine miles north. So for people to go anywhere other than that is a 60-mile or 80-mile round trip.

(GP, area D)

We analysed survey responses to see if some patients were more likely to be offered a choice than others. The survey data was analysed using binary logistic regression to explore the factors that influenced whether patients said they were offered a choice of hospital. The results of this analysis are presented in Table 9 overleaf. The dependent variable in this analysis is patient recall that choice was offered when referred for treatment, and the model looks at which factors predict whether patients recall being offered a choice after controlling for other variables. The variables listed in the table had a significant impact on whether patients recalled being offered a choice. The results are expressed as the odds ratio that a particular category of patient was offered a choice compared to the comparison group (in brackets).

Table 9 Binary logistic regression model of recall of choice

Variable	(Comparison group) Response category	Odds ratio	Significance	Lower 95% CI	Upper 95% CI	Interpretation
Gender	(Female) Male*	0.79	0.03	0.64	0.97	Men were significantly less likely to be offered a choice than women.
Referral priority	(Routine) Urgent**	0.60	0.00	0.44	0.83	Respondents whose referral was routine were significantly more likely to be offered a choice than those with urgent referrals.
EQ-VAS self-rated health status	(Healthiest quartile) 2nd quartile** 3rd quartile** Unhealthiest quartile	0.72 0.67 0.59	0.01 0.01 0.07	0.57 0.50 0.34	0.91 0.89 1.04	The healthiest respondents were significantly more likely to be offered a choice than those who rated their health in the 2nd or 3rd quartile.
Urban/rural	(City/large town/suburbs) Small town** Village/rural*	1.71 1.42	0.00 0.02	1.32 1.07	2.23 1.89	Respondents living in small towns and villages or rural settings were significantly more likely to be offered a choice than those in cities/ large towns or suburbs.
Anticipate an operation or inpatient stay	(No) Yes** Don't know	1.52 0.91	0.00 0.51	1.21 0.68	1.91 1.21	Those who anticipated that they would need an operation or inpatient stay were significantly more likely to be offered a choice than those who did not.
Resident PCT	(PCT A) PCT B** PCT C** PCT D** Other PCTs**	0.30 0.22 0.20 0.32	0.00 0.00 0.00 0.00	0.16 0.13 0.11 0.20	0.56 0.38 0.36 0.53	Respondents who lived in PCT A were significantly more likely to be offered a choice than those living in any other PCT.
Constant		3.38	0.00			

Note: Dependent variable: Recall that a choice was offered. Other variables included in the model were: age group; ethnicity (white and mixed/non-white); level of education; gender; EQ-VAS self-rated health status; PCT of residence; past experience of local hospital; urban/rural; anticipation of needing an operation or inpatient stay; referral priority; frequency of GP attendance.

** significant at 1 per cent level

* significant at 5 per cent level

Although GPs thought that older patients and those with lower levels of education may not want to choose, a patient's age and level of education did not significantly influence whether choice was offered. Men were less likely to be offered a choice than women (*see* Table 9, above), but ethnicity was not a significant predictor. Unfortunately, it is not possible to establish with these data whether patients with language difficulties or mental health problems are less likely to be offered a choice. Despite translation services being available, patients who had difficulties understanding English are under-represented in the sample (*see* Appendix A for a fuller discussion of the limitations of the study).

Similarly, although GPs thought that choice was more applicable in urban centres, patients living in a small town were significantly more likely to be offered a choice than those living in a city, large town or suburb (*see* Table 9 above). To a lesser extent, patients living in villages and rural areas were also more likely to be offered a choice, although this result dropped out of the model when the data was weighted to account for over-sampling of ISTCs (*see* Appendix A).

Some GPs said they were less likely to offer choice for a 'serious' referral that required urgent treatment. Our results show that patients whose referral was classed as urgent were indeed less likely to be offered a choice than those needing a routine referral. The results also show that patients with a lower self-reported health status were less likely to be offered a choice than those who placed themselves in the healthiest quartile. However, patients who anticipated needing an operation or inpatient stay were significantly more likely to be offered a choice.

The way that choice was implemented locally had an impact on the number of patients offered a choice. The results show that respondents who lived in PCT A were far more likely to be offered a choice than those in other PCTs, when controlling for differences in patient characteristics. This backs up findings from bivariate analysis shown in Figure 9 (*see* p 54).

When the regression is run with data that has been weighted for the over-sampling of ISTCs (*see* Appendix A), the results remain largely the same, but one additional variable becomes significant. Patients who had a bad past experience of their local hospital were significantly less likely to be offered a choice (significant at 1 per cent level).

Despite concerns expressed by GPs and providers, younger, highly educated patients were no more likely to be offered a choice than older and less educated patients. Although many of the GPs and providers we interviewed regarded choice as only relevant in large metropolitan areas, patients in small towns were more likely to be offered a choice, possibly because choice was more relevant to them if they had a number of providers located at an equal distance from their home. In this regard, there appears to be a discrepancy between the views and opinions of GPs and providers and the way choice is operating in practice.

Patients who have more serious treatment needs and are aware of this before being referred are more likely to be offered a choice. But when the health need is urgent, they are less likely to be offered a choice, possibly due to GPs prioritising speed of access.

In the next section, we consider whether those patients who were offered a choice took the opportunity to access care from an alternative to their local provider. We also examine in more detail which patients take up the opportunity to choose.

Are patients exercising choice?

Theory and policy assume that at least a proportion of patients who are offered a choice will choose to travel further (ie, to a non-local provider) in order to access higher-quality services. These so-called 'switchers' are the ones whose preferences are in theory supposed to signal to providers what is important to patients (*see* Section 1).

However, when patients are offered a choice, many may actively choose their local hospital. Conversely, even when patients are not offered a choice, some may be referred to a non-local provider for a number of reasons – the range of treatments available locally, the GP's view of the best place to receive treatment, or the GP's habitual referral patterns. For this reason, it is not easy to identify how many patients are exercising choice to bypass their local provider. For example, we do not know which of those attending their local provider made an active decision to do so. In this section, we analyse a number of different data sources to understand whether patients are exercising choice to attend a non-local provider, and which patients are exercising choice. We examine the factors that influence patients' choices and the preferences of different groups of patients.

We draw on data from a number of sources: the questionnaire, which asked whether respondents were treated at their local hospital and whether they were offered a choice; postcode data, to examine whether patients attended the hospital nearest to their home; data on GPs' views of where their patients attended hospital; and finally, provider perspectives on this.

Patients' responses

Seventy-three per cent of respondents said they had been referred to their local hospital. Twenty-one per cent of those not offered a choice were referred to a non-local hospital compared with 29 per cent of those offered a choice. In other words, an additional 8 per cent of patients travelled to a non-local provider when offered a choice (*see* Figure 11 below). This figure reduces to 5 per cent when the data is weighted to compensate for the over-sampling of ISTCs (*see* Appendix A). The difference in the weighted data occurs because ISTCs were not generally considered by patients to be their local hospital. Just 20 per cent of ISTC patients compared with 77 per cent of those attending NHS trusts said they were attending their local hospital.

In addition to asking patients if they were attending their local hospital, they were also asked for some postcode data, which allowed travel distances to be calculated to show whether patients attended the hospital that was nearest to their home. Thirty-nine per cent of respondents who were not offered a choice and 53 per cent of those who were travelled beyond their nearest hospital. In other words, 14 per cent more patients travel further than the nearest hospital when choice is offered. This figure reduces to 12 per cent when the data is weighted to compensate for the over-sampling of ISTCs.

To summarise, the data suggests that between 5 and 14 per cent more patients travel beyond their local or nearest provider when choice is offered.

Figure 11 Offer of choice and location of treatment

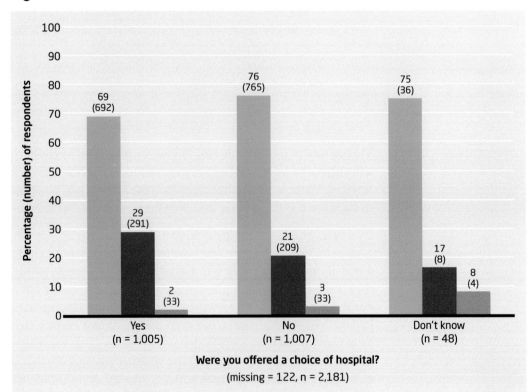

Travelling to a non-local provider may not always be what a patient wants, and many will choose to be treated locally. We asked patients whether they went to the hospital they wanted. The results in Figure 12, below, show that, as would be expected, allowing patients to choose their hospital increases the chance of their being treated at the hospital they want: 91 per cent of patients who were offered a choice went to the hospital they wanted, compared with 52 per cent of those not offered a choice. However, only 10 per cent of those not offered a choice did not go to the hospital they wanted, compared to 4 per cent of those who were offered a choice. The main difference was that over a third of those who were not offered a choice had no preference over where they were treated. This suggests that patients who have a preference may be more likely to be offered a choice or, indeed, request to be referred elsewhere, and that those who are not offered a choice may have been happy to go with the suggestion made by the GP.

Figure 12 Offer of choice and attending the hospital the patient wanted

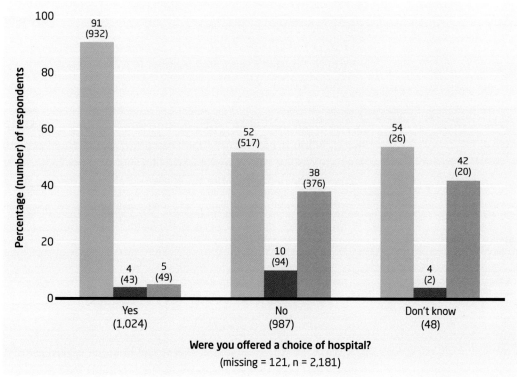

GPs and providers' views

Many of the providers we interviewed said patients were very loyal to their local hospital. One trust had found it difficult to persuade patients on their waiting list to receive quicker treatment at another hospital.

> *Our local people are very, very loyal to us and actually want to be treated at a local hospital.*

(NHS provider, area C)

> *We did some work trying to move, I think it was the orthopaedic patients out, and actually 70 or 80 per cent of them – I can't remember the exact figures – didn't want to go anywhere else other than here anyway, even when we were trying to put them out somewhere else to hit targets and waits… So they still wanted to stay locally.*

(Foundation trust provider, area B)

In a few interviews, GPs also spoke about the importance of loyalty to local health services and familiarity with particular hospitals.

There's a hospital loyalty... I'm thinking of a few people who say 'I only like to go to [local hospital name]...' They feel comfortable there.

(GP, area B)

And another thing you've got to remember is, people have quite an allegiance to the local health providers, that there's a strong feeling that people should support the local hospitals.

(GP, area A)

Some interviewees explained patients' 'stickiness' to the local provider as a result of factors such as ease of access, travel time and public transport.

If you talk to people, they don't want to go to [name of ISTC], it's too far. They really seriously just don't want to go there because it feels like the back of beyond for them and, of course, they feel very confident in their local hospital.

(Foundation trust provider, area D)

I still think it's down to locality. People want to come local. They don't want to have to travel, they don't want their families to have to travel far to visit them, so the locality is important.

(Foundation trust provider, area B)

In two trusts, providers spoke about patients feeling a connection to their local hospital through family members being treated there or having been born there. One trust with four sites found that patients were reluctant to move between them. 'Local' in this area seemed to be defined by the small town that each hospital site served.

When I come here it is very much like, my, you know, people's mothers were born in the hospital, they were born in the hospital, will always come to the hospital, they still call it by its old name.

(NHS provider, area B)

Most patients are treated at their local hospital regardless of choice. This may be because (as both GPs and providers explained) patients are loyal to their local trust and reluctant to consider travelling further. Patients were more likely to get to the hospital they wanted when they were offered a choice, although in general, those not offered a choice were happy with where they had been referred to, or had no preference.

When given a choice, at least some patients take the opportunity to be referred to a provider other than their local hospital. Somewhere between 5 and 14 per cent more of those offered a choice choose to be treated beyond their local or nearest provider compared to those not offered a choice. These are the patients we would expect to provoke a response in providers if they were systematically moving away from poor providers because of specific deficiencies in their services. Whether providers are actively seeking to understand why patients choose to bypass them in favour of other, more distant providers, and adjusting their services in response, is considered in Section 5. Before that, the report now considers whether patients with particular characteristics are more likely to travel to a non-local provider.

Who is exercising choice?

This report has discussed concerns from policy commentators and academics (Section 1) as well as the GPs and providers involved in the study (Section 2) that patient choice would increase inequity in the NHS, with some patients more able to travel to access higher-quality care from a non-local provider. There was an expectation that wealthier, healthier, younger patients would be more willing and able to travel beyond their local hospital, and that more educated patients would be better equipped to compare hospitals and select a higher-quality alternative. The fear is that poorer, older, less-educated patients would be left to be treated by poorer services.

There have also been concerns that choice was only really relevant for patients in London and other urban centres, as those in more rural areas would have to travel further to access alternatives to their local provider.

This section of the report uses data collected on the demographic characteristics of survey respondents and their health status to explore whether some patients are more likely to travel beyond their local provider than others. This analysis focuses on those who chose a non-local hospital. We begin by looking at which patients chose a non-local provider, and then consider patients who chose a non-local provider when presented with hypothetical choice sets.

Real choices

To gain a better understanding of which patients chose a non-local provider (while controlling for other factors), we tested a model of factors thought to influence the choice of non-local providers. Data from patients who said they were offered a choice was analysed using a binary logistic regression with the dependent variable being patient-reported attendance at a non-local hospital (*see* Appendix A). The results, in Table 10 overleaf, are expressed as the odds ratio that a particular category of patients travelled away from their local hospital compared with the comparison group.

Table 10 shows that patients aged 51–65 were more likely than younger patients (aged 16–35) to travel to a non-local provider. There is some indication that patients who held a degree were more likely to choose a non-local provider (significant at 5 per cent level). Gender and ethnicity made no significant impact on whether a patient chose a non-local provider. As previously noted, we were not able to examine whether patients who have difficulties speaking English are less likely to choose a non-local provider.

Although results outlined in 'Who is offered a choice?' (pp 56–9) showed that a patient's age and level of education had no impact on the likelihood of their being offered a choice, it does seem that these characteristics affect the likelihood a patient chooses an alternative to their local provider.

Patients who live in small towns and villages or rural locations were also more likely to choose a non-local provider rather than those in cities, large towns or suburbs. When the data is weighted to control for ISTC over-sampling (*see* Appendix A), the impact of living in a small town is no longer significant, although living in a village and rural location remains so. Patients who relied on public transport to travel to a non-local hospital were less likely to travel to a non-local provider (although only significant at 5 per cent level and drops out of the model when the data is weighted). A patient's PCT of residence did not have a significant impact on whether they travelled beyond their local hospital.

These results run counter to the views of many of the providers and GPs we spoke to, who felt that choice was only relevant in metropolitan areas where patients had many

Table 10 Binary logistic regression model of travelling beyond the local provider for treatment

Variable	(Comparison group) Response category	Odds ratio	Significance	Lower 95% CI	Upper 95% CI	Interpretation
Age group	(16–35)					Respondents aged between
	36–50	1.93	0.07	0.94	3.93	51 and 65 were significantly
	51–65**	2.67	0.01	1.32	5.39	more likely to choose a
	66–80	1.84	0.11	0.87	3.00	non-local hospital than those
	81+	1.22	0.70	0.44	3.45	aged 16–35.
Gender	(Female)					
	Male	1.39	0.08	0.96	2.01	
Frequency of	(Once)					
GP attendance	2–5 times	1.28	0.55	0.57	2.84	
in last	6–10 times	0.84	0.67	0.36	1.92	
12 months	More than 10 times	0.62	0.34	0.23	1.66	
Urban/rural	(City/large town/suburbs)					Those living in small towns,
	Small town **	2.09	0.00	1.35	3.23	villages and rural locations
	Village/rural **	2.48	0.00	1.53	4.03	were significantly more likely
						to choose a non-local hospital
						than those in cities, large
						towns or suburbs.
Education	(No formal qualifications)					Those holding a degree were
	Below degree level	1.23	0.35	0.80	1.89	significantly more likely to
	Degree level and higher*	1.86	0.02	1.08	3.20	choose a non-local hospital
						than those with no formal
						qualifications.
Usual way to	(By car)					Those who usually travelled
travel to a	Public transport*	0.47	0.03	0.23	0.93	to a non-local hospital by
non-local	Taxi	1.07	0.90	0.39	2.95	public transport were
hospital	Other	0.27	0.13	0.05	1.47	significantly less likely to
						choose a non-local hospital
						than those who usually
						travelled by car.
Past experience	(Generally good)					Those with bad or mixed
of local	Generally bad**	24.94	0.00	4.96	125.31	past experience at their local
hospital	Mixed **	2.87	0.00	1.88	4.36	hospital were significantly
	No past experience	1.73	0.14	0.84	3.58	more likely to choose a
						non-local hospital than
						those who had a generally
						good experience.
Resident PCT	(PCT B)					
	PCT A	1.19	0.77	0.36	3.96	
	PCT C	1.16	0.80	0.37	3.66	
	PCT D	0.97	0.96	0.29	3.21	
	Any other PCT	2.74	0.06	0.98	7.70	
Constant		0.03	0.00			

Note: dependent variable: attending a non-local hospital (respondents were asked whether the hospital they were attending was their local one). Other variables included in the model were: age group; ethnicity (white and mixed/non-white); level of education; gender; EQ-VAS self-rated health status; PCT of residence; past experience of local hospital; urban/rural; anticipation of needing an operation or inpatient stay; frequency of GP attendance; referral priority; mode of travel to non-local hospital. Only respondents who were offered a choice were included in the analysis.

** significant at 1 per cent level

* significant at 5 per cent level

providers nearby and access was easier. One trust with sites in a number of towns as well as on the edge of a metropolitan area felt that patients and GPs had greater loyalty in the large towns than in the suburbs.

We have a very loyal clientele generally, their people in [PCT A] go to[hospital A1 NHS] because it's where you go. And the GPs again want to refer to [hospital A1 NHS], [small town name]. GPs generally want to refer to [small town hospital name], and the patients want to go there. So in some senses they're very loyal, loyal to the extent of some initial resistance to change, even if the service was only five more miles down the road and was actually a lot, lot better. [The big city] has been a bit different, because although there is quite a lot of loyalty, [the big city] hasn't got the same loyalty as the townships if you like around [the big city].

(NHS provider, area A)

There was a clear link between past experience of a hospital and propensity to travel beyond the local provider for treatment. A patient with a bad experience of their local hospital was much more likely to choose a non-local provider compared with someone who had a positive experience at their local hospital (odds ratio of 24.94, 95 per cent CI of 4.96 to 125.31). To a lesser extent, someone with mixed past experience at the local hospital was more likely to choose to be treated elsewhere.

Anticipating the need for an operation or inpatient treatment, referral priority and self-reported health status did not affect patients' likelihood of travelling non-local. Frequency of GP attendance remained in the model but did not have a significant impact on whether patients went non-local. Although results in Section 3 'Who is offered a choice?' Table 9, (p 58) showed that GPs were more likely to offer a choice to patients who anticipated needing an operation (although were less likely to offer choice if the treatment need was urgent, or if the patient was less healthy), these factors did not influence whether the patient travelled to a non-local hospital.

When patients are offered a choice, most choose their local provider, but older patients, those living outside of cities and large towns, those educated to degree level and those with a bad past experience of the local hospital are more likely to choose care from a non-local provider. When the analysis was repeated for those not offered a choice, the only variable that affected whether patients travelled to a non-local provider was their past experience of the local hospital.

Revealed preferences

To understand more about the impact of location, distance and hospital characteristics on patients' choice of hospital, a multinomial logit (MNL) model was developed as an extension of the previous logistic regression. Rather than modelling a binary decision of choosing to stay local or move to an alternative, this probabilistic choice model, based on revealed preference data, represented the choice between a large number of possible hospitals, each of which had different characteristics that may (or may not) have influenced the decision to choose them (*see* Appendix A, 'Questionnaire data analysis', pp 168–71).

This model showed that distance is an important factor influencing choice of hospital. The model suggests that patients living in local health economy D were more tolerant towards the travel distance to a hospital. The area has a lower density of hospitals, and patients will on average already need to travel further to reach their local provider. We also identify a very strong preference for remaining at the local hospital, which is to be anticipated given that 70 per cent of the patients in our sample believed that they were attending their local hospital.

Stated preferences

Analysis of the choices made by patients presented with the hypothetical choices (*see* Appendix A) allows us to gain an understanding of whether certain groups of respondents showed a greater propensity through their choices to stay at the local provider, and whether some patients outside of the constraints of the current situation (where many are not offered a choice and little information is available) are more likely to choose care from a non-local provider. One hospital in each hypothetical choice set was labelled 'local provider'.

When all of the data is looked at together, respondents chose to stay at the local provider in 61 per cent of the choice scenarios rather than selecting either of the two alternative providers offered. All other things being equal, it would be expected that respondents would choose each of the three hospitals in approximately equal proportions, so this level of preference for the local provider suggests that respondents view the local provider as having an attraction over and above the information presented on performance.

Figure 13, below, summarises the stated preference choice behaviour of the respondents across their sequence of choice scenarios. We see that 25 per cent of respondents opted to stay with the local provider in all of the choice scenarios they were presented with. This lack of discrimination in the responses might suggest that some of these respondents were not engaging with the exercise. However, it may also indicate that there is a sizeable proportion of patients who, regardless of the options presented to them, always choose to go to the local hospital.[3]

Figure 13 Responses over the sequence of stated preference choices

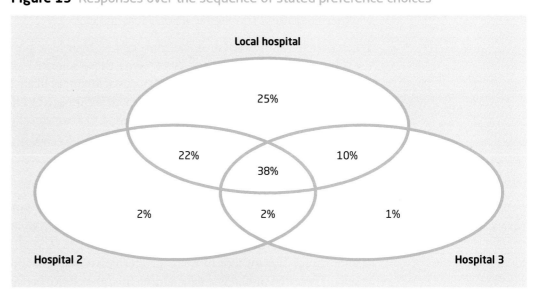

The overlap between the local hospital and the other two hospitals in Figure 13, above, shows that 70 per cent of the respondents sometimes chose the local hospital and sometimes chose an alternative provider across the sequence of choice scenarios. This suggests that, with these hypothetical choices, a large proportion of patients are willing to weigh up the performance of available hospitals and are willing to move away from their local provider.

All other things being equal, when given a choice between three hospitals with identical attributes, except that one is designated as the 'local' hospital, some groups of people are more likely to choose their local hospital and some are more likely to consider an alternative.

In Figure 14, opposite, we show the value placed on staying with the local provider for those characteristics that are associated with a propensity to stay with the local hospital.

---

[3] This is similar to the findings from previous studies of patient choice, where 20 per cent of the survey respondents consistently chose the local provider in all of the choice scenarios offered (Burge *et al* 2006). In this previous study, the position of the alternatives within the choice task were varied between respondents, and the model developed demonstrated that the position of the local hospital within the task had no significant impact on the probability of it being chosen – ie, respondents did not choose the hospital presented first in the choice more than the other options offered.

The figure presents these values in units of equivalent hours of travel time – that is, the travel time that would need to be saved to make an alternative hospital more attractive. The error bars are the 95 per cent confidence intervals on these estimates. It should also be noted that the terms are additive, and any single patient may fall into multiple groups and hence have a higher propensity to stay at the local hospital.

Figure 14, below, shows that the following groups of people would be more likely to stay with their local hospital (irrespective of that hospital's characteristics):

- those without internet access

- those with a low level of formal education (no formal qualification or GCSE/O level equivalent)

- those that normally do not travel by car to their local hospital

- those living in a city or large town

- those who knew about their right to choose a hospital before visiting their GP.

This suggests that, when looking across all of the characteristics of the respondents, the absence of internet access had the strongest relationship with the decision to stay with the local provider.

Conversely, Figure 15, overleaf, shows that the following groups would be more likely to attend an alternative to the local hospital:

- those who would like more information to help them choose a hospital

- those with either bad or mixed past experience of their local hospital

- those who have heard about the performance of hospitals in their area from the local media

- those attending their chosen hospital in local health economy A

- those being referred for trauma or orthopaedics

- those who have visited their GP six times or more in the last 12 months.

Figure 14 Characteristics of respondents more likely to choose their local hospital in the discrete choice experiment

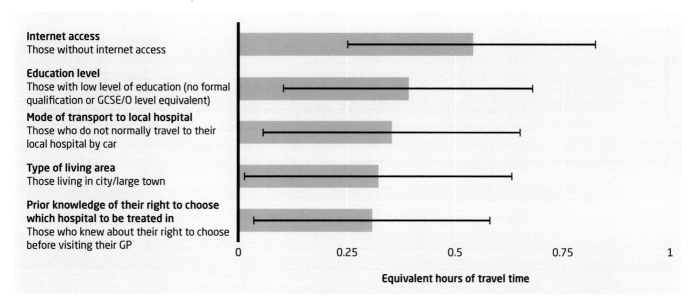

Figure 15 Characteristics of respondents more likely to choose a non-local hospital in the discrete choice experiment

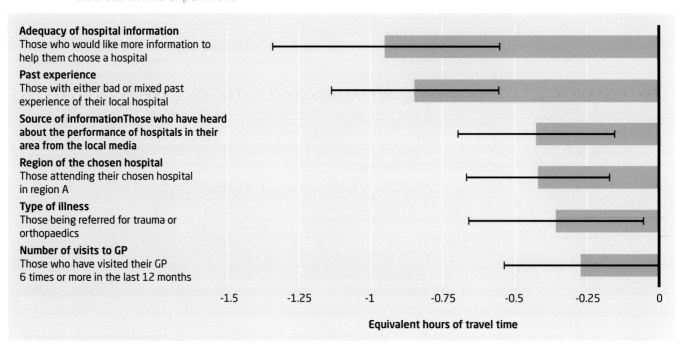

There appears to be some connection between income and education and those selecting their local hospital. Respondents without internet access, with lower levels of education and who did not travel to hospital by car were more likely to select their local trust irrespective of performance or other attributes.

Respondents who lived in cities or large towns were also more likely to select the local provider (*see* Figure 14, p 67), which is consistent with the survey results presented in Table 10, p 64.

The data on hypothetical choices shows a clear relationship between perceived performance of the local hospital and the willingness to continue to attend this provider. Within the discrete choice experiment, there were a number of reputation attributes that were varied, including the opinions of the GP, the patient's friends and family, and the local press. These all act in the expected direction, with patients indicating that they would be more likely to choose a hospital with better reputation.

However, in addition to this information, we have also been able to incorporate patients' own stated perceptions of their local provider. Here we see that, as might be expected, those patients who have had a generally bad or mixed experience of their local hospital in reality are more likely to choose a non-local hospital in hypothetical situations. We also see that those patients who report that they have heard about the performance of hospitals in their area from the local media are more likely to choose to travel to an alternative hospital (which makes sense as local media reports typically cover poor performance).

Although the expectation is that choice is more likely to be exercised in urban centres than rural areas, our analysis shows that, when offered a choice, patients from villages and rural areas were most likely to opt to be treated at a non-local provider. Analysis of the choices made by patients within the discrete choice experiment suggests that practicalities and real world constraints (such as their dependency on public transport to reach the hospital) may influence patients' choices. Another explanation is that those living in large towns and cities have a greater affinity to their local provider, whereas in small towns and villages, patients may have a number of equidistant providers and therefore have less affinity with any single hospital.

The results raise some concerns about the impact of patient choice on equity. Patients with lower levels of education were less likely to opt for alternative providers, while those educated to degree level or above were more likely to travel beyond their local provider for treatment. In hypothetical situations, patients without internet access, with lower levels of education and who normally do not travel by car to hospital were most likely to select their local hospital. These findings suggest that some people face constraints on their ability or willingness to exercise choice to be referred beyond their local area. Although younger patients were anticipated to be more interested in choice and the opportunity to travel beyond their local provider, older patients (aged 51–80) were most likely to do so. One possible reason for this is that older patients may be more likely to need specialist care or have more regular contact with health services, and are therefore more familiar with other hospitals and willing to travel further. Conversely, younger patients may be more interested in convenient care that is closer to home.

Finally, patients who had a bad experience of a local hospital were much more likely to go to a non-local provider. It appears that the ability to exercise choice and 'exit' from the local hospital is important for those patients who have had a previous (negative) experience with their local provider. This suggests that experience is a key factor in determining a patient's choice of hospital. We now explore these underlying factors that drive patient choice in more detail.

Why are patients choosing particular providers?

We have discussed whether patients were offered a choice and whether they considered exercising that choice and travelling beyond their local provider. We now consider what factors influence the choices patients make. These are the factors about which we would expect providers to compete, and expect GPs to provide information to patients to help them choose.

We begin by considering the factors that patients said were important to them when choosing a hospital, along with GPs and providers' perceptions. Each factor is discussed in turn. We then look at revealed preference data on the characteristics of the hospitals patients chose to attend, and discuss what this tells us about their preferences. Finally, we consider which factors were important to patients when making choices in hypothetical situations, and how they traded off one factor for another.

The views of patients, GPs and providers

Our survey asked patients directly what factors they considered when choosing a hospital for their recent referral. Those who had been offered a choice were asked to state how important various factors were in influencing which hospital they chose. The list of factors was developed following interviews with patients about how they made their choice (*see* Appendix A).

The factors are not mutually exclusive: hospital reputation, for example, may be influenced by the standard of the hospital's facilities and the quality of care provided. Quality of care may encompass the friendliness of staff, organisation of the clinic, and clinical aspects of quality. In Figure 16, below, factors rated as 'essential' were scored as 3, 'very important' as 2, 'somewhat important' as 1 and 'not important' as 0. The scores shown are the mean score given by respondents for each factor. The list gives an indication of how important the survey respondents felt these factors were – factors that others had identified as influencing choice.

Figure 16 Factors that influence patients' choice of hospital

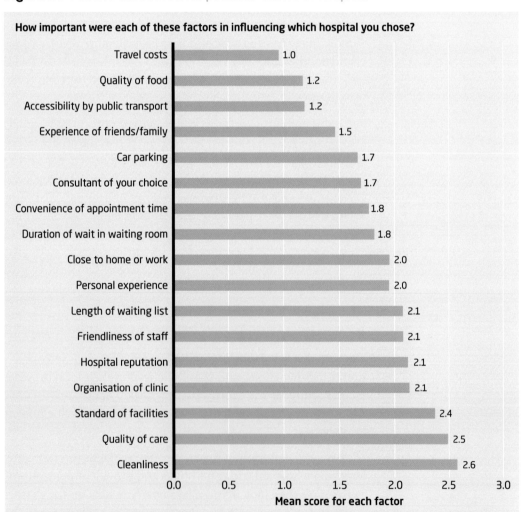

Note: In this figure, factors rated as 'essential' were scored as 3, 'very important' as 2, 'somewhat important' as 1 and 'not important' as 0. The scores shown are the mean score given by respondents for each factor.

Scores for each factor have been rounded to one decimal place. The length of the bar represents the non-rounded score.

Cleanliness

Cleanliness and quality of care were rated as the two most important factors for patients when choosing a hospital. This is in line with the findings of recent patient choice monitoring surveys carried out by the Department of Health (Department of Health 2009a).

The GPs and providers we spoke to had mixed views on whether infection rates influenced patients' choices. A hospital's level of cleanliness does not reflect its rates of hospital-acquired infections, but the two are closely connected in patients' minds, and there is evidence that hospitals where patients rate cleanliness higher have lower infection rates (Trucano and Kaldenberg 2007). In one of the local health economies studied, two GPs operating within the same PCT stated:

Out of every 100 referrals I do, probably one or two people will say… 'What are my chances of getting MRSA?'

(GP, area C)

They want somewhere with a low hospital-acquired infection rate. That's top of the pops normally, they normally say about MRSA, they all tend to know about that.

(GP, area C)

Overall, providers were more aware than GPs of potential patient concerns, which were partly due to national press coverage of MRSA outbreaks:

Infection and common courtesy. That's what patients think, that's what matters to patients.

(Foundation trust provider, area D)

So, I think it's an expectation… to come into a hospital and it's safe... I think there still is a trust with a consultant... and the cleanliness thing is probably the only thing that they probably might have a different view about because there's been so much national press about that.

(Foundation trust provider, area D)

Infection rates and cleanliness were seen as a particularly important factor to patients choosing private providers. ISTC survey respondents placed more importance on cleanliness than NHS respondents, giving the factor an average score of 2.9 compared with 2.5.[4] Two of the private providers interviewed felt that patients were choosing to be treated by them because of their low infection rates, and one respondent mentioned this explicitly:

I get phone calls from private patients saying, 'What's your MRSA rate, what's your C diff rate?'

(Independent sector provider, area C)

One of the elements of [name of ISTC]'s reputation in this part of the world is that the infection rate there is very low, whereas [another NHS hospital], for example, is, well, it's relatively low but not so low. I mean, you're much more likely to get infection at [that NHS hospital] than you are just at [name of ISTC], and it's just a fact in the community quite frankly, once you start talking about hospitals.

(Female patient, age 78, area D)

Those who anticipated needing an operation also gave cleanliness a slightly higher importance score on average than those who did not (2.7 vs 2.5).[5]

---

[4] Differences significant at 1 per cent level.

[5] Differences significant at 1 per cent level in the unweighted data and 5 per cent level in the weighted data.

Quality of care

The second most important factor to patients was quality of care. We did not define 'quality' in our questionnaire; therefore, we do not know whether patients interpreted this to mean clinical effectiveness or a wider view of quality encompassing aspects of the patient experience. GPs suggested that, in practice, they did not believe that patients made choices based on clinical outcomes.

> *I don't think I've ever had a patient say 'I don't want to go there because I've looked at their outcome figures and I don't like the look of it'.*
>
> (GP, area B)

> *I think only one of the five partners has had one patient who actually wanted to look at that and go through various… data sheets to actually look at the figures before they make their choice.*
>
> (GP, area A)

Providers also indicated that, in general, they felt that patients did not consider quality in terms of clinical outcomes when choosing where to have treatment. Moreover, a number of interviewees said they believed there was an assumption that care would be of a similar clinical quality whichever hospital was chosen. A number of patients also held this view. However, one private provider described patients phoning up and asking for clinical information such as readmission and mortality rates.

> *[Are there any differences do you think in the cleanliness of hospitals locally?] No. [What about the quality of care that's provided?] Oh, they're both the same, it's very, very good.*
>
> (Female patient, age 50, area D)

> *They challenge now, inpatients ring up and say, both NHS and private, 'How many operations… how many readmissions has she had? What's the mortality rate, what's your infection rate like?*
>
> (Independent sector provider, area C)

Patients report that their choice of hospital was guided by standards of cleanliness and quality of care. While GPs and providers consider that infection rates are important to patients, they are sceptical about whether patients are interested in clinical outcomes as the basis for choosing a hospital, instead assuming that all hospitals provide equally good clinical care.

Standard of facilities

The standard of facilities was the third most important factor cited by patients when choosing a hospital. It was rated as more important by respondents who chose an ISTC (2.6) than those attending an NHS trust (2.3) – an unsurprising finding, as both of the ISTCs involved in our study were located in newly built premises.[6] While this was not something that was mentioned by GPs, it appears that hospital providers were aware that the age and appearance of the buildings in which services are delivered is a key factor in their success.

One trust dismissed a nearby trust as not posing any competitive threat due to its poor premises and staff retention problems.

> *I probably very arrogantly would say that they're not really in the best position to compete with us, their premises are worse than ours, they're finding it difficult to retain*

---

[6] Differences significant at 5 per cent level.

experienced consultants and nurses… So they're not really in a position to compete and, in fact, a lot of our patients will initially go to [hospital name] and [hospital name] and then choose to be referred here.

(Foundation trust provider, area B)

This same trust had recently completed its own private finance initiative (PFI) new build, and this was seen to be potentially threatening by a neighbouring trust.

I think one of the big things that has influenced the strategy at the moment is a new hospital at [name of site], so a brand new, state of the art facility, massive new hospital, that people may well choose to go there because you just drive past it and it looks impressive. So we recognise that we need to compete from a quality point of view.

(Foundation trust provider, area B)

Another trust in the same area felt that other hospitals with new facilities had the competitive advantage over them.

I think there is a more immediate one [threat], which is that, particularly because some of our competitors have new buildings in place faster than us and therefore are offering patients a better physical environment, we find we lose work to competitors faster than we can cope with in the short term. We've not seen any sign of that happening yet but it's a possibility.

(NHS provider, area B)

One trust had experienced a reduction in referrals following the opening of a new hospital, but this had only been temporary.

On our western border is [small town] and [small town] group of hospitals, and they opened their new acute hospital… about two years ago. And for six to eight months after the opening of that facility we saw an impact on the flow of work into our hospital… Since then, it's kind of swung back to sort of where it was beforehand, so it sort of suggests it was a kind of temporary, 'let's go and try out the new building' sort of phenomenon.

(NHS provider, area B)

Customer service

In addition to the standard of facilities, patients also felt that it was important to go to a hospital that provided a smoothly run service with well-organised clinics (ranked 4th) and friendly staff (ranked 6th). Patients who chose ISTCs placed more importance on how organised the clinic was than those referred to NHS trusts (2.3 vs 2.1).[7]

A number of patients mentioned differences in the way they were treated by staff at different hospitals, and the importance of friendly staff who had time to talk to them.

And the staff, being able to talk to the staff about… like in [NHS hospital name] you feel as if you can't say anything to them because they're just too busy, whereas both in [another NHS hospital] and [ISTC] they have the time to sit and talk to you and if you've got any… If you're feeling a little bit concerned, they will talk you through everything there is to talk you through.

(Female patient, age 46, area D)

The quality of food was less important overall, although those who anticipated needing an operation ranked this higher (1.3) than those who did not (1.0).[8]

[7] Differences significant at 5 per cent level.

[8] Differences significant at 1 per cent level.

Convenience and transport

Issues relating to convenience and transport were relatively unimportant to patients, who rated them lower than some other factors. For example, travel costs and accessibility on public transport were rated on average as 'somewhat important'. Car parking and being 'close to your work or home' ranked higher – on average, they were 'very important'. However, they still only ranked 13th and 9th respectively.

These ratings differed by local health economy area. For example, in area B, where patients tended to rely on public transport, convenience was rated as more important than in area D, where patients more often travelled by car (*see* 'Differences by local health economy area', pp 77–8). Patients attending ISTCs were significantly[9] less concerned about these factors than those attending NHS trusts. On average, they rated travel costs as 0.6 (compared with 1 for patients treated in the NHS), accessibility on public transport as 0.5 (compared with 1.3 for patients treated in the NHS) and 'close to home or work' as 1.2 (compared with 2.1 for patients treated in the NHS).

Although when presented with a list of factors, patients gave convenience and transport a relatively low ranking, when interviewed about which hospital they chose and why, proximity to their home was often the first factor mentioned.

> *He mentioned that I could have it done at [local hospital name] and I said 'Well, that'll do me', I said, 'You know, that's the easiest one for me to get to', I said, I'll go there.*
>
> (Male patient, age 61, area A)

GPs regarded transport as one of the biggest factors that influences patients when choosing a hospital, not only because of convenience for them but also because of the ease with which family and friends can visit.

> *I think in reality, apart from the wealthy, not many people are going to be wandering away from their locality because their family are here… So their support is local.*
>
> (GP, area B)

> *So when I offer patients choice, their decisions seem to be made on the basis of how close the hospital or clinic is to their home, really.*
>
> (GP, area D)

In area C in particular, GPs thought that convenience was often more important than the quality of care.

> *People seem to value the car park above the quality of the consultant sometimes… because actually the teaching, the big hospital in [town name] has got terrible parking and it's quite expensive, whereas [NHS hospital]'s a bit easier. So a lot of people don't want to go to [town name] because the parking's bad.*
>
> (GP, area C)

> *I mean, people don't want to go to [hospital name] in [small town] because it's hopeless to get into the place, the car parking is about eight pounds I think, and, you know, it's new and it's a government flagship, but… People go to [foundation trust hospital] or [other foundation trust hospital] or they like going to [another foundation trust hospital] because that's a smaller one and they can park there. Very often, people are more concerned about things like parking than they are about the clinical quality of the place.*
>
> (GP, area C)

Waiting times

We found that although waiting time was 'very important' to patients, they ranked it 7th behind factors relating to the patient's experience in the hospital, hospital reputation,

---

[9] Differences significant at the 1 per cent level.

quality of care and cleanliness (*see* Figure 16, p 70). Waiting times were more important to patients attending ISTCs than those at NHS trusts (average score 2.3 vs 2.0),[10] and a number of the patients interviewed who were treated at ISTCs had been attracted by their shorter waiting times.

> *They did discuss with me things like, there were different hospitals I could go to, but the [ISTC] was quicker, basically. They said I'd be on a waiting list for others. And that's about it.*
>
> (Female patient, age 24, area A)

Previous patient surveys and discrete choice experiments also found that waiting times were an important factor in determining where patients chose to attend hospital (see Section 1). The 18-week target from referral to treatment has reduced waiting times to first outpatient appointment dramatically, and may have resulted in choice being less influenced by this aspect of a provider's performance. Waiting times were slightly more important to respondents who chose a non-local hospital (average score 2.2 vs 2.0), showing that some patients may choose to travel beyond their local provider for this reason.

When GPs were questioned about the importance of waiting times to patients, they expressed different views. One GP felt that location far outweighed waiting times for his patients, and another felt that they were not an issue in his area. However, most other GPs identified waiting times as the second biggest factor influencing patient choice (after location). A few GPs thought that these two considerations tended to split between young and old, reflecting degrees of mobility and extent of other commitments like jobs and school holidays.

> *I did a survey of 100 of my patients around where they would choose to go… and by far and away the majority of them, the top priority around choice was the geographic location of the provider, and not the length of time they were having to wait.*
>
> (GP, area A)

> *I think what patients want mainly are two things. One is, in the elderly, they want it to be their local hospital… And with generally most other age groups, they want it to be as soon as possible.*
>
> (GP, area C)

> *I equate it to you or I going to Specsavers… If we're busy and we're desperate to get our eyes checked, we might go to Specsavers because we could probably walk in to that service and get it done there and then. But actually, if we possibly had a bit more time, we might go to our regular trusted opticians rather than, sort of, a high street chain. And it's the same for patients really, it depends what their life priorities are at the time.*
>
> (GP, area D)

A number of providers in local health economies B and C felt that waiting times were an important influence on patients' choice, be this through the patient choosing a shorter wait or the GP directing patients to a hospital with a shorter wait.

> *I think the other thing we can see is our call centre is getting a steady stream of people ringing in and saying, 'If I were to come to you for a gastroenterology appointment or an orthopaedic appointment, how long would I have to wait?' And then, in effect, the response is, 'Ok, thank you, I'll get back to you'.*
>
> (NHS provider, area B)

It appeared that those hospitals with shorter waiting times felt they had a competitive edge over other providers with longer waiting times. Some providers were using their

[10] Differences significant at 5 per cent level.

comparatively short waiting times to try 'picking up some new markets'. Surprisingly, one ISTC had been unable to gain a comparative advantage over the NHS by offering shorter waiting times.

My understanding… was that, in the first year, the [ISTC] wasn't as utilised as it was hoped to be. I don't know, again, how that looks and feels now. I know their access times aren't remarkably different to ours in most cases.

(Foundation trust provider, area D)

Reputation of the hospital

A hospital's reputation was rated as a 'very important' factor by patients, who said it was the 5th most important influence on their choices. GPs also thought it was an important factor to patients and gave examples where patients had demonstrated a preference for, or aversion to, a local hospital because of reputation – often based on scares in the local press or a previous personal experience.

…it is a negative choice in the sense of, they choose not to go to the closest because they don't trust it or they had a bad experience or, you know, 'that's where my mother died'.

(GP, area B)

So a lot of people will say, '[Hospital name]'s fine, that's where I had my baby and that's where my son had this done'.

(GP, area C)

One of the hospitals does have a bit of a reputation in the media and people do say 'Well, actually, I would rather go to [another hospital name] because of that'.

(GP, area A)

Two of the providers interviewed also identified stories in the local press as a factor influencing patients' choices. One patient described press stories about cleanliness contributing to a local hospital's poor reputation.

It's got a bit of a bad reputation lately. And I think things like that do put me off. [Is that from stories in the press or just generally that you hear locally?] Word of mouth, people I've known use the hospital. But then other people sing its praises. And I think maybe things I have read in the paper, and, of course, you do read things like cleanliness and stuff like that, which, I think, straight away does put you off.

(Female patient, age 57, area B)

There is an indication from the patient survey data that some patients seek out hospitals with a better reputation. Respondents who chose a non-local provider said that reputation was, on average, more important in their choice than those attending their local trust (rated 2.2 vs 2.0).[11] The key is to understand what it is that creates a good reputation for a hospital. The way patients form opinions about local hospitals is considered in more detail in 'What support, advice and information do patients receive?', pp 86–92.

Personal experience and experience of family and friends

Providers identified word of mouth and recommendations from family and friends as another factor affecting patients' choices, particularly in privately run centres, where establishing a good reputation was key to drawing in NHS patients.

NHS patients come here that have never been before and they go away and they've had such a positive experience, that… they go back and they tell their families, their

---

[11] Differences significant at 1 per cent level.

neighbours, 'Oh, that was fantastic', and it has had an impact on private patients coming here... increased our private business through word of mouth really.

(Independent sector provider, area C)

I think they will always ask around, you know... 'Who's had a similar procedure or has been in this hospital', or whatever. And I think they do listen very carefully and look at those sort of experiences.

(NHS provider, area C)

Personal experience was more important to survey respondents at NHS trusts, who were more likely to have been treated there before, than at the relatively new ISTCs (average score 2.0 vs 1.6).[12] Despite provider views, the experience of family and friends was ranked, on average, as only 'somewhat important' by patients treated at NHS hospitals and those treated at ISTCs.

Probably if it was a hospital I hadn't been to before, I would try and ask around from people who had had previous experience at that place. I would be a bit nervous about going somewhere I had no knowledge of at all.

(Male patient, age 59, area D)

Ability to see consultant of choice

Seeing a particular consultant was ranked as only the 12th most important factor by patients, and although GPs did not identify this as a key factor in patients' choices, they did talk of a few individuals who expressed a wish to be referred to consultants they had seen before or to units that specialised in particular conditions.

Some patients come along and say... 'I'd like to go to consultant X because... my neighbour saw him and he was fantastic'.

(GP, area A)

I had one patient recently and I mean, in a way, it was a good example of the way the system worked... He'd had an operation done four or five years ago... He remembered which hospital it was but he knew that the consultant who did it had left the hospital... and he wanted to go and see him.

(GP, area B)

Differences by local health economy area

When results of the patient survey were analysed by local health economy (LHE) area, cleanliness, quality of care and the standard of facilities came out as the three most important factors in each area and were ranked in the same order of importance. This implies that these were universal priorities for patients, irrespective of context. There was also little difference between the rating of waiting times across our areas, with ratings of 2.1 or 2.2 across all LHEs. This perhaps reflects the convergence in waiting times as a result of the nationally set waiting-time targets.

However, as would be expected, there were some differences between the four areas, particularly regarding the importance of factors relating to transport. For example, in LHE B, situated in a major metropolitan area where 19 per cent of patients travel to their local hospital by public transport, accessibility on public transport was rated as 'very important' (average rating 1.6). In LHE D, a more rural area, where just 9 per cent of patients use public transport to travel to their local hospital, accessibility on public transport was only 'somewhat important' (average rating 0.9).[13] Respondents in LHE

---

[12] Differences are significant at 1 per cent level.

[13] Differences significant at 1 per cent level.

D were also less concerned with whether the hospital was close to their work or home (average rating 1.8 compared to ratings of between 2 and 2.2 in other areas[14]). Despite a greater use of cars to travel to hospital, patients in LHE D rated car parking as no more important than respondents in other areas, with all of the ratings being 1.6 except LHE C, which was 1.8.

Private providers

The motivation among patients who chose a private sector hospital appeared to be slightly different from those who chose care provided by an NHS provider. Although the survey does not provide information on patients attending private hospitals, it does include responses from NHS patients who were treated at ISTCs. As described above, patients at ISTCs placed more importance on cleanliness, the standard of facilities, how well the clinic was organised, and waiting times, than patients treated at NHS trusts. They were less concerned with personal experience of the centre and factors related to convenience (travel costs, access on public transport, and whether the hospital was close to their work or home).

GPs understood that speed, cleanliness and a more personal service attracted some NHS patients to the new independent treatment centres, but felt that negative press coverage was deterring others.

> *We do have an orthopaedic treatment centre which is further from our local provider but where waiting times are significantly less… People, as a whole, once I have the discussion with them, are choosing the time of access rather than the ease of access… And another factor that patients liked significantly was the very personal touch that they received.*
>
> (GP, area D)

> *If they can have cold surgery on bones, to be able to go to a hospital, for example, [ISTC], where it's a new hospital and probably has a lower MRSA level… It's fantastic really… I can get hips done in six weeks… and they provide a fantastic transport service.*
>
> (GP, area D)

> *It's not an attractive option… They're too far away and they have a poor reputation… It's been in the local press… The complication rates, the lack of follow-up.*
>
> (GP, area D)

Interviewees from private providers believed that patients were attracted by their hotel-type facilities such as a private room, good car parking, the ability to see a consultant rather than a more junior doctor, short waiting times, the cleanliness of the newer facilities, and low infection rates. As new market entrants, word of mouth was particularly important in attracting patients.

> *The bigger our bank of past NHS choice patients, the more salespeople we've got out there telling their family and friends, 'Go to the [independent sector clinic], because I went there and it was fantastic…' There's no doubt in my mind that that is one of the biggest driving forces in sending people here… And the other one is the consultants, they're known among opticians and GPs for what they do, and that generates referrals, and they'll refer to us.*
>
> (Independent sector provider, area B)

---

[14] Differences significant at 1 per cent level.

Because it's private, because they will believe they're coming to a hotel environment as opposed to a hospital. They believe they'll get in quicker, without a doubt. Sometimes it's convenience... Why wouldn't they want to come to the private sector?

(Independent sector provider, area C)

The differences in terms of waiting list is a big issue... They've got single rooms and a TV, etc, here so there are some major differences. Surgically, there isn't, the docs work here, the docs work there.

(Independent sector provider, area C)

The factors that GPs and providers believe are most important to patients in their choice of hospital differ from the factors patients say are important to them. Patients said that cleanliness, quality of care, and the standard of facilities were the most important factors that influenced which hospital they chose. Although GPs and providers did recognise that infection rates were an important influence on patients' choices, they did not think that patients were comparing hospitals based on their clinical quality of care or, indeed, other aspects that patients may consider to be part of quality, such as the friendliness of staff or how organised the clinic is. GPs and providers felt that patients chose a hospital based on location and convenience (including ease of car parking and travel distance), and waiting times, which the survey showed to be relatively unimportant to patients.

In interviews, patients often said they chose a particular hospital because it was near to their home, but when prompted with a list of factors in the patient survey, they were more concerned with quality of care, cleanliness and the standard of hospital facilities. Similarly, in early versions of the Department of Health's patient choice monitoring survey, location and convenience were the most common factors volunteered by patients as influences on their choice (Department of Health 2006). However, when presented with a list of options in later surveys, quality of care and cleanliness ranked highest (Department of Health 2009a). These differences between unprompted and prompted responses may go some way to explaining the differences between GPs and patients' perceptions of the factors that influence choice.

The ranking of factors was similar across local health economies, showing cleanliness, quality of care and the standard of facilities to be universal priorities for patients when choosing where to receive treatment. There was some difference in the importance attached to transport considerations, with these factors being more important to patients in areas that were reliant on public transport. In these areas, respondents were more concerned with whether a hospital was close to their work or home, and its accessibility on public transport.

Patients appear to choose private providers for a slightly different set of reasons to those choosing to be treated at NHS hospitals. Waiting times, cleanliness, the standards of facilities and how well organised the clinic was were more important to patients attending the newly built ISTCs.

Those who anticipated needing an operation or hospital stay were more concerned about cleanliness, the quality of food and the quality of care than those who did not anticipate inpatient treatment. They were less concerned about whether the hospital was near to their home or work than other patients. This implies that choice of hospital is to some extent affected by the point in the pathway at which the choice is offered. When a patient already knows they will need an operation, their priorities are slightly different from patients who do not know this.

Revealed preferences

Analysis of the characteristics of the hospitals actually chosen by respondents can be compared with the characteristics of nearby hospitals they could have chosen. This gives some insight into the trade-offs patients made, although clearly, results must be interpreted with caution, as patients may not have been aware of the comparative performance of local hospitals on all or any of the factors we consider in the model (for more detail, *see* Appendix A).

From revealed preference analysis, the factors that were found to be statistically significant in our model can be split between characteristics of the hospital and its environment, and aspects of hospital performance.

Figure 17, opposite, shows that, among the factors relating to the hospital environment, patients prefer to attend hospitals that have been rated by other patients as having a good or excellent environment, are larger, have more parking available, and have higher doctor-to-nurse ratios.

In Figure 18, the values are presented in units of equivalent miles of travel distance – that is, the distance that would need to be saved to make an alternative hospital more attractive than another with the stated characteristics, or the distance they would travel to get to a hospital with these characteristics. For example, on average, and with all other things being equal, patients would travel an additional 12 miles to be treated at a hospital that has been rated as having a good or excellent hospital environment rather than one that is only rated as acceptable.

In terms of hospital performance (*see* Figure 18 opposite), all other things being equal, patients will seek to attend hospitals with lower *Clostridium difficile* infection rates, which perform better on national targets such as those relating to the proportion of patients seen within four hours in accident and emergency (A&E), and the cancer-related waiting-time targets, and have shorter average waiting times. For example, hospitals within our choice model had infection rates between 0.19 and 1.56 per 1,000 bed days for people aged 65 and over, staying in hospital for three or more days. The trade-offs that patients were observed to make suggest that, on average, a patient would travel an additional 12 miles to be treated at a hospital which had an infection rate that is 1 in 1,000 bed days lower than another hospital.

In contrast, the choices patients made suggest a relatively low value of waiting time relative to travel distance, with patients appearing to be willing to travel between 3.5 and 6 miles to obtain treatment one month sooner (*see* Figure 18 opposite). This is in line with results from the patient survey, where waiting times were ranked as less important than factors such as quality of care, cleanliness and the standard of facilities. It is also noteworthy that the revealed preferences show that the retired patients in the sample were more sensitive to waiting times than patients of working age.

Stated preferences

The analysis of the discrete choice experiment provides insights into how patients trade off a range of different factors, as they cannot choose to have everything at the best possible level (as opposed to ranking each factor independently, *see* Figure 16, p 70). Patients were presented with six choice sets, and in each set they were given three hospitals with different characteristics to choose between. For more information on the discrete choice experiment methodology, *see* Appendix A, 'Questionnaire data analysis', pp 173–76.

Figure 17 Characteristics of the hospital and its environment, and the relationship with choice of hospital

Figure 18 Hospital performance and the relationship with choice of hospital

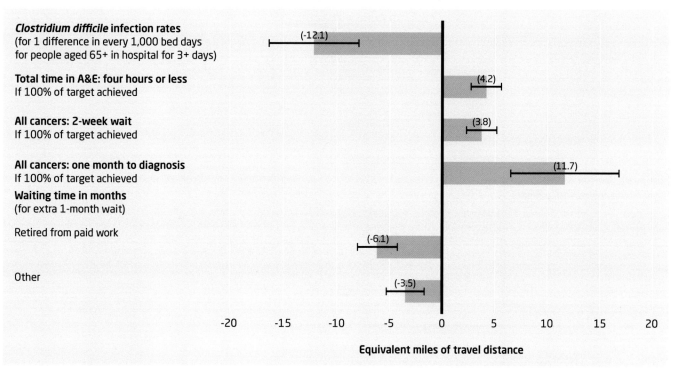

Quality

Figure 19, below, shows the values placed on hospital performance ratings when patients trade them off against increases in travel time. When interpreting this figure, it should be noted that each of the performance ratings is estimated relative to a base level – for example, the figure reports the value placed on medium, low, or unknown hospital infection rates relative to high hospital infection rates. This does not imply that respondents have no preferences with regards to high infection rates, but rather shows the value placed on the other levels of performance relative to this level of the attribute.

Patients were willing to travel for almost two hours to attend a hospital with a low rather than high infection rate (although the absolute values of the rates were undefined) and up to an extra hour and 15 minutes for a hospital rated 'good' rather than 'poor' on cleanliness and standard of facilities. Patients were prepared to travel on average up to 1 hour 45 minutes longer to receive treatment at a hospital rated 'good' rather than 'poor' on a measure of improvements in health (similar to patient-reported outcome measures

Figure 19 Trade-off between hospital performance ratings and travel time

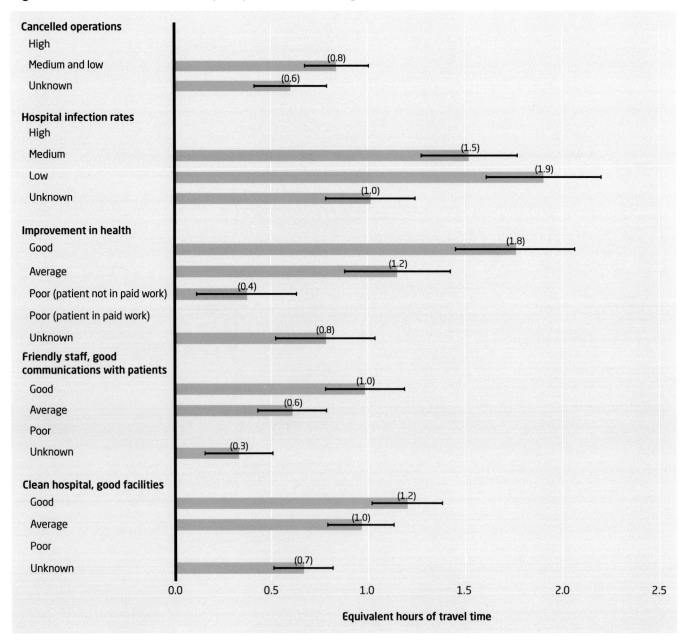

(PROMs)). Patients who were not in paid work placed a lower value on 'improvement in health' than those who were in paid work (ie, the difference in value between 'poor' and 'good' is smaller than for those in paid work), with the difference between 'good' and 'poor' valued at 22 minutes less than those in paid work. On average, patients are willing to travel an extra hour to be seen at a hospital rated 'good' on communication and friendly staff compared to one rated 'poor'.

Waiting times

Using the results from the discrete choice experiment, we can also estimate the relative importance patients place on waiting times vs travel times (*see* Figure 20 below). We find that there is a difference in the value placed on waiting time according to age and level of education, with those patients aged 20–59 placing more value on lower waiting times for outpatient appointments than others. Within this age group, patients with a higher level of education (ie, degree-level qualification or higher degree) value each week of waiting time as worth 20 minutes of travel time (meaning they are willing to travel another 20 minutes to reduce their waiting time by one week); by contrast, patients in the same age group who do not hold a degree value each week of waiting time as worth 14 minutes of travel time. Patients in other age groups value each week of waiting time as worth 10 minutes of travel time.[15]

In other words, all other things being equal, patients aged 20–59 and with higher levels of education would be prepared to travel about 1 hour 20 minutes to gain treatment a month sooner. On the other hand, patients in the same age group but with no degree would only be prepared to travel an additional 56 minutes for a similar reduction in waiting time. Patients of other ages would only be prepared to travel an additional 40 minutes to be treated a month sooner.

Figure 20 Trade-off between waiting times and travel time

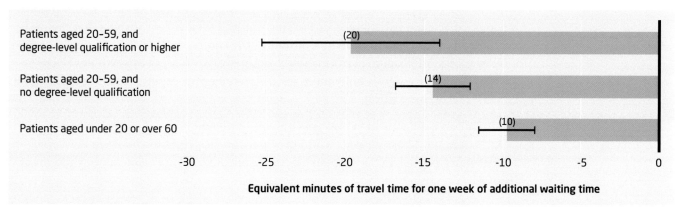

Equivalent minutes of travel time for one week of additional waiting time

Reputation

To understand how patients trade off their GP's opinion with other factors, we examine data on the impact of the GP's opinion when this is traded off alongside other information about the hospitals on offer (*see* Figure 21 overleaf). Their GP's opinion is clearly important in shaping the choices patients make, although analysis later in this section shows that many patients do not receive advice from their GP (*see* 'What support, advice and information do patients receive', p 86).

[15] The final models reported only include statistically significant differences, so, for example, the model incorporates a distinction on the basis of education for those in the 20–59 age group but not for other age groups.

Figure 21 The importance of different sources of opinion on choice of hospital

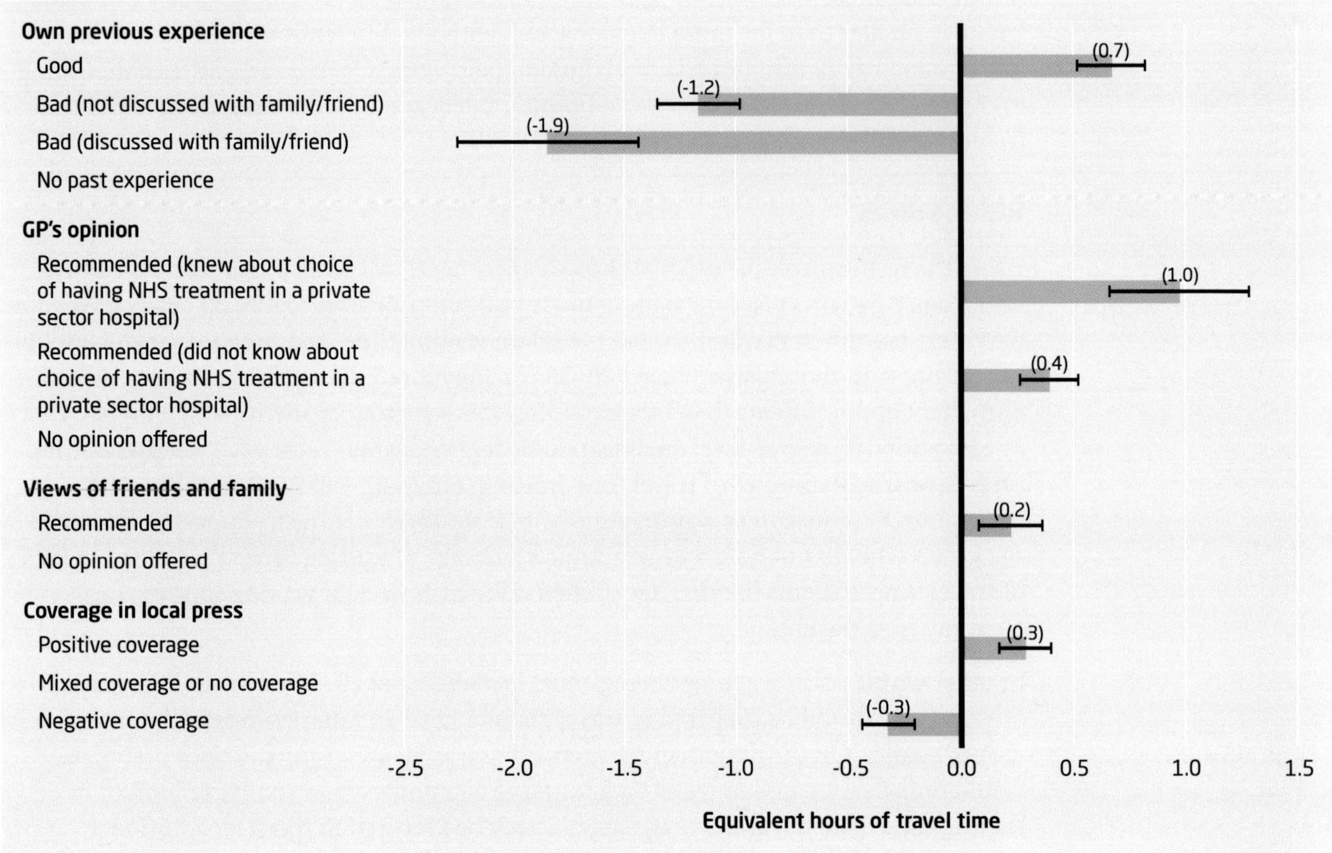

We can observe that, all other things being equal, respondents would be prepared to travel an additional 40 minutes for referral to a hospital they know to be good from their own previous experience. Patients are also willing to travel further to a hospital that their GP recommends. However, this does not dominate the choices and can be offset by a number of other aspects of hospital performance. It is noteworthy that, all other things being equal, patients place significantly more weight on their own experience of a hospital than their GP's recommendation.

We also observe differences in how much weight different types of patients attach to the GP's opinion. Those patients who were aware of their right to choose to have NHS treatment in a private sector hospital placed significantly higher value on the opinion of their GP.

The analysis shows that the patient's own experience of the provider is key, and patients would travel very significant distances to avoid providers where they have previously had bad experiences. The impacts of the opinions of GPs and friends and family and coverage in the press are smaller, but are also significant in terms of the choices being made.

Missing data

Some of the hospitals included in the hypothetical choices presented to patients had information listed as 'data not available'. It is interesting to note that the values patients placed on certain factors in the absence of information suggest that where data is not available, patients assume the hospitals provide a service that falls somewhere between 'poor' and 'average'. This is consistent across all five factors for which data was not always available. For example, patients place a value equivalent to one and a half hours of travel time on a hospital having 'medium' rather than 'high' infection rates, but only a value equivalent to one hour of travel time for the hospital having an 'unknown' rather than a 'high' infection rate (*see* Figure 19, p 82).

This suggests that those hospitals performing above average would be well advised to make their performance data publicly available, otherwise prospective patients may assume poor or average performance.

There are a core set of factors that are important to patients when making decisions about which hospital to be referred to: cleanliness, quality of care and the standard of facilities. This is consistent with patients' revealed preferences, which show that they chose to attend hospitals with lower *C difficile* rates (a factor closely related to cleanliness in patients' minds), higher ratings of quality (by the Care Quality Commission), and higher patient ratings of the quality of the hospital environment. In hypothetical choice sets, patients similarly placed a high value on infection rates, outcomes and good hospital environment.

Except for a few GPs who thought that patients were interested in infection rates and some private providers who indicated that patients were actively choosing private facilities due to their lower infection rates, most GPs and providers thought that other factors such as transport, location and waiting times were more important. In fact, these factors were ranked lower by patients.

Providers made almost no mention of clinical quality as a dimension on which they were competing for patients. The main focus was on the standard of the facilities – hospitals with new facilities were seen to have a competitive advantage. Waiting times were also important in the competition between some private sector providers and the NHS.

Our results suggest that when patients are presented with information on the factors that are important to them, they give more weight to those factors in their decision-making. For example, patients place more value on infection rates in their hypothetical choices than in the choices they are shown to make in the revealed preference analysis. This disparity may suggest that patients are quite sensitised to the issue of infection rates, but in practice are relatively unaware of the infection rates at the hospitals they can choose between.

The discrepancy between the factors that patients believe to be important and GPs and providers' perceptions of what is important to patients may be influenced by the system and information that is available to support choice. Information on distance, location and waiting times is embedded within the Choose and Book system and is accessible at the time that GPs/patients are selecting a provider. To access information on clinical quality or infection rates, GPs/patients must go onto the NHS Choices website or consult printed performance tables. Much of the information is presented at trust level rather than clinic or consultant level (although more condition-specific information is being developed). Although patients think these factors are important, they may not be using them to discriminate between hospitals due to lack of information, and this may explain why providers do not recognise them as patient priorities.

Having established the factors that patients say are important in their decision-making, we now look in more detail at the support and information patients are given to help them choose a hospital that meets with their preferences.

What support, advice and information do patients receive?

Consumers need accurate and comprehensible information on hospital performance to help them choose if choice is to act as an effective mechanism for improving hospital performance. However, information that accurately reflects each hospital's characteristics and performance is not available in practice. Empirical literature on the operation of choice found that equity issues were minimised when patients were supported by patient choice advisers as part of the choice pilots (*see* 'Theory and evidence of patient choice', p 19).

As the agents of choice at the point of referral, GPs play a key role in advising patients and directing them to available information sources. It is the responsibility of PCTs to ensure that information about local providers is available to help patients choose. Further support may also be made available to patients from other practice staff or telephone booking advisers.

The evidence presented so far has shown that, in most cases, it is the GP who offers patients a choice about where to receive treatment (*see* 'Are patients offered a choice?', p 49). However, both patients and GPs described a mechanistic or tokenistic offer of choice, with little discussion of the options available. We also know that for many patients, choice and appointment booking happen over the telephone after the GP consultation. We now consider in more detail whether the level of support and information provided for choice to be exercised is sufficient.

Advice

Of patients who had been offered a choice, Figure 22, opposite, shows that 40 per cent received advice from their GP, 35 per cent consulted their family and friends and 14 per cent received advice from a telephone booking adviser. The GP's advice and recommendation was important, as confirmed by many of the survey respondents when interviewed.

> *I assumed it would be [hospital name]. And she [the GP] said, 'Actually, I've referred you to [hospital name]? Is that OK?' And I said, 'Yes, that's fine'. And she said that she thought the [hospital name] consultant was very good. And, obviously, I said, 'Yes. Go there.'… I could have insisted on [another hospital] if I'd wanted it but I took their recommendation that the [hospital name] consultant was very good.*
>
> (Female patient, age 55, area D)

Looking just at those patients who were offered a choice by their GP, over half (54 per cent) also received advice from the GP. Put another way, just under half of patients who were offered a choice by their GP received no advice from them. Also, nearly three-quarters (69 per cent) of those who were offered choice by a telephone booking adviser received no advice from them.

Most GPs interviewed said patients tended to ask them for advice when offered a choice of provider and, with one exception, saw it as part of their role to provide that advice. Some GPs found it difficult to support all of their patients equally. GPs and their practice staff generally offered practical assistance to elderly or non-English speaking patients when booking appointments. But it seemed that these patients might receive less information to support choice. Even though interpreters were provided, very little written information was available in languages other than English, and in the more ethnically diverse practices, this was clearly a concern.

> *Choice is there, available, but… they're not able to avail it… because of… the language barrier that is restricting their rights really.*
>
> (GP, area A)

Figure 22 Sources of advice to help patients choose

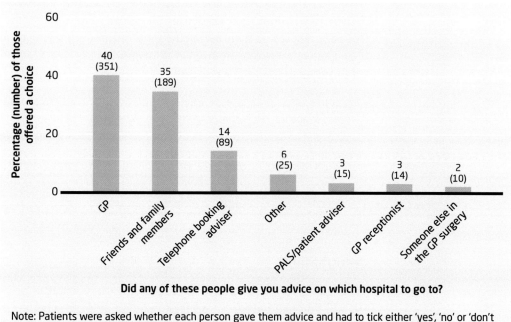

Did any of these people give you advice on which hospital to go to?

Note: Patients were asked whether each person gave them advice and had to tick either 'yes', 'no' or 'don't know'. The figures shown are the percentage of respondents to each question who ticked 'yes'.

It is perhaps not surprising, therefore, that the one area where GPs were more likely to feel that they did offer all patients an equal opportunity to choose was local health economy D – the least ethnically diverse and possibly most socially advantaged of the four areas studied.

Many GPs described a rather paternalistic approach to their patients, which was often driven by a belief that in their role as patient advocate, it would be a dereliction of their duty not to guide patients, and older patients in particular.

> *Well, really, we shouldn't influence them at all… if they're well informed enough… But I think you've got to take the role of the GP, they trust us, don't they, the older patients to know where to refer people… In an ideal world, they should be able to decide for themselves, but they can't… some aren't capable of it either, are they?*
>
> (GP, area C)

> *In terms of being the patient's advocate… steering them through, otherwise if we weren't to do that and they went on NHS Choices, they'd spend hours and be in real danger of making the wrong… they could end up missing out on someone who's right on their doorstep.*
>
> (GP, area D)

GPs were asked how they advised patients, and they said that the advice was often based on knowledge and relationships built up over a number of years in practice, encompassing consultants' personal as well as professional skills, feedback from previous patients, awareness of specialist procedures and experience of systemic problems at different hospitals.

> *It's purely, sort of, local knowledge, and also I think the most valuable thing is actually feedback from previous referrals.*
>
> (GP, area C)

> *We'll stick to consultants that we're happy with… We just tend to stick to people that we know… We've had good positive experiences in the past.*
>
> (GP, area C)

Providers felt that the GP's opinion was key to patients' choices, and described the efforts they were putting into maintaining good relationships between consultants and GPs. When asked about their marketing strategies, all of the organisations interviewed were focusing on GPs as their main customer rather than trying to directly influence patients (*see* 'Collecting and using market information', pp 116–22, for a more detailed description of provider marketing activities).

> *...but I sense that we still have a population who believe that doctor knows best and that the choice for the patients will largely be dictated by what the GP advises the patient.*
>
> (Foundation trust provider, area D)

> *Yes, while they're giving patients choice I get the impression from GPs that they have a lot of influence in that choice, you know, a lot of patients will say, 'Where do you go, doctor?'*
>
> (Foundation trust provider, area D)

Information

There are a range of resources that patients can consult to help them choose a hospital in addition to advice from professionals. To find out whether these were being used, our survey asked patients which sources of information they consulted to help them choose. Figure 23, below, shows that the NHS Choices website, which was set up to provide information on comparative hospital performance, was only consulted by 4 per cent of patients who were offered a choice; 3 per cent consulted hospital or treatment centre

Figure 23 Sources of information to help patients choose

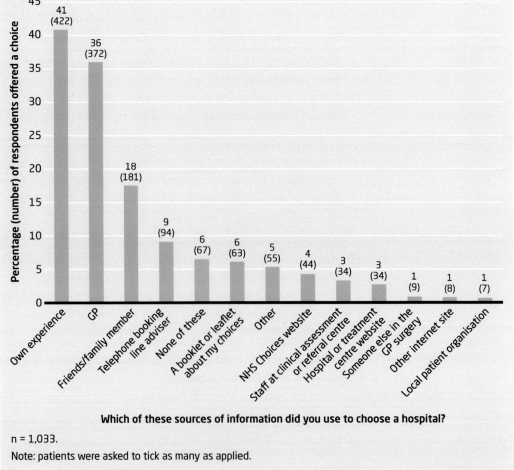

Which of these sources of information did you use to choose a hospital?

n = 1,033.

Note: patients were asked to tick as many as applied.

websites, and 1 per cent consulted other websites. Some of the respondents who consulted websites may have been looking at information on location or treatment options rather than performance. One patient reaffirmed the importance of past experience over information gained from internet sites:

> I don't look up anything on the internet because I wouldn't want to start travelling to a... I tend to stick with a local one because I think I wouldn't want to be travelling and I wouldn't want anybody else to have to travel if I was in hospital. So really no, I just base my opinions on my own experience, experience of close family, probably don't take too much notice... I do read bits in the press but then I think it doesn't surprise me because they're all under so much pressure. They're not on their own so I don't just single out that particular hospital for that. I'd rather, if I've got the choice, I'd rather go, say, to the [hospital name] because I just regard that it's the main hospital and we've had a lot of experiences with my husband when he had to go in.
>
> (Female patient, age 57, area B)

Performance information is also available in printed booklets that are produced by PCTs and distributed by GPs. The results show that only 6 per cent of patients consulted these booklets when choosing where to be treated. The Department of Health's own survey similarly found that only 5 per cent of patients consulted the NHS Choices website, 1 per cent looked at another internet site, and 7 per cent consulted a booklet (Department of Health 2009a).

Responses to a general question asked of all respondents (and not just those offered a choice) about how they had heard about the performance of local hospitals in their area underlined the importance of experience over published performance information (*see* Figure 24 below). Only 7 per cent of survey respondents knew about hospitals from performance reports. Instead, they relied on their own experience (56 per cent), the experience of family and friends (52 per cent) and reports in the media (50 per cent) for information about their local hospitals.

Several people we interviewed at provider organisations felt that patients did not have access to sufficient information to make a choice based on quality, and that the information currently available to patients meant that decisions were more influenced by waiting times than quality.

Figure 24 Sources of information on the performance of local hospitals

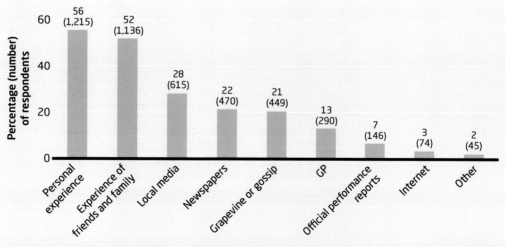

Have you heard about the performance of hospitals in your area from any of these sources?

n = 2,181.

Note: patients were asked to tick as many answers as applied.

You're getting quicker access but you're not quite sure what you're getting for your deal.

(Foundation trust provider, area D)

If it was working properly then patients would have a genuine choice of three or four and possibly five providers, and they would make that choice on the basis of a whole range of indicators in terms of patient experience and what matters most, and that's from car parking to clinical outcomes.

(Foundation trust provider, area D)

I think it's very difficult at the moment to get comprehensive information for patients to access that gives them that sort of detail.

(NHS trust provider, area C)

Despite what would seem like a lack of information and support to help patients choose, Figure 25, below, shows that just 14 per cent of those offered a choice said they would have liked more information. Most said the amount of information they were given was 'about right' (60 per cent) or they did not want any information to help them choose (22 per cent). Almost no one who responded felt they had too much information (0.5 per cent).

Table 11, opposite, shows that patients who received their choice in a letter after their GP consultation were most likely to want more information, while those who spoke to a member of the Patient Advice and Liaison Services (PALS) or a patient adviser were most satisfied with the amount of information they were given (although the numbers were small).

Some GPs talked of their difficulty in keeping up to date with information on local providers.

Hospitals... don't seem to... publish, even to GPs, a sort of list of consultants' interests and which consultant particularly likes to do what or what they're skilled up to do.

(GP, area B)

We have to rely on individual bulletins from individual providers, some on paper, some by email, and try and hold all that information in our head. And the reality is, we don't bother... Unless the service across the road from where I work is bad, I tend to use the service across the road.

(GP, area B)

Figure 25 Patients' views on the amount of information given

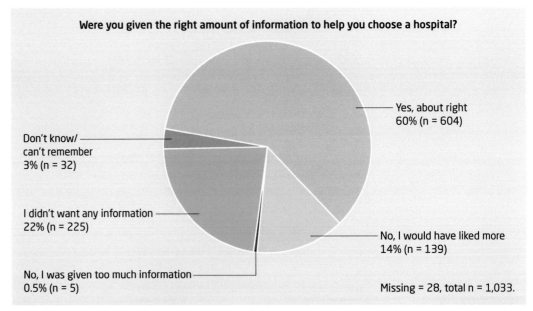

Were you given the right amount of information to help you choose a hospital?

Yes, about right 60% (n = 604)

Don't know/ can't remember 3% (n = 32)

I didn't want any information 22% (n = 225)

No, I would have liked more 14% (n = 139)

No, I was given too much information 0.5% (n = 5)

Missing = 28, total n = 1,033.

Table 11 Offer of choice and the amount of information wanted to help respondents choose

Who offered the choice?	Were you satisfied with the amount of information given to help you choose?				
	Yes – about right (% (number))	No – I would have liked more (% (number))	No, I was given too much information (% (number))	I did not want any information (% (number))	Don't know/ can't remember (% (number))
In a letter received after GP consultation	50 (118)	27 (63)	0 (1)	19 (46)	4 (10)
Telephone booking adviser	54 (115)	17 (37)	1 (2)	24 (50)	4 (9)
PALS/patient adviser	82 (14)	12 (2)	0 (0)	6 (1)	0 (0)
Someone else in the GP surgery	50 (7)	21 (3)	0 (0)	29 (4)	0 (0)
GP receptionist	59 (20)	12 (4)	0 (0)	27 (9)	3 (1)
GP in the consulting room	63 (418)	11 (75)	0 (2)	22 (145)	4 (23)

Note: Some patients were offered choice through more than one route.

More general marketing material from providers was regarded with disdain.

I mean, providers are into selling things, aren't they?… In fact, my practice manager of 25 years… is now a commercial director of the hospitals. So she's in the game of selling services and proving they're the best thing since sliced bread.

(GP, area C)

Never used marketing material and I've never really had any… I think it's really from personal experience of the hospitals and consultants.

(GP, area D)

When patients were considering more distant providers, GPs became concerned about their ability to offer any guidance at all.

The difficulty is… if we leave it up to patients, we'll get these situations where they'll go to a far-flung clinic or whatever and we'll think, well, actually, I know nothing about these people.

(GP, area C)

It seemed relatively unusual for the GPs interviewed to offer information or support beyond their own advice unless patients specifically requested it. A few GPs handed out Choosing Your Hospital or other booklets, and some directed patients to the NHS Choices website or individual providers' websites, but they expressed doubts that patients wanted this much information or that they would be able to interpret it in a meaningful way. This perhaps explains the very low number of patients who report using these resources in our survey.

We did, I think, have a period where we directed people to the website… but again, we found the take-up was very, very poor and patients just felt they were bombarded with too much information.

(GP, area A)

And the majority of patients, we don't sort of direct them to NHS Choices website or anything… If they ask questions, then I may need to direct them to it… If they don't ask questions, they don't exhibit the need to know any more… therefore it's not an issue.

(GP, area B)

There is currently no performance information, aside from waiting time, displayed in the Choose and Book system. The possibility of more clinical outcome data being included in Choose and Book was welcomed by one GP, although he feared that he would then have to devote more of his time to explaining it to his patients. However, at the moment, it seems that in most cases, referrals for standard procedures involve few discussions about clinical outcomes, and some GPs clearly mistrust performance data.

> *No one's ever asked me about quality in terms of published outcomes… It's just who you think's best… and who I think's best is just purely based on… talking to colleagues… It's not based on any objective evidence.*
>
> (GP, area B)

> *And we don't give them lots of, sort of, statistical information about hospitals. I'd have very little faith in it, personally.*
>
> (GP, area C)

> *I suppose there's the odd one that looks at statistics put out by hospitals… but they're going to be fiddled anyway.*
>
> (GP, area C)

Patients saw GPs as the main source of professional support and advice when choosing a provider (40 per cent received advice from their GP when choosing), and GPs saw this as part of their role, although they did not always feel equipped to offer advice. Some patients were offered choice after the GP consultation and received advice from a telephone booking adviser (14 per cent). GPs said they used their knowledge from relationships with specific consultants, feedback from patients, and their experience of systematic problems at particular hospitals to help them advise patients. The 'soft' intelligence used by GPs may provide information to aid choices locally but this means that GPs are unable to advise patients who want to travel beyond the one or two providers about which they have information.

Very few patients consulted the NHS Choices website (4 per cent) or leaflets (6 per cent), which both provide information on hospital performance. GPs did not think patients were interested in comparative performance information about hospitals and they themselves distrusted it, so rarely directed their patients to this information. Despite what might be regarded as a lack of comparative material on which to base their decisions, only a small percentage of patients reported that they would have liked more information.

Patients mostly considered their own past experiences when choosing where to be treated, along with advice from professionals and their family and friends. Analysis of the choices patients made in hypothetical situations (*see* 'Why are patients choosing particular providers', pp 81–5) shows that although their GP's recommendation is important to them, they put more weight on their own past experience.

Summary

Our evidence suggests that although there has been some progress, choice has not been fully implemented in the way the policy envisaged. Although most of the GPs we spoke to said they offered patients a choice, only around half of patients recalled being offered a choice. Choice was sometimes offered in a tokenistic way that patients did not interpret as a meaningful discussion of options. Choice was also offered in some cases by telephone booking advisers or in a letter received after the GP consultation. Patients' recall of choice may have been affected by how that choice was offered.

The policy of 'free choice' should enable patients to choose any eligible NHS or private sector provider; however, most were offered between two and five choices and very few remembered privately run options being available. The way local incentive payments to GPs were structured appeared to have some influence on the number of patients who recalled being offered a choice.

We found that most patients were treated at their local hospital, and, irrespective of choice, were happy with the hospital they were referred to or had no preference. However, patients who were offered a choice were 5 to 14 per cent more likely to travel to a non-local provider than those not offered a choice. The ability to exercise choice seemed to be particularly important for patients who had had a bad experience at their local hospital.

Despite GP and provider expectations that choice would be exercised more in urban centres, patients who lived outside urban centres were more likely to be offered a choice and more likely to choose a non-local provider. This may be because patients in large towns and cities have a greater affinity to one local provider whereas those living outside urban areas may have a number of providers equidistant from their home.

The results do raise some concerns about the impact of choice on equity. Although there were no differences in who was offered a choice by age or level of education, there were some inequities apparent in who was exercising choice; older patients and those educated to degree level were more likely to travel to a non-local provider. Also, GPs working in areas of greater ethnic diversity felt that non-English speakers were disenfranchised by the choice process. In hypothetical situations there were also indications of inequities which might affect real choices; patients without internet access, with lower levels of education, and who normally do not travel by car to hospital were most likely to select their local hospital.

A core set of factors were important to patients when choosing a hospital: cleanliness, quality of care and the standard of facilities. This was shown in analysis of: patients' responses about their recent referrals, data on revealed preferences, and analysis of choice in hypothetical situations. Patients attending ISTCs placed slightly more importance than those attending NHS-run hospitals on waiting times, cleanliness, the standard of facilities and how well organised the clinic was.

GPs and providers identified a different set of factors that they felt influenced patients' choices. Although they recognised that infection rates were important, they did not think that patients were comparing hospitals on either clinical quality or other aspects of quality, such as the friendliness of staff or how organised the clinic was. GPs and providers felt that patients chose a hospital based on location and convenience (including ease of car parking and travel distance) and waiting times, which in fact were relatively unimportant to patients.

This discrepancy may be partly explained by differences between patients' prompted and unprompted responses. They were more likely to cite transport and location considerations as important in unprompted responses, whereas when presented with a list of options, they cited factors relating to quality. Another explanation may relate to sources of information patients access. Information on distance and location is embedded in the Choose and Book system, but to access information on clinical quality patients must look at websites such as NHS Choices or leaflets on hospital performance, which our data shows few did. GPs did not think patients were interested in this information and distrusted it so rarely directed them to it. Past experience was the factor most cited by patients when asked what information sources they consulted ; advice from the GP and experience of family and friends were also important.

Most often GPs based their advice to patients on their knowledge of specific consultants, feedback from patients and their experience of systemic problems at particular hospitals. This reliance on local 'soft' intelligence meant that it was difficult for GPs to provide advice to patients about hospitals outside the local area. Although patients were most likely to seek advice from their GP, telephone booking advisers also had an important role to play.

The model of patient choice envisaged by policy, which would promote competition between providers based on aspects of care that are important to patients, requires patients to be offered a choice and to use that opportunity to select high-performing providers. Although we found that half of patients are offered a choice and that they value quality of care when choosing between hospitals (in both real life and hypothetical situations), they (and their GPs) judge that quality on 'soft' intelligence rather than on published performance measures.

In the next section, we explore the extent to which competition was operating in the four local health economies we studied, and whether this is being driven by patients switching or by other drivers.

4 Does patient choice create competition between providers?

As set out in the analytical framework at the beginning of this report, patient choice at the point of referral was designed to create competition for NHS patients between NHS organisations and between the NHS and the independent sector. Competition, in turn, is supposed to result in providers improving the quality of their services. This section focuses on the extent to which patient choice is creating competition between providers (analysis of providers' responses to competition is dealt with in the next section). In the interviews with providers, we asked them whether they had experienced any changes in market share and whether this was a result of patient choice, who they perceived their competitors to be, and how competition might develop in future.

We analyse providers' perceptions of the markets within which they operate, and assess the extent to which competition appears to be operating in practice. Using interview data means we can only judge competition from the providers' perspective; however, we supplement this with a basic analysis of changes in market share using routine data.

Extent of competition in local areas

Each of our local health economy areas was selected on the basis of the potential for competition and the penetration of choice. Through the interviews, we gained a picture of the local configuration of providers and the competitive dynamics (as seen through the eyes of those we interviewed). These features are summarised in Table 12, overleaf, and described in more detail below. We also present some data on the relative market share of outpatient referrals received by NHS hospitals in each area (based on the primary care trust (PCT) of interest).

Local health economy A

One large trust dominates this area, with facilities on five sites after previous mergers. There is no sense of threat from other local NHS providers, as the catchment population is perceived to be very loyal. Indeed, this loyalty is proving a barrier to reconfiguration and concentration of services across the sites the trust manages. Although they are part of a larger conurbation where there is a high concentration of hospital facilities and plans for reconfiguration, they serve a population with high levels of need, and currently, demand outstrips supply. They are quite confident, therefore, of their own 'survival'.

> So some clearly aren't big enough to survive, I don't think... So dotted around [nearby big city] are 10 DGHs [district general hospitals]... Why have we got 10 DGHs? I don't know... You think that's an awful lot of hospitals, but most of them, apart from mine, are in reasonable physical nick. But I've got the population, nobody else has got the population, and I'm not sure that anyone strategically has worked that one out in the longer term... And you think, well, I'm sure somebody ought to have done something more radical.
>
> (NHS provider, area A)

Table 12 Description of nature of competition in each local health economy (LHE) as described by providers

	LHE A	LHE B	LHE C	LHE D
Market characteristics	Dominated by single trust with several sites, offering DGH-level services	Concentration of tertiary, specialist and DGH providers, including university hospital with PFI NHS treatment centre	Concentration of tertiary and DGH providers, including university hospital with PFI DGH with co-dependency on PCT Other peripheral smaller DGHs in process of downsizing	Concentration of DGHs Aggressive NHS provider
Independent sector	ISTC Regional CATS using mobile units	ISTC Specialist niche provider of ophthalmology services 2 established independent providers	No ISTC Plans for new private hospital shelved Up to 6 established independent providers New market entrants in primary and community services	Some independent sector entrants, including possible new hospital
PCT	Weak commissioning	Some tendering of community contracts	Active tendering of contracts to shift services into the community	Active
Partnerships	Partnership with CATS using facilities and renting space	PCT encouraging collaboration between NHS providers Between large acute providers (two foundation trusts) Sharing of facilities/capacity with independent providers	Joint strategic planning group between 3 local hospitals Use of capacity in independent provider	Between NHS providers
Primary care		Smaller DGH looking to expand into community services		PCT provider services and primary care seen as a threat

DGH: district general hospital
PFI: private finance initiative
CATS: clinical assessment and treatment services

The trust is establishing partnerships with local specialist providers in order to 'franchise' some of its services. The main focus is on delivering DGH-type services, with some interest in expanding into the community using new NHS Local Improvement Finance Trust (LIFT) facilities to provide services closer to patients. The PCT appears to have been unsuccessful in developing community-based services, and the demands on the hospital continue to exceed planned volumes.

There is a large independent sector treatment centre (ISTC) in the wider metropolitan area to which local patients are referred, but this has not resulted in a drop in referrals to the trust. The ISTC is, therefore, not perceived as a significant competitive threat; indeed, the trust has, on occasion, sought to encourage patients to attend in order to reduce pressure on their own facilities. The ISTC is primarily focused on operating to a contract and treating whoever is referred (if eligible), rather than competing for patients. This may be because it is a Wave 1 ISTC, with a national contract and volume guarantees.

The trust does feel somewhat threatened by private sector market entrants into diagnostic and outpatient services – so-called Clinical Assessment and Treatment Services (CATS). These mobile clinical units, designed to provide rapid clinical triage, access to diagnostics and some treatments, are being used across the area and are delivered by a private sector company. They estimated that the planned volumes by the CATS was equivalent to a potential loss of around 35,000 outpatients and around 9,000 surgical cases from the trust. The trust is trying to minimise the impact of these facilities by having their own staff working some sessions, with the proviso that they would be able to refer those patients to the trust for more complex treatments. They also feel threatened by the PCT

Figure 26 Proportion of outpatient referrals for PCT A received by the main NHS providers and overall referral numbers 2005/6-2008/9

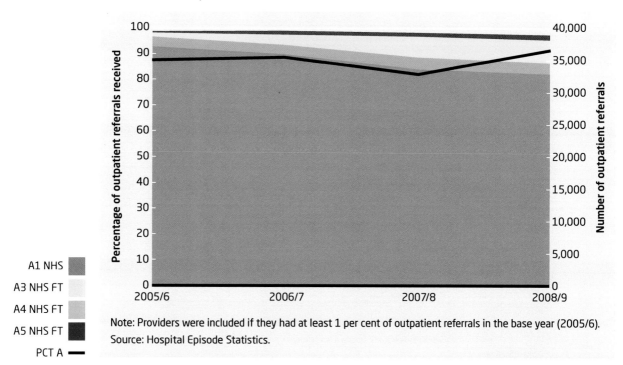

Note: Providers were included if they had at least 1 per cent of outpatient referrals in the base year (2005/6).
Source: Hospital Episode Statistics.

provider arm, which they are not convinced will be subject to fair competition but will remain 'feather bedded' by the PCT.

In local health economy A, the volume of outpatient referrals made by the PCT has remained relatively stable at around 35,000 consultations per annum. There has been a slight shift in activity away from the dominant NHS trust (A1 NHS), with some of the additional market share picked up by a NHS foundation trust (A3), whose proportion of activity rose from less than 2 per cent in 2005 to more than 9 per cent in 2008/9 (*see* Figure 26 above).

Local health economy B

There are several NHS hospitals in this area, which means there is potential for competition.

> *Because we're basically running hospitals right at the middle of the [regional area] conurbation and on all of our borders, there is another big acute trust. I think we worked it out not long ago, all of our patients have another acute hospital within five miles of them that they could choose to go to. Some of them have two or three.*
>
> (NHS provider, area B)

However, a number of these providers are competing in different markets. There is a university hospital with a new private finance initiative (PFI) build, which is focused on expanding its tertiary services. The other local provider was dismissed as not being a competitive threat because of its poor facilities. This smaller hospital was focused on expanding into community services and therefore felt in competition with other organisations bidding for community tenders. It appears that there are high levels of demand, and with the 18-week target, spare capacity was not yet an issue for these providers.

In addition, there are a number of collaborations across the local health economy. Providers were part of a system-wide strategy led by PCTs, which aimed to co-ordinate

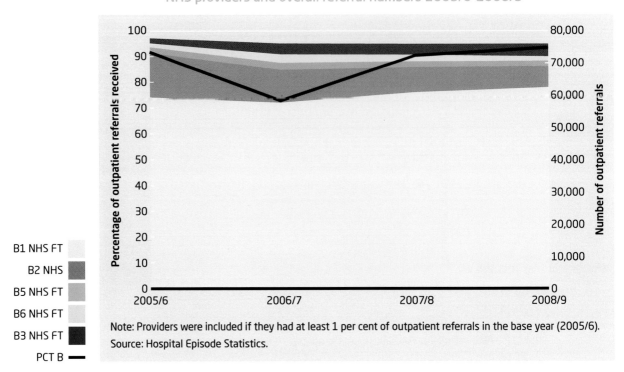

Figure 27 Proportion of outpatient referrals for PCT B received by the main NHS providers and overall referral numbers 2005/6–2008/9

B1 NHS FT

B2 NHS

B5 NHS FT

B6 NHS FT

B3 NHS FT

PCT B

Note: Providers were included if they had at least 1 per cent of outpatient referrals in the base year (2005/6).
Source: Hospital Episode Statistics.

the development of services across the area. The two large acute providers had a very close relationship and were working together to address common challenges rather than competing.

No providers in the area reported facing a competitive threat from the private sector. The district general hospital (DGH) had won the contract to run the local Treatment Centre, thus minimising the potential threat to the hospital's income if a private provider had taken on this activity. The large acute trusts faced with excess demand currently had co-operative relationships with established independent providers in the area who could provide additional capacity and with whom they shared some facilities.

The dominant NHS foundation trust (B1) has increased its market share, even during a period when the total volume of outpatient referrals has risen from a low of 60,000 in 2006/7 to nearly 80,000 in 2008/9. It has taken market share from another NHS foundation trust (B3 NHS FT), whose market share fell from about 17 per cent in 2005/6 to less than 8 per cent in 2008/9 (*see* Figure 27, above).

Local health economy C

The local DGH hospital (C3 NHS) takes the majority of referrals from the local PCT and does not feel that there is much competition for these. One other DGH in the periphery of their catchment area is being downsized and another is seen to have a poor reputation (C2 NHS). The main DGH is seeking to expand its catchment area for routine elective referrals to parts of other PCTs' patches, although capacity issues limit the extent to which it can do this. The PCT is actively tendering for services traditionally delivered in hospital, and some private sector organisations have bid successfully for these contracts. This poses the greatest threat.

There are good relationships between the local DGH (C3 NHS) and the main university hospital (C4 NHS), and there is a growing recognition that they can collaborate rather than compete for patients. Indeed, there have been discussions to strengthen and increase the number of referrals to this hospital rather than tertiary referrals being made to another (almost equidistant) university hospital, where historically some referrals have gone.

> ...*what we're doing is working quite collaboratively with them at the moment to try and see whether we can... if they develop the right services, whether our consultants here will make their tertiary referrals into [hospital C4 NHS] rather than [a university hospital]... So that's really where they're looking to develop, so... there's no way we're looking to develop tertiary services, so we're not looking at the same market.*

(NHS provider, area C)

While the university hospital can largely guarantee they will get tertiary referrals from their own facilities located in nearby towns, they are keen to secure these referrals from other local providers.

> *So ensuring that this is the way they send them for their specialist patients, I mean for the District General work in [town name] and [another town name] we have by far the large, the majority and very few leakage out... But it's about, particularly on the tertiary services, that we want them to come here.*

(NHS provider, area C)

There is no local ISTC, and plans for a new private hospital were shelved because of the recession. This would have taken about £5 million of business from one of the local trusts equivalent to about 10 per cent of their elective activity in three specialties. There is no competitive threat from the established independent providers, and again, they are used as additional capacity to help deal with excess demand. Indeed, there is a private hospital co-located with the university hospital, and the two have a very good relationship. For the many independent providers in the area, the main competition is with each other, for private, paying patients. Their main threat from the NHS is a reduction in the use of capacity for 'waiting list' patients.

Figure 28 Proportion of outpatient referrals for PCT C received by the main NHS providers and overall referral numbers 2005/6–2008/9

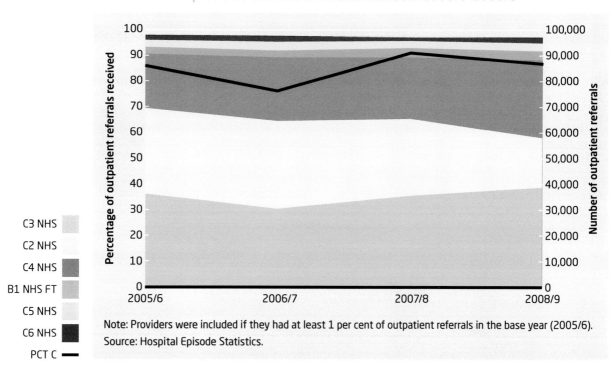

Note: Providers were included if they had at least 1 per cent of outpatient referrals in the base year (2005/6).

Source: Hospital Episode Statistics.

In local health economy C, two NHS trusts (C2 NHS and C3 NHS) shared about two-thirds of the market, with a third provider (C4 NHS) picking up 20 per cent of outpatient referrals from PCT C in 2005/6. The market share of C2 NHS reduced from 33 per cent to less than 20 per cent from 2005/6 to 2008/9. It appears that most of this activity has been picked up by the university hospital (C4 NHS), whose market share increased during this time by 10 percentage points.

Local health economy D

There are a number of foundation trust hospitals in this rural area, each providing some specialist services but with no single dominant tertiary provider. There is loyalty from local patients living in the towns where the hospitals are based, and a sense that other hospitals would find it difficult to attract patients away from these localities. However, patients living in the surrounding rural areas on the boundaries of hospital catchment areas were seen to be easier to attract away to another hospital. There have been some attempts to forge co-operative relationships between NHS providers in the area but hospitals had not always found this easy. Two of the local foundation trust providers had an informal agreement not to compete for services. These hospitals differed in their profile of activity, with one dominated by elective work and the other by emergency work. One of these hospitals has plans to become a university hospital and was seeking to invest in new facilities for maternity services and accident and emergency (A&E).

There was an ISTC in the area, but in a relatively rural location, and due to its distance was not seen to be a threat, though hospitals admitted they had been worried when it first opened. The ISTC itself did not feel it was competing with the NHS but providing additional capacity through its contract. Plans for another private hospital in the area do not appear to concern NHS providers at present. The existing private hospitals were seen as partners rather than competitors, and one trust benefited from their relationship by renting facilities to the private sector. Many of the general hospitals felt more threatened

Figure 29 Proportion of outpatient referrals for PCT D received by the main NHS providers and overall referral numbers 2005/6-2008/9

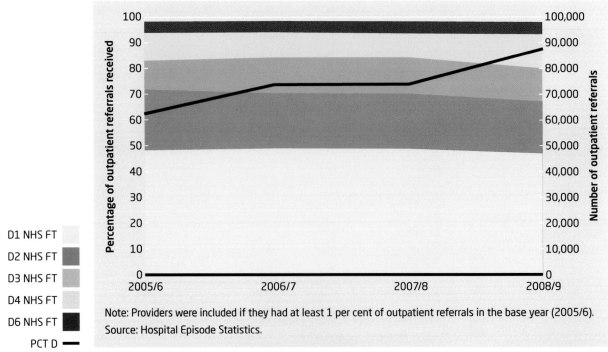

Note: Providers were included if they had at least 1 per cent of outpatient referrals in the base year (2005/6).

Source: Hospital Episode Statistics.

by GPs with special interests, practice-based commissioners, PCT provider arms and other providers competing for community-based services.

Local health economy D has seen a large increase in the volume of outpatient referrals, from 60,000 in 2005/6 to close to 90,000 in 2008/9. The market share of local providers has been relatively stable during this period. One of the local NHS foundation trusts (D1 NHS FT) has largely maintained its 48 per cent market share of referrals. There has been a small shift in market share between two other foundation trusts (D2 NHS FT and D4 NHS FT), with the latter gaining about 3 percentage points over the period.

While there appears to have been little change in market share in local health economy D, some providers appear to have lost market share in these PCTs: A1 NHS –11 per cent, B2 NHS – 9 per cent, and C2 NHS –14 per cent. In particular, it is interesting to note that several of the hospitals that have gained market share are either foundation trusts (A4 NHS FT And D4 NHS FT) or university hospitals (B3 NHS FT and C4 NHS). While it is not possible to attribute these changes to patient choice alone – there are a range of factors that determine where patients are referred for outpatient consultations – it does appear that since patient choice at the point of referral was introduced, some hospitals have lost market share relative to other local providers. We also cannot observe from this analysis whether trusts have gained market share from other neighbouring PCTs or made up the activity in other areas of their business (for example, emergency or elective inpatient activity).

The dynamics of competition appear to differ depending on the local configuration of providers, their proximity to each other, the population they serve, the type of services they provide, and whether there are local agreements in place. We now look at some of these issues in more depth as they play out across the areas we studied, and discuss the extent to which choice appears to be driving competition.

Are providers competing for patients?

Local providers

For most providers, geographical proximity was a key factor in defining their competitors. There were some differences here between DGHs and those trusts that were niche or specialist providers (see below). In general, the view was that competition is defined by distance because of the limits to patients' willingness to travel.

> *The ones that are nearer to us are technically, as far as the patient's concerned, I think, bigger competitors.*
>
> (Foundation trust provider, area D)

Some hospitals that were initially mentioned as possible competitors were then dismissed because they were too 'far away'. One hospital that was 15 miles away was described in this way. Distance was also cited as a reason why an ISTC had had only minimal impact on one provider's market share.

> *The ISTC… is too far away… We thought we might lose things but our radiology, our diagnostic services are just excellent, so I think people think we don't need to drive all the way up there… We didn't see wholesale changes when that was set up.*
>
> (Foundation trust provider, area D)

The number of providers locally also made a difference to how competitive the market felt to NHS providers.

> *But around this area, because we do have other providers, both from the public sector and for ISTCs and other neighbouring trusts, there is a slight competitive edge out there.*
>
> (Foundation trust provider, area B)

One chief executive felt that the competition between hospitals was linked to an ingrained culture of competition between local communities.

> *I have a theory that the hospital is, of course, only part of the wider health community, and because there is such competition between two communities, people who work for the hospital and people who support the hospital always want us to be better than [other foundation trust hospital].*
>
> (Foundation trust provider, area D)

From the perspective of providers, the definition of the market was geographical and the intensity of competition was largely dictated by the geographical proximity of similar providers. Their perception of the (limited) willingness of patients to travel meant that the market area was drawn quite narrowly in their minds, although as we have seen earlier, at least some patients are willing to travel further.

Interviewees talked about a number of other organisations in their locality who they viewed as collaborators rather than competitors. They talked of the common challenges they faced and implied that these are better solved collaboratively rather than through a competitive relationship.

> *Certainly, the chief executives from both [foundation trust hospital] and [other foundation trust hospital] have developed a much closer working relationship in this last year or two because basically we're facing the same sort of challenges and the same sort of issues in terms of meeting the 18-week target, meeting the A&E target, meeting the agenda on patient choice, providing capacity, trying to recruit experienced doctors and nurses… So it's almost a case of, 'How can we work together to actually resolve some of these issues?', rather than actually competing with each other.*
>
> (Foundation trust provider, area B)

Two trusts we spoke to had signed a formal memorandum of understanding and there was regular contact between the chief executives. According to this agreement, they do not compete on existing services but compete where there is increased activity or for new services.

> *We… have spent the last three years trying to get that relationship right, because he's [the other hospital's chief exec] very, very competitive. We now have a memorandum of understanding that the two boards have signed up to about where we're going to compete and where we're not, because actually you can spend far too much time competing over stuff that actually is just… either us or them are doing it well. So he and I have an understanding that where we have services in place, historic services in place, and let's use ENT and ophthalmology as examples, neither hospital are going to be competing on that basis because actually why would we? But where we see huge activity swings, so increased activity, or where there is a need for a new service, we will definitely fight like the death to deliver it.*
>
> (Foundation trust provider, area D)

The chief executive of this foundation trust provider talked about their personal relationship with the chief executive of another foundation trust hospital, stating that they 'have a fairly loose agreement that actually we're not going to tread on each other's territories'.

In area C, a strategic planning group comprising chief executives and medical directors from three NHS hospitals meets monthly to discuss how to work together and how to develop services.

> *…it was about saying, 'How do we work together to develop services in a way that's right for the whole of [town name] and [area c] economy, and not just right for one of us and not the other?'*
>
> (NHS provider, area C)

Several local trusts in and around area B were working closely with each other and the PCT in a major service development programme.

> *We have a very good working relationship with our PCTs, and we have a programme of work… where the chief executives are like that [gestures to show close relationship] together… And I think their closeness and consistency reflects within both organisations.*
>
> (Foundation trust provider, area B)

Some trusts were quite overt about the fact that they did not want to 'fight over' patients and, as a consequence, had divided things up so that they would concentrate on providing the services they already provide well.

> *So I think we've developed our own niche markets within the city, and there's almost like an acceptance that we wouldn't want to do that anyway, so we'll concentrate on our bread and butter and you concentrate on yours. So that's interesting. And in terms of patient choice, it doesn't help patients actually fighting over who is going to provide a service, because it doesn't really give them much in the way of choice.*
>
> (Foundation trust provider, area B)

Several hospitals had apparently taken a strategic decision not to enter into direct open competition with other local providers out of a concern not to destabilise other providers or provoke a reaction. This was true of a local community hospital *'to which people are loyal'* as well as a neighbouring district general hospital.

> *Why would we try and divert people away from the community hospital, which could lead to its closure? I think it would be a difficult job, I don't know how morally correct it would be.*
>
> (Foundation trust provider, area D)

> *I mean, our preferred strategy is not to get into outright competition with neighbouring organisations. We've done exceedingly well, as I said, in the current environment, and we're quite keen to continue that. And in a sense, part of our strategy is not to threaten other people's income streams on the basis then that we don't actually get some counter reaction. So we are keen to develop some of our tertiary services further, such as interventional cardiology, but we're not specifically going out simply to increase volume, partly because I think it's destabilising to other sectors of the health economy, and that really isn't very helpful.*
>
> (Foundation trust provider, area D)

In developing a new service, one provider had met with another local provider to discuss their plans before going ahead. This meant they could identify a gap in services and rather than both try to introduce a new service and compete for patients, they agreed that just one site would develop the service.

> *I sat down with their chief operating officer and a couple of their managers with me and one of my surgeons and everything else, and said 'Right, let's agree a strategy here, we don't want to shaft you and we don't want you to shaft us. So there's enough work*

*out there, let's agree how we're going to do this…' And we did actually, and we've
developed a breast reconstruction plastic surgery service.*

(Foundation trust provider, area B)

Such relationships were not always easy to broker, though, with a general suspicion about
the intentions of their neighbouring hospital.

*By the end of the conversation, instead of him thinking I was just trying to hold onto
my market share, it's about actually, there's room for both of us, it's just that you're
dealing with one end of the market and we're dealing with the other, you know.
Sometimes it's about having sensible, adult conversations, but they're really hard with
your local competitors because of the dose of paranoia everybody's got.*

(NHS provider, area C)

One trust had made attempts to forge collaborative relationships, particularly to solve
problems around staffing issues, but had not found their neighbouring trusts responsive.

*I think they were trying very hard with [hospital name] to get some links for
paediatrics because there are problems with the junior on-call cover, etc, but they all
just start to get a bit difficult, a bit territorial.*

(Foundation trust provider, area D)

In other cases, there was no evidence of collusion but rather a historical pattern of
service delivery, with services divided up in a way that meant hospitals were not directly
competing for patients or activity.

*But the vast majority of elective services are actually split in a complementary
way, so, for example, as a trust we provide elective orthopaedics to the whole of
the conurbation, we provide all of the ophthalmology, all of the urology, all of the
interventional cardiology, all of the vascular surgery. So it isn't a truly competitive
environment in that sense.*

(Foundation trust provider, area D)

Another example of collaboration arises from past joint planning to reconfigure services.
In the large city that is close to area A, for example, reconfiguration plans have involved all
PCTs and virtually all providers at one stage or another, with the result that as plans move
into the implementation stage, it assumes a collaborative approach to decisions about the
type and location of services.

Foundation trusts

There was a perception among a few NHS providers that foundation trusts were more
competitive than non-foundation trusts. One trust had identified that the business plan
submitted by a neighbouring foundation trust applicant included assumptions that they
would take volume from them.

*There's one particular provider who has, in its foundation trust application, set out to
pinch a [X thousand] of our catchment.*

(NHS provider, area B)

One trust that was among the first to become a foundation trust in its area felt that
competition would increase when other neighbouring trusts gained foundation status.

*So the situation is changing, so our kind of honeymoon period, if you like, of having
been pretty much the only, one of only two foundation trusts in town, is changing, so
that's a threat.*

(Foundation trust provider, area D)

Others felt that the approach to competition was largely dictated by the chief executive, regardless of whether they were a foundation trust or not. One foundation trust hospital described its neighbour as having a very different philosophy.

We always think our main threat is our rivals down the road [foundation trust hospital name], because they have a different philosophy to us. Their philosophy is quite simple: 'what is ours is ours and what is yours is up for grabs'.

(Foundation trust provider, area D)

Specialist or tertiary services

There were a few examples of where neighbouring NHS providers had made agreements not to compete in particular service areas; instead, they had 'carved up' the market so that they were offering different and complementary services. Co-operative relationships focused on, for example, establishing pathways covering tertiary and step-down care, for example, through a cardiac network, and two hospitals had put in a joint bid for a stroke unit.

The relationships between tertiary providers and DGHs were seen to be complementary rather than competitive.

We don't really compete with them because we've got a different sort of patient class. They're much more of a tertiary specialist centre... and so, interestingly, our patient portfolio is quite different, and we've agreed not to go robbing each other's activity, so we tend not to.

(Foundation trust provider, area B)

Another trust that was focused on tertiary care did not perceive a hospital interested in 'DGH-type' work as a competitor.

[Hospital name] are particularly looking at not developing their district general hospital side of things, they're looking for tertiary work. The way they see their future is actually becoming a true tertiary centre, and we can kind of help with that in a way, because a lot of our tertiary referrals go to [foundation trust hospital], and what we're doing is working quite collaboratively with them.

(NHS provider, area C)

Providers that were offering a niche service (such as specialist ophthalmology) or were established as specialist hospitals (eg, children's or orthopaedics) were not seen to be in direct competition with local providers. In fact, neighbouring hospitals seemed to wish to co-operate with such providers in order to attract better staff (some of whom were in shared posts), or use their facilities.

So we work very much with them as a trust in terms of some of our trauma consultants have honorary contracts at the [specialist hospital] and some of the [specialist hospital] consultants have honorary contracts to come and work here... We actually use their facilities and we pay them for their theatres and some of our consultants, so that's very much a partnership working in terms of orthopaedic services. We have similar service-level agreement arrangements with [name of children's hospital] in the centre of town.

(Foundation trust provider, area B)

[Name of specialist hospital] is just around the corner, it's in our patch. They're very specialist and very elitist, and in actual fact our waiting times are lower than theirs, so they don't really pull work from us.

(Foundation trust provider, area B)

Since I've been here I haven't really spent a lot of time worrying too much about competitors, so I couldn't off the top of my head tell you who I think our main competitors are... We are the only specialist ophthalmic facility in the area, which makes a big difference, because we concentrate purely on ophthalmology, whereas our competitors will offer it, or some even don't, some now refer their ophthalmic patients to us for choice, but in terms of our activity, because we concentrate on that, it's very specialist.

(Independent sector provider, area B)

There was some evidence of potential competition between tertiary hospitals and medium-sized hospitals that had some limited specialist services. Some of these providers were actively seeking to repatriate patients and develop and invest in services locally.

Certainly, in terms of our strategic development, as I say, our clear ethos is around being a local provider of care to our population so we haven't got an ambition to develop large tertiary services. But we have got an ambition to repatriate services which are currently tertiary services but we think we can do.

(NHS provider, area C)

However, these providers were not mentioned by the larger tertiary institutions as competitors. Either they were not yet aware of their plans or felt that they were only likely to result in a limited shift in activity. It may also reflect the fact that these centres of excellence are increasingly focused on quaternary services.

The independent sector

The established private independent sector hospitals we spoke to felt that competition was with other private providers for paying patients, not with the NHS or other private providers for NHS-funded patients. The loss of customers to other nearby private hospitals was their greatest worry.

The biggest worry for us... is if they're nicking our private patients rather than taking NHS... So our focus is on who's got what share of the market for private patients, and that, we've got quite a lot of information about.

(Independent sector provider, area C)

Even the ISTCs saw themselves as providing complementary services to the NHS rather than as competitors. They still had national contracts at the time of our interviews, and therefore there was no real competitive threat as long as they were working at capacity and in line with their contractual obligations.

However, there was recognition that in some very particular areas of care, the NHS provided an excellent service locally, and this meant it was difficult for the private sector to compete.

[Day care endoscopy and colonoscopy] are just absolutely fantastic in this area, you can get quicker in the NHS than you get here, without a doubt.

(Independent sector provider, area C)

One of the main threats mentioned by the private sector was reduced waiting times in the NHS. Ironically, this was not because it would reduce their competitive advantage in the eyes of patients or because patients will choose to stay in the NHS rather than go private (both as private payers or as NHS-funded patients) but because it will reduce the need for waiting list initiatives whereby local trusts send patients who will breach waiting-time targets to be treated privately. This spot purchasing of care appears to continue and is often at more lucrative rates than the tariff for directly referred 'choice' patients.

Independent sector providers were also concerned about the impact of the recession on their private market share. Their NHS work was, in part, seen as a steady income, albeit one which they assessed in terms of profitability.

If we can take private patients, then we would back off on NHS patients.

We actually only undertook those [NHS paid] procedures that we thought gave us a margin.

It has to be financially viable for us… In the case of total knee replacements, the tariff has been reduced substantially, which makes it non-viable for us…

There were a number of examples where NHS providers were expanding in order to repatriate activity that they currently contract out to independent sector providers (usually under pressure to meet waiting-time targets). One private hospital felt that a local hospital had made an active business decision to reduce the number of patients they send to the independent sector. They have built a modular build theatre in the car park, referred to negatively as the 'portacabin'.

They're very pro-private sector and then they're very anti… us at the moment because they've built a portable operating theatre in the car park.

(Independent sector provider, area C)

The general feel we've got is that they certainly don't want to offload any patients to the private sector.

(Independent sector provider, area C)

Indeed, this was confirmed when we spoke to the trust. The trust had actively sought to expand its own capacity to reduce dependence on the private sector for treating patients.

We did used to send a lot of orthopaedic stuff out, and then we had a brainwave, or my director manager for orthopaedics had a brainwave, and we bought a modular theatre, and we've tagged it on the back of… [one of our hospitals], and we've now brought it all back in house. We've actually gone into direct competition with the private sector, because our waiting times are pretty low in comparison anyway.

(Foundation trust provider, area B)

Almost no one we spoke to in the NHS saw the presence of the private sector as posing a real threat to their business.

I don't see a threat at all from them [the private sector].

(Foundation trust provider, area B)

There are some private hospitals but I wouldn't say we really felt the threat from the independent sector.

(NHS provider, area B)

The general perception among NHS organisations we spoke to is that the volume of activity in the private sector is small, and has not presented a threat to date. However, trusts were watching new developments closely and there was wariness that if the private sector were to grow, they might start to feel an effect.

The independent sector is moving in a bit more than it has done previously. Up until now it's been really, really peripheral to our core business and represents 0.01 per cent or something… But it is starting to crank up a bit with a new independent sector treatment hub. It's 25 miles away, so it's a fair distance, but it could draw in patients that would otherwise have come here.

(Foundation trust provider, area D)

In some places, the NHS had responded to the threat of market entry by developing their own services, thus limiting market entry opportunities for the private sector. This was true where the NHS had developed treatment centres or bid to run them.

At the time we opened the treatment centre, there was a bit more of a worry because if the independent sector had been awarded contracts for all the day case stuff that's going through the treatment centre, we would have had a problem.

(NHS provider, area B)

The level of competition with the private sector for elective activity was also dependent on the profile of the hospital in terms of emergency and non-elective activity. For example, one NHS provider with large volumes of emergency and high-risk work and maternity care did not feel under threat from a nearby ISTC.

Because of my case mix, the private sector is much less of a risk for me because, actually, the private sector doesn't want to do big volume emergency work, and it doesn't do radiotherapy and all of the stuff, so it doesn't do a big volume of obstetrics. So the private sector is not so much of an issue for us.

(Foundation trust provider, area D)

The private sector (particularly established independent hospitals) were viewed by most NHS organisations as collaborators, providing extra capacity when needed or sharing facilities or equipment. They acted as a release valve when internal capacity was proving difficult to manage.

Again, we use both hospitals in terms of providing additional capacity when we have issues about theatre capacity here… I think we work very collaboratively with the private sector, we don't view them as competition… I think there's more than enough to go round.

(Foundation trust provider, area B)

We've worked with [nearby private hospital], or they've worked in the patch for a very, very long time, and so I think we've got some sort of equilibrium there.

(NHS provider, area C)

There's quite a wealthy population, there's a strong private sector market but actually, we find, we've used them when we need extra capacity rather than taking work away from us. We haven't seen any major flows towards them away from us in anything so far.

(NHS provider, area C)

We're full to bursting, the demand through the front doors just keeps coming and coming and coming – for emergency patients – and rather than cancel them all we sent particularly urgent… and some of these were urgent breast cancers and stuff that there's no way we're going to cancel, but to take the pressure out of the acute hospitals we did send some of those to the private sector around Christmas and New Year. Other than that, we haven't sent any.

(Foundation trust provider, area B)

Another trust with significant elective activity, despite operating at capacity, was keen to ensure that its staff were working with private sector entrants in the diagnostics and outpatient market in order to protect referral and elective surgery volumes. There were other examples where providers were looking for opportunities to place consultants in community facilities in order to protect referral volumes.

One foundation trust in area D had visited a nearby ISTC to see whether they could form a partnership and have their clinicians do some sessions at their site. The same trust was considering something similar with another private sector provider that was opening a new hospital nearby.

In area A, a consortium of local PCTs had commissioned a seven-year contract with a private provider of outpatient and diagnostic services – endoscopy and five surgical specialties. The volumes of outpatient work this would take from one of the NHS trusts in the area were significant.

> *We have taken the view that that's too much of a threat, we can't afford to lose 35,000 outpatients and 9,000 surgical treatments.*
>
> (NHS provider, area A)

The trust's response to this has been to investigate possible collaboration with the private provider. The idea is that NHS nursing staff would be taken on by the private provider, along with the transfer of outpatient sessions (and some consequent transfer of costs), but coupled with an understanding that referrals for surgery would come to the trust.

> *We'll lose some of the profit element round the outpatients, but we won't lose the surgery, and keeping the surgery going is quite critical for us.*
>
> (NHS provider, area A)

The stakes, according to one interviewee, are high:

> *I don't think we can afford not to be there, because if they [the private provider] make it work, we'll get crucified in the process, absolutely crucified... If this is made to work, it will devastate, devastate outpatient departments around [large metropolitan area]. But some of my colleagues [in other trusts] are still refusing to have anything to do with them.*
>
> (NHS provider, area A)

PCT providers and primary care

As well as competing with other local hospitals, providers increasingly felt that they were competing with primary and community care providers.

Smaller hospitals were looking to develop more services in the community. For some, this meant bidding for PCT tenders for new community-based services. One trust was planning to respond to a local tender *'for the Darzi Centre'*. Interviewees reported difficulties in forming a consortium as *'we did not really have some of the experience that would have probably put us above the line'* (foundation trust provider, area D).

As a result of practice-based commissioning, GPs are increasingly organising themselves to deliver what were traditionally hospital-based services. Other developments such as minor injury units and GP-led health centres were also seen to be competitors.

> *GPs [are] putting themselves together in groups to deliver the services that we've done previously.*
>
> (Foundation trust provider, area D)

Some of these GP consortia are organised as private companies. This *'commercialisation of the local health economy'* (foundation trust provider, area D) was seen as further increasing the threat from primary care. As well as competing for outpatient activity, these companies are expected to compete against the hospital for PCT tenders (*see* 'commissioning contracts' pp 112–14 below for more on competition for the market). The provider arms of PCTs were also seen as competitors. One hospital saw the PCT provider arm as the *'scariest competitor'* (foundation trust provider, area D), in part, because before 'any willing provider' choice was introduced, the PCT could exclude services from the 'choice' list and *'shut us off'* (foundation trust provider, area D). Another hospital provider regarded the PCT provider arm as a threat because they were unlikely to be given a chance to compete on a level playing field.

> *At the moment, the PCT provider arms are [the most threatening] because I'm not quite sure what the PCTs are doing with their provider arms, how feather bedding they are of them, and my suspicion is that they will be, they're bound to be, because they're responsible for them still.*
>
> (NHS provider, area A)

The need for PCTs to separate their provider and commissioner functions has provided an opportunity for hospitals to take over community services. Several trusts were interested in vertical integration with PCT provider services and one foundation trust (area D) was considering buying a community hospital. One trust interested in this possibility was clear that they would only do so where they could see patient benefit; they were not interested in 'chasing turnover' (foundation trust provider, area D).

Interestingly, when discussing the possibility of vertical integration, providers also talked about the need for good relations and partnership working with primary care.

> *There's also an issue about good relations in primary care with the GPs, for example, and lots of these things are partnership issues between ourselves and GPs, and that makes good clinical sense.*
>
> (Foundation trust provider, area D)

However, there were also examples where hospitals' collaboration with primary care could be seen as anti-competitive. Hospitals talked of placing consultants in outpatient facilities or doing remote clinics in order to get referrals channelled into their hospital. Consultants practising at one of the private hospitals were building relationships with a local GP practice opposite the hospital, offering outreach clinics, with the anticipation that if patients needed further treatment they would refer to themselves and carry out the work at the private hospital (presumably funded by the NHS through choice).

In general, smaller hospitals felt somewhat threatened by PCT provider arms, private sector organisations, and GP enterprises who may be better placed to bid successfully for PCT contracts.

NHS providers appeared to be competing with each other to some extent. Perhaps surprisingly, given the subject of our interviews, there were many examples of how different providers (both NHS and private sector) were co-operating and collaborating. In other markets (if NHS providers were deemed to be 'undertakings'), some of the more formal agreements to 'carve up' the market might be deemed collusive. Indeed, it is likely that some of these agreements are in breach of the principles and rules for co-operation and competition (PRCC). Most providers generally did not view foundation trusts as more competitive than other NHS trusts. Specialist providers and those providing tertiary services were developing relationships with local referring hospitals rather than competing with them.

The independent sector was not perceived as much of a threat but has been used as a key partner in providing much-needed extra capacity to get waiting times down.

While the creation of PCT provider services and changes in primary care were seen as potentially threatening, several smaller hospitals were seeking opportunities to integrate more closely with community services and primary care.

What are providers competing over?

Patients

Some providers spoke about actively seeking to attract patients away from other providers in particular geographical areas. However, some were wary of trying to compete with other providers that had good reputations.

> *Certainly from [small town] up to the north east we are keen to pick up more orthopaedic work… We have already been attracting orthopaedic work to us from there very successfully and we are looking to maintain that. Then to the east we are looking at whether there is potential to attract more dermatology work...*
>
> (NHS provider, area C)

> *…the big thing is location of other hospitals because, you know, [foundation trust hospital] is not that far from us but it's got a very good hospital of its own. So those patients, if we were to try and increase market share there, it would be very difficult, whereas if we go to [another area] which is closer to [foundation trust hospital] but traditional referral patterns have involved [another foundation trust hospital] then we can look at market share.*
>
> (Foundation trust provider, area D)

One provider expressed concern at the possibility of losing patients from clinics that were equidistant from other local providers.

> *You feel much safer with the patients in the local area… We've always had concern about the [another area] clinics we do because that's equidistant from [foundation trust hospital], [other foundation trust hospital] and us, and very easy for patients to start drifting to other hospitals.*
>
> (Foundation trust provider, area D)

Being on or near the coast created a natural geographical boundary to some market areas and limited the expansion of a provider's market area in some directions, thus increasing the chances of competition with other neighbouring areas.

> *So if they want to expand their catchment area, they can't go south because it's the sea, so they'll come north. So that would be a concern really… [Nearby hospital] and [another nearby hospital] are our closest hospitals in the north.*
>
> (Foundation trust provider, area D)

GP referrals

The majority of trusts we spoke to were more concerned about GP referrals than about patient choice. Where competition was in evidence, it was for GP referrals, and there was quite a lot of activity around marketing services to GPs (*see* 'Collecting and using market information', pp 118–9). But providers recognised that GPs were often loyal to their local hospital and found that it was difficult to challenge their referral patterns and persuade GPs to refer elsewhere.

> *…we want to increase the number of patients that are referred here within the capacity that we've got, and our market share on the whole is very, very good for our surrounding GP practices. For GP practices, more on the kind of periphery of our core catchment population, it's more variable and so there are some practices that do refer to us… for certain things, and so we're trying to understand what that is and why that is and trying to influence that…*
>
> (Foundation trust provider, area D)

There is no point sending it to GPs based right next door to [foundation trust hospital] because, you know, with the best will in the world, he's never going to refer for anything other than something that's particularly specialist.

(Foundation trust provider, area D)

Tertiary referrals

While many trusts were full to capacity and managing their 18-week target, some were seeking to expand their market share. However, this was often about 'repatriating' patients who were otherwise being treated out of area and 'capturing' referrals from new geographical areas.

In these times of Payment by Results, our main aim is protecting our activity, because now that money follows the patient, we have to make sure that we hold onto the activity that we're doing. The flipside to that is that we are also probably looking to increase our activity in areas where we can, either by taking little bits of market share from other providers or by providing new services that either aren't on offer or are on offer out of the region that we can repatriate here. So those are probably the main drivers, because really, the finance is so key, but patient choice is also part of that.

(Foundation trust provider, area B)

…our clear ethos is around being a local provider of care to our population, so we haven't got an ambition to develop large tertiary services. But we have got an ambition to repatriate services which are currently tertiary services.

(NHS provider, area C)

Hospitals were assessing which areas were easier to compete in. Areas that were ripe for expansion were those where there were gaps in services and they could pick up tertiary referrals that were currently going to another provider.

[We] look at the gaps in what [foundation trust hospital] provides. They don't provide children's services, so we can go there and start, you know, trying to build relationships there… and we have a few consultants who go down and hold clinics in [nearby area].

(Foundation trust provider, area D)

Commissioning contracts

'Any willing provider' contracts for elective care and 'free' choice mean there has been little payer-driven competition in this sector. However, some PCTs, particularly where they account for a significant proportion of a provider's referrals, may use their purchasing power. One PCT that accounted for 50 per cent of referrals at one provider was acting as a strong commissioner, frequently mentioning the possibility of using other providers during contract negotiations.

So in discussions with [PCT name] it is a real issue. They not infrequently point out to us that they have alternatives, and in some cases, our competitors are doing things we're not.

(NHS provider, area B)

Most of the examples where providers were competing for PCT tenders involved community-based services. Trusts had met with varying degrees of success, and this coloured their view of how much of a threat the increasing use of competitive tendering by PCTs was. This competition for the market seemed to be of most concern for district general hospitals, which were not established as tertiary centres, and in those areas where the PCT was actively using competitive tendering as the mechanism for developing new community-based services.

One provider that had been successful in winning community tenders felt that other trusts were threatened by their success.

> *I think we are probably more threatening to other hospitals. We've already won the PCT B dermatology service, which theoretically stole work off another hospital, and we've won [another PCT's] community ophthalmology services, so we're probably more seen as threatening to some of our neighbours.*
>
> (NHS provider, area B)

Another provider who had been successful in winning PCT tenders said '*[the private sector will] always be a threat, we'll just be one step ahead, or work with them*' (NHS provider, area C).

One NHS hospital thought that the tendering of services and price competition would open up opportunities for the private sector.

> *Where PCTs are obviously looking at the price and looking at tendering things out, or certainly diagnostic services, 50–50. Some of that's in-house driven, some of it's externally driven, those things can be quite easily picked up and taken to the private sector.*
>
> (Foundation trust provider, area D)

For the smaller district general hospital, the threat from the private sector was in primary care and in areas where the PCT was deciding to tender services to provide clinical services in the community rather than at the hospital.

> *The... threat I think is more to do with the tendering process set up by commissioning and the potential to lose tenders.*
>
> (Foundation trust provider, area D)

Another trust had lost out on a contract which they had previously held for GP out-of-hours services to a private company. They saw PCT tendering of services as the biggest competitive threat, with a number of other contracts up for tender in the near future.

> *The PCT is looking at tendering genito-urinary medicine, which is a service that we run, and they are looking at diabetes and having a community-based diabetes service. Again, that may end up going to tender, so there is some potential we might start to lose business to those... There are competitive forces but it is forced more through the PCT re-tendering things than it is, in a sense, from other providers.*
>
> (NHS provider, area C)

In contrast to those who talked about the PCT as a threat because of aggressive approaches to tendering services, some trusts had established a more collaborative relationship with the PCT. Other providers were seen to be unco-operative, simply sending commissioners the bill for activity.

> *I think the PCT... is the strong partner and we seem to be popular because we co-operate with them, whereas [foundation trust hospital] do their own thing and then charge them for it.*
>
> (Foundation trust provider, area D)

One trust appeared to be particularly engaged with the local health community and was co-operating with the local PCT and local authority. One interviewee talked about other providers feeling they have an unfair advantage from having 'struck a deal' with the PCT. The collaborative working between the PCT and local providers on service redesign was seen to insulate the provider from choice, because the PCT was unlikely to actively encourage patients to go elsewhere.

> *There is a bit of anxiety, I think, from some of the people around our edges that we might have developed a relationship and struck a deal with PCTs that provides us with*

an advantage that they might not have in their areas. We're within the rules, we've been through all of this with the SHA [strategic health authority], they understand the context within which we're operating, so if we can pull off a relationship like this, then that's great. And, of course, within it we're not constraining patient choice, so if patients like the model we are developing... then they can choose to use it.

(NHS provider, area B)

They wouldn't want to be encouraging patients not to use us, would they, because we're all working together.

(NHS provider, area B)

Some providers were actively seeking to establish good relationships with neighbouring PCTs in order to expand market area to those where waiting lists are longer.

...where we've got referrals... that come from a wider geographical area, we've been responding to those areas, so, for example, in [a nearby county] we know that they've got pressure on access times in certain specialties, like endoscopy and orthopaedics, so we've been working with that PCT and actually going into [name of county] and picking up some new markets.

(NHS provider, area C)

There is clearly a tension in some areas between the PCT's role in ensuring the efficient and cost-effective provision of services locally, and in facilitating patient choice. In one area, where two providers were located close together, services had been historically distributed between the two organisations to avoid duplication. Although the local PCT was described as having choice 'very, very high up their agenda', they were keen to avoid duplication. So their focus on choice often resulted in promoting competition for local community service contracts rather than promoting what one interviewee described as a 'real choice' for patients (foundation trust provider, area D).

A GP in the same area commented on similar tensions between practice-based commissioning and choice.

Groups of GPs are being encouraged to commission services that are designed to deliver the most efficient, the most close to home, etc... So if they have been involved in the commissioning of this service... it's quite difficult then to offer choice.

(GP, area D)

For most providers, their market is defined geographically and their competitors within the NHS were neighbouring hospitals. Generally, providers were only directly competing for patients at the boundaries of their catchment areas, where providers were equidistant for patients in that locality. However, the main focus of competitive activity was securing GP referrals and repatriating tertiary referrals from other areas.

While most providers recognised that PCTs were increasingly using competitive tendering for clinical services, there were mixed reactions to this. Some saw it as an opportunity to expand into community services, while others saw it as a direct threat, particularly where private sector companies were involved in bidding.

Summary

The potential for competition existed across each of our four local health economies, with several NHS hospitals in close proximity. However, competition for patients was limited to the periphery of catchment areas. This is consistent with spatial models of competition (where location of the firm is important to the customer), which predict that competition arises at the margins of geographic boundaries where the cost of switching is lowest.

As well as differences in how competition was operating across the four areas, it became clear that different types of providers were experiencing competition differently depending on their scope (secondary or tertiary) and type (elective or emergency) of activity. Among the organisations we interviewed, we were able to distinguish four different types of provider.

- Large trusts (often including a university teaching hospital) focused on tertiary and specialist activity.

- Medium-sized trusts looking to develop their tertiary services in niche specialties in order to 'repatriate' patients currently receiving specialist treatment elsewhere.

- Medium-sized trusts looking to increase or protect referrals to their elective services – focusing on putting consultants in the community to 'feed' referrals to the trust.

- Small and medium-sized trusts operating over capacity, just seeking to treat patients within waiting-time targets rather than expand and develop services. Possibly looking to expand into delivery of community services.

Tertiary hospitals are clearly less focused on patient choice, largely relying on consultant-to-consultant referrals from local feeder hospitals. While they might face some competition from other regional tertiary centres or specialist units within local hospitals, at present, this is not driven by patients' preferences. In general, the market in health services was divided up by specialty and severity, with niche providers, specialist hospitals and tertiary centres not appearing to directly compete with local DGH-type providers. There was a small amount of activity to repatriate some tertiary referrals by local hospitals, though there was little sign of overt competition.

Hospitals whose activity is dominated by emergency care and admissions are also less focused on choice as are those who are operating at or above capacity and continue to face rising demand. They are more interested in demand management than in patient choice.

The medium-sized hospitals varied in their approach to choice depending on whether they were operating at or over capacity, and the proportion of elective and non-elective work. In hospitals where the workload was dominated by emergency activity or where referral volumes were high and rising, there was little incentive for providers to compete for patients. The difficulties of expanding facilities and securing adequate staff to increase supply mean that most hospitals are operating at or near capacity. The additional requirement for hospitals to meet waiting-time targets meant that providers were focused on demand management rather than market expansion.

For smaller hospitals, the increasing use of competitive tendering by PCTs for new community-based services appears to present both an opportunity and a threat. Certainly, competition for the market appears to be a stronger driver than competition within the market.

Finally, providers saw GPs as a significant barrier to the development of patient choice and the establishment of a competitive market for health care services. They perceived that GPs' referral patterns tend to be fairly stable and that they pay attention to quality. With practice-based commissioning and the development of community-based services run by GPs, there is also a potential conflict of interest. A number of primary care practices have also developed referral management centres, which potentially reduce the volume of referrals to hospitals (threatening their income) but also redirect patients to community-based services (Imison and Naylor, forthcoming).

Despite the presence of the private sector in each area, including ISTCs, competition between NHS providers and the private sector was not felt to be a threat. Indeed, in some areas, it appears that actions were taken to restrict competition. The nature of ISTC contracts limited the extent of competition for elective activity, and in one area, the NHS provider had successfully bid to run the Treatment Centre. Established independent sector providers were, on the whole, more interested in protecting their 'waiting list' patients and their private-pay patients, with only moderate interest in the 'recession proof' NHS choice patients.

Relationships both within the NHS and with the private sector were mainly collaborative, and sometimes even bordered on the collusive. In general, organisations were seeking to form partnerships where these benefited the organisations themselves, with little reference to the benefits for quality or value for money. Examples of partnerships included those designed to help meet waiting-time targets, to protect referral volumes, to extend reach into the community and primary care, or to ensure that investments in niche specialist services were not duplicated locally.

However, there were also agreements (both formal and informal) not to compete, or to allocate patients, services or geographic areas between providers. The existence of such agreements implies that providers are prepared to go to some lengths to avoid competition. Some of the agreements and relationships described in this report are, therefore, likely to be inconsistent with the principles and rules for co-operation and competition, and where these involve 'undertakings', would be defined as anti-competitive activity.

5 How providers have responded to choice, competition and other factors

In principle, being able to choose a hospital for diagnosis and/or treatment has two benefits for patients. For individual patients, there is a direct benefit of choosing a hospital which best caters for their needs – such as ease of access, short waits, and so on. Different patients will place different weight on each hospital's attributes and make different decisions concerning the trade-offs they are willing to make between these attributes (as we have seen in Section 3).

The second benefit for patients is that the policy of choice (combined with the financial incentives of Payment by Results) gives hospitals an incentive to compete for activity (as discussed in Section 4). Again, in principle, the choices patients make send a signal to providers, which can provoke actions by individual hospitals: for example, to improve the quality of services.

So, in theory, and as with private markets, the aggregate actions of patients should lead to a continuous process of responses by providers as they react to losses in custom (and hence income) by investigating the reasons and responding appropriately. Providers may also respond to a potential loss of income as a result of patient choice by improving quality or other aspects of patient care before any such losses are sustained.

In practice, however, how providers respond to patient choice, and to what extent, will depend on a number of assumptions. Previous sections have reported on a prerequisite – that patients have been given the opportunity to choose in the first place, and that when they do make their choice, it is an informed and rational one.[13] On the supply side, if providers are to improve services in line with patients' preferences the following conditions need to hold:

- the signal that patients send through the choices they make is sufficiently strong (for example, there will be a minimum actual or anticipated loss of activity before a provider deems it necessary to react)

- the provider correctly interprets the crude increase/decrease in referrals arising from choice (for example, investigating why patients are choosing alternative hospitals)

- providers have the capability and resources to respond appropriately.

The extent to which providers take up the incentives embodied in choice (including the financial incentives), and to which the assumptions underpinning choice hold in practice, will determine how far choice can act as a lever to improve providers' performance and quality of services.[14]

---

[13] 'Rational' in the sense that each individual's choice best meets their particular desires and needs - which may not appear rational to others with different views, attitudes and values.

[14] It is worth noting, of course, that there may be potentially adverse responses to the choices patients make - for example, a provider may, in the face of a loss of activity in one area, simply withdraw from the market for that service. This will adversely affect those patients who do not want to switch to alternative providers (on the assumption that they have assessed that the existing provider best meets their needs).

In this section, we explore our interviewees' responses to these issues. We investigate their views about the factors – including choice – that drive service changes, from external factors such as centrally imposed targets, to intrinsic motivational factors associated with professionalism (*see* Figure 4, p 7). But first, we look at the market information and intelligence that providers collect and use, the extent to which they monitor referral volumes and changes in market share, and what actions they have taken in response to such information.

Collecting and using market information

As noted above, a key aspect of how providers respond to patient choice is how they interpret the signals that patients implicitly send through the choices they make. In broad and basic terms, providers need to understand and monitor changes in referrals, workload and the general market conditions in which they operate. Here, we report on the sources of market information and intelligence that providers in the four local health economies are using, as well as the extent to which they are investigating changes in market conditions.

Sources of market information

While most providers we spoke to relied on external data sources, these were often supplemented with data produced internally or collected by the trusts. Most providers were using products offered by Dr Foster, which use routinely available data and allow trusts to examine referral patterns by practice. However, a number of interviewees questioned the timeliness and accuracy of this data.

> *I use Dr Foster… but I also use our information services department because I want to validate… Sometimes the Dr Foster information isn't as up to date or there can be glitches where one trust hasn't submitted their information… It might seem that we go from, I don't know, say from [local community hospital] having a 20 per cent market share to having 88 per cent one month, which obviously isn't right.*
>
> (Foundation trust provider, area D)

There were also concerns expressed about the usefulness of this data due to differences in the way hospitals use coding. For example, one interviewee pointed out how different hospitals record specialties in different ways, either using a catch-all category such as 'general medicine' or specific categories such as 'gastroenterology' and 'endocrinology'. The implication is that it is hard to distinguish whether patients are going somewhere else or whether movements are the artefact of coding practices.

One interviewee warns that Dr Foster data should be treated with caution, as it is based on the number of patients seen rather than referrals; increases in activity may be due to a trust clearing their waiting list backlog rather than gaining market share. This suggests that such data need to be used together with information on referrals.

> *Dr Foster works on the numbers of patients seen, to give you your market share information. But the numbers of patients that you see might go up because you've got waiting times issues or you're trying to reduce your wait. So it may look like you've been losing market share but it's just that another trust is catching up with their waiting times. So you just have to be sensitive, how you look at the information.*
>
> (NHS provider, area B)

As well as examining shifts in numbers of patients and referrals, most trusts were collecting information about the quality of their services, from the perspective of patients,

GPs, practice managers, and their own staff. One hospital had set up a group of practices which provided external monitoring of discharge information. This trust, together with others we spoke to, were generally keen to understand what GPs wanted and their views as referrers.

There was no sense that data availability was a problem; indeed, one person observed that the availability of market information was as good, if not better than, that available in the private sector.

> *Certainly, our non-executives who are from the private sector are really just blown away and are saying this is better marketing information than you would get anywhere in the private sector. It is really powerful stuff, really detailed.*
>
> (NHS provider, area C)

In terms of private sector activity, trusts had no routine information other than that gleaned from Choose and Book. They were most interested in comparative waiting times. One trust was monitoring the activities of local independent providers but this was due to a concern that hospital consultants were making themselves available at the private hospital through Choose and Book. This gave rise to a potential financial conflict of interest, with the possibility of consultants recommending that patients are treated by them at a private hospital.

> *I know that one of the things that I've been asked to keep my eye on is provision of services from Choose and Book by private sector hospitals, specifically the [large private hospital provider] and [another large private hospital] organisations... I'm not convinced that's because we're too concerned about the competitiveness, because they tend to do elective stuff and our elective access is actually quite good... I think I've been asked to keep an eye to see if our consultants themselves are publishing themselves onto Choose and Book.*
>
> (Foundation trust provider, area D)

The independent sector did not seem to be collecting information about their competitors with respect to NHS patients. While one said they had the capability to extract information about referral flows and where their patients are coming from (eg, primary care trust (PCT) of residence), they are not doing this at the moment.

Monitoring the market

In general, most trusts we spoke to were doing some analysis of the market. However, there was considerable variation in who was monitoring this data, how frequently and for what purposes.

> *We have a full market analysis of every... square inch that we serve.*
>
> (NHS provider, area C)

> *We keep a close eye on what's happening on the market situation... and we look at it on a monthly basis. 'Are we getting our share of the market?' 'Is it going up, is it going down?' What's happening, basically.*
>
> (NHS provider, area C)

Trusts do appear to be keeping an eye on nearby hospitals to see if they become more competitive and start to expand their current market area.

> *Currently, we're looking at other hospitals and I would say [name of foundation hospital trust] is our closest high-performing trust with a good reputation.*
>
> (Foundation trust provider, area D)

There were several comments from different trusts that suggest they are taking a more proactive view of the market and their business. This involved benchmarking performance against neighbouring trusts, including infection rates, waiting times and ratings by the regulator (the Healthcare Commission at the time of our research).

One large teaching hospital had its own data and informatics department. Operational managers looked at the data weekly and used it for capacity planning. Activity reports were presented to the chief executive's advisory board each month. There was also a six-monthly review of performance, which considered changes in activity and looked in detail at market share data, using it for strategic planning.

> *We're looking at trends and [ask]: 'If it continues to grow like this, why is it growing at this rate, what are the causes for this, what impact is this having on patient choice in terms of slot availability, do we invest now in terms of increasing capacity?'*
>
> (Foundation trust provider, area B)

One trust that had received the majority of its referrals (95 per cent) from one PCT found it easy to undertake useful, detailed activity analysis.

> *We're quite lucky here I think, 95 per cent of our business comes from [PCT C]. So if I had 10 different PCTs, it would be much harder to do some of that analysis I guess, and you get to know the GPs very well in the patch, and you get a real flavour for what's happening just because it's contained.*
>
> (NHS provider, area C)

Some trusts mentioned that their board considered these data – for example, they might feature in a market intelligence report to the board. At other trusts, a sub-committee such as a business development group looked at the data.

Despite having access to the Dr Foster data, one trust appeared not to use it for any systematic analysis or reporting of market performance. This trust had appointed a management consultancy firm to review their market analysis.

> *Well, our assessments are in and the model that we use is currently under review. After that there'll be at least quarterly reports going to the board and there'll be monthly reports going to the executive.*
>
> (NHS provider, area C)

In most trusts, there was an identified position (often quite senior) which was responsible for understanding the market and referral flows. One trust was taking the opportunity of appointing a new marketing director, whose role was to include looking at the market and how they can attract more patients.

> *I think that will be work I would expect the marketing director to undertake to get a better handle on the accuracy of patient flow data.*
>
> (NHS provider, area C)

At a couple of trusts, data was being used at a more operational level by divisional managers and clinical directors. In one foundation trust in area B, the medical director was most conversant with the Dr Foster tools and information on referrals. At another, the information was used to support clinical directorates in becoming more business-like.

> *So people who've got the operational responsibility, so they can see their specialities and… referrals, what have you, it's trying to engage them in thinking about running their service in a different way – in a more business-like way – than perhaps NHS managers traditionally have done.*
>
> (NHS provider, area B)

You can look at it by specialty and HRG [Healthcare Resource Group], which all of our CDs [clinical directors] and DMs [divisional managers] have access to. So, for example, I'm the director manager for orthopaedics and I wanted to look at hips and knees and where they're coming from, and thinking right, ok, well [area C] and [another area], what sort of activity flows did we get there? And you can actually click on it and it shows you exactly which GP practices have referred to you.

(Foundation trust provider, area B)

Investigating changes in market share

We asked providers to describe how and why referral patterns had changed. Many of them reported that they were experiencing high and increasing referral volumes overall. However, most providers felt the increases were not primarily due to patients actively choosing their trust.

I question how much it [patient choice] actually is moving patient flows.

(NHS provider, area C)

We're seeing a continual increase in referrals but would that be choice? … I'm trying to understand why referrals are increasing across the board, and is that patient expectation, patient demand, earlier referral?

(NHS provider, area C)

Changes in referral volumes were put down to other factors such as a decrease in orthopaedic referrals, which one trust speculated was due to more patients being treated in the community. Another trust felt that changes in referrals were due to different demand management initiatives from surrounding PCTs. Another felt that demand had increased as patients who previously paid for treatment privately were seeking treatment in the NHS.

We've had some little bit of movement… However, I'm not sure we can attribute it to patient choice. We certainly haven't seen a major exodus of patients leaving the area… We would have expected to have seen a reduction in outpatient referrals, because that's being managed in primary care now.

(Foundation trust provider, area B)

Sometimes they have one eye done privately and then obviously, with the introduction of choice, they have their second eye done on the NHS… Six months ago, somebody may have thought 'I've got some savings, I'll pay to have my cataracts done privately', and now they wait a little bit. They are coming to the same place, still being treated here, but as an NHS patient.

(Independent sector provider, area B)

In general, it was easier for hospitals to see if they were losing patients (ie, reductions in referrals) in certain specialties or from particular GPs. If such falls in activity were identified, then often further investigations would be made to find out why.

…market share is a slightly more difficult thing to quantify because the information is not as readily accessible [or] timely as we would like it to be… Where our activity is decreasing, we're obviously then trying to find out why, and if there are services that we're not offering in other areas that we could and therefore ought to be offering, and similarly, if we build into that our service development.

(Foundation trust provider, area B)

One trust with increased referrals to their dermatology service felt that this was due to its excellent reputation. Another made a clear link between increased referral volumes and their early introduction of directly bookable appointments in Choose and Book.

We have seen some evidence that referrals are rising faster from outside our traditional catchment than they are from inside it, and I can't explain that beyond the sort of positive hypothesis from our end is, people understand we are the regional providers of ophthalmology, we are the experts in the field, and so are increasingly shifting towards us.

(NHS provider, area B)

Partly because I think a lot of referrals are going up anyway, but partly because our reputation has improved as a result of various things that we've put into place, reduction of infection and that sort of thing. So we can see that patient choice is having an effect on our referral numbers.

(NHS provider, area C)

So our referrals have gone up and I think some of that is to do with the fact that we pushed Choose and Book very early.

(Foundation trust provider, area B)

There were also examples of increased referrals due to trusts opening new services, although it was not clear whether these were due to patients actively choosing the trust, or GPs or PCTs directing referrals there.

The independent sector organisations interviewed had all seen steadily increasing referral volumes since they started treating NHS patients. But they were not able to identify whether this was because of patients actively choosing their organisation or other factors.

Our choice throughput increased even in the short time I've been here... It's increasing, and it has been since it started.

(Independent sector provider, area B)

Where there had been changes in a hospital's share of the market for particular specialties, these were usually small and interviewees generally felt they were not linked to patients actively choosing their trust. The changes in patient flows that were experienced were usually attributed either to changes in PCT commissioning or general, provider-driven, changes in patient pathways and service redesign – not to patient choice.

There are some changes in patient flows where they have commissioned alternative models, so the model's being commissioned differently, so somebody else is providing it. We just see work go to them.

(NHS provider, area A)

Interviewees gave a number of examples of actions that were taken as a result of the kind of market intelligence noted above. One trust had used referral data to set up an extra clinic in order to ensure that referrals lost due to longer waiting times were regained.

They were offering appointments within a very short time of receiving the referrals. In other words, they were seeing patients within about a week of referral, whereas we were seeing patients within about three weeks, and that was driving down the number of referrals we were receiving.

(NHS provider, area C)

Another trust was using information to decide where to concentrate potential expansion efforts – for example, whether and where to do consultant community clinics and where to locate new community diagnostic facilities. Such decisions did not rest solely on market information but were also informed by discussions with GP surgeries. In addition, this information is being used to understand the potential consequences of a new treatment centre.

...so that's significant, and that would inform where we send our consultants to do peripheral clinics and where we invest our resources. There's some talk of us working with surgeries in this area to have a primary care sector where we can do diagnostic work and they want to talk to us about staffing that. So we'd look at that from a feasibility point of view, as well as patient numbers and convenience and where the roads are, where the patients come from... But there are limitations, and that's where speaking to the surgeries can be a lot more beneficial.

(Foundation trust provider, area D)

If we're looking at service development of facilities, then that's what we will look at [referring to Dr Foster information]. There's a new treatment centre opening... so we're looking at what we get from there, what we might lose and what we could perhaps gain.

(Foundation trust provider, area D)

Providers use data on referrals to inform their marketing strategies. Some used it to identify GPs not currently referring to the trust in order to target these practices so they could discuss reasons for low referrals.

We know which practices we've got that lower our [referral] rates, so we go and talk with the specialty leads to [find out] what we are not doing, what is not working... and modify our services accordingly. So we're using quite a bit of feedback.

(NHS provider, area C)

They also follow up on their referral analysis by going out to GPs and investigating whether there are other issues involved.

Where we believe that we're losing market share from a particular practice, [the medical director] will go out and say 'You're not referring as many people into the services, is there an issue?'

(Foundation trust provider, area D)

One interviewee from an NHS provider in area B stated that if they saw a sudden drop in referrals, they would want to investigate and act on it. They also stated that they visit GP practices they feel may potentially refer elsewhere – but it is not clear that this is a direct response to data.

The independent sector was also monitoring the pattern of GP referrals. However, it did not appear that they were as active as NHS providers in approaching GPs in practices from which they were getting few referrals.

Very, very few GPs would refer from that area, and I don't understand why, because we are their local independent sector... We've got all the data [so] that we can say where they've come from, got all that.

(Independent sector provider, area C)

Most trusts were actively monitoring referral volumes, and at least some were acting on this information to investigate the reasons for low volumes. As well as patient choice, there are many other factors that influence the volume of referrals received by a trust. These include overall demand for services locally, GP referral patterns and PCT referral management initiatives. During this period when activity was rising or at least stable, any changes in market share experienced by providers do not appear to have had a major impact.

Patient choice and quality improvements

While we found some evidence (albeit variable) that providers were actively gathering and analysing market data and using it to improve services, there were also many examples of ongoing and planned service developments. In this section, we report on the factors driving these changes in each of the four areas studied. We also explore providers' views and attitudes about the broader influences on their organisation's behaviour, mission and strategy. We look at some examples of service improvements and the factors influencing them. We then address the most important question: the extent to which patient choice has driven improvements in the quality of providers' services.

It is worth noting that the aim of the interviews was not to generate, by definition, quantitative evidence of providers' response to choice, but rather to gain insights into their attitudes and views. We were also interested in what managers and clinicians see as the main drivers of service change in their organisation.

Local health economy A

Mission and strategy

The mission of the NHS trust in area A was typified as providing good care for every patient on every visit. Given a history of poor performance on quality and finances, there has also been a focus on improving patient safety and eliminating accumulated debt problems. However, it was clear that the strategy was overwhelmingly driven by the need to reconfigure almost all of the trust's services following a merger of four trusts in 2002. Service reconfiguration issues are compounded by other long-term plans for service change involving four local PCTs. As a consequence, strategic direction is overwhelmed by the capital and service operational needs to see through major service changes that will take some years.

Despite these planned changes, there remain, according to some interviewees, major unresolved issues concerning mission and strategy. Chief among these is that there are possibly too many district general hospitals in the locality.

> There's an awful lot of hospitals in [big city], what on earth are they all doing here?
>
> ...some clearly aren't big enough to survive.
>
> (NHS provider, area A)

For the local independent sector treatment centre (ISTC), their mission was straightforward:

> ...[to] treat patients with dignity and respect... and to give them the ultimate service [possible].
>
> (ISTC provider, area A)

Unlike the NHS trusts, the ISTC's mission and strategy appeared not to be bound up with the reconfiguration plans in the area.

Specific service developments

Planned and ongoing service developments were numerous and major, and in general arose from the NHS trusts' amalgamation of four previous district general hospitals coupled with the city-wide reconfiguration plans.

Service development examples from local health economy A

Service development	Main drivers
Major reconfiguration of acute and maternity services	Merger of four trusts into one; city-wide plans for reconfiguration of services; care closer to home
Plan for bariatric services (possible joint venture with private company)	High demand, not enough supply
MRSA/*C difficile* reduction plan	National targets; professional desire to improve service quality
Patient pathway redesign	To help meet 18-week waiting-time target
CAT scanner	To help meet 18-week waiting-time target

The role of choice

The role of patient choice in directly driving service changes was, according to interviewees, very limited. First, given the nature of the area and the population, a number of interviewees noted that there was a strong loyalty to each of the four hospitals which now constitute the whole trust, and patients apparently have little appetite to travel or to exercise their right to choose.

> *So most people carry on coming to their local hospital because they know it and their GPs know the people there and they refer to them.*
>
> (NHS provider, area A)

> *...the experience we have had in practice is that although choice is there and although there are a number of other providers that people could easily choose, typically they've not done that and, indeed, quite the opposite.*
>
> (NHS provider, area A)

On the other hand, the counter view from the local ISTC was that patients are willing to travel.

> *...providing they get a good service, they're quite prepared to travel, whereas people say patients won't travel, but that's a misconception I think... People think they won't travel but it depends on how they offer the facility and also what the facility offers the patient.*
>
> (ISTC provider, area A)

Second, the big service reconfiguration agenda currently facing the trust was historic (arising from the need to rationalise services across four hospital sites and the city-wide plans for reconfiguration). Third, from the trust's point of view, there is little motivation to attract more patients as they are struggling with current workloads.

> *We're really struggling with 18 weeks at the moment and the reason is, as we start to reduce our waiting time, we get loads more referrals in...*
>
> (NHS provider, area A)

However, there was also a recognition that choice, and the threat of losing work, acts in an indirect way (at least at present).

What's important for us as an organisation is that it's always in our mindset, in our psyche...

(NHS provider, area A)

For the local ISTC provider, choice was obviously central to their work and their very existence. However, their contract was with the local PCT and referrals were in line with contracted activity, so there was no motivation to attract more patients. Interestingly too, the ISTC interviewee felt that the threat of losing patients would not affect the way they worked; their mission and basic view would remain: that they aimed to provide the quality of care they would want for themselves. Clearly, however, once contract guarantees expired loss of revenue due to switching of patients would have an impact on such providers' ability to meet their mission and overall goals.

Local health economy B

Mission and strategy

Interviewees from the three NHS providers in this area taking part in our research expressed the general sentiment that their organisations were striving to improve patients' health, to serve their local populations and create good services. For some, their ambitions were global.

[The hospital's mission] is to be the most exciting and successful health care organisation worldwide.

(Foundation trust provider, area B)

How these ambitions would be achieved differed between organisations due, in part, to a 'path dependency' – that is, a particular local history and local circumstances – and to the different strategic plans adopted. For example, one trust was preparing to apply for foundation trust status and this was a significant factor driving current management efforts – mainly with internal reorganisation and detailed financial planning. For another trust, their new hospital, funded through a private finance initiative (PFI) and due to open in 2010, significantly shaped actions and views across a range of the trust's planning and service developments – from a need to secure sufficient finances in the future, through to ensuring their hospital was the hospital of choice for patients.

The biggest risk is around finances. It's about maintaining our position in terms of patient choice and maintaining our level of activity and increasing it because we've... got a mortgage to pay in terms of our PFI.

(Foundation trust provider, area B)

However, there were also similar factors influencing change. For two trusts, for example, an important driver of planned changes was a desire to develop more community-based services and to look beyond the physical boundaries of the hospital.

I think we're very clear that we're trying to turn ourselves into an acute hospital that looks outside of its boundaries and towards primary care; [a trust] that works closely with GPs, that has consultants out in a range of locations in the community, and, as a result, has a much smaller acute hospital at its core.

(NHS provider, area B)

This reflects an important set of external, national influences on providers, including the general strategy from the Department of Health as reflected by Lord Darzi's report

(Department of Health 2008a), which called for a stronger focus on improving quality and re-engineering services. Specific national targets are also an important influence – particularly the maximum 18-week wait and reductions in health care associated infections such as MRSA and *C difficile*.

> *Targets are absolutely key… Some people think, 'Oh my God, not another target', but actually, targets keep you focused… on what you are trying to achieve. So it is a very targeted organisation, but in my opinion that is not a bad thing.*
>
> (Foundation trust provider, area B)

Specific service developments

We also sought examples of current or planned service developments and explored what factors interviewees felt were driving these changes. Examples are summarised in the box below.

Service development examples from local health economy B

Service development	Main drivers
New (PFI-funded) hospital	Long-planned replacement for outmoded Victorian buildings
Dermatology clinics located in the community	General desire to move services closer to patients' homes; enhance hospital's attractiveness to patients
New clinic slots in the evenings and at weekends	Response to increase in referrals (arising from Choose and Book and need to meet 18-week wait target)
New outpatient facility	Desire to improve patient experience at the 'front door'
Future plans to expand bariatric services	Desire to increase income
Increase in phlebotomy service capacity	Response to complaints by GPs of need for increase in service availability
Various activities to reduce waiting times	Meeting 18-week target

The role of choice

While none of the interviewees stated that these developments were a direct response to patients choosing alternative hospitals, some did refer to choice as a factor, in the sense that many of the developments were designed to make the hospital more attractive to patients.

A number of providers felt that investment in facilities would attract patients.

> *In terms of providing the best in care for patients, obviously choice is a main factor… The reason that we're reconfiguring services is to provide the best services for patients so that they choose to come and be treated here, so that this hospital will be their place of choice for treatment. So certainly, choice was part of that strategic thinking.*
>
> (Foundation trust provider, area B)

We're having a major investment on our site strategy, and one of our first priorities is a brand new outpatient facility with patient testing and minor theatres and all sorts of stuff. And from a patient choice perspective, that's the one that I think... because people do expect decent facilities and we're not providing them.

(Foundation trust provider, area B)

The new hospital is a huge incentive for us in terms of patient choice because we will have absolutely state of the art facilities with very good levels of single occupancy or low number occupancy rooms, which is going to make it a very attractive prospect in terms of attracting patients.

(Foundation trust provider, area B)

Others were aware of the general threat, even if patients were not exercising choice.

Yes, I think actually, in some ways, the threat [of patients choosing to go elsewhere] is sort of almost as powerful as the reality. And I think we're more conscious of the threat [even though we haven't] actually seen changes in practice on a large scale yet, but that doesn't mean they won't crop up at some point.

(NHS provider, area B)

We've had whole sets of conversations about we've got to try to make sure our services are sufficiently attractive to our patients, just in case they start to exercise choice in a way they currently don't seem to be.

(NHS provider, area B)

I think we've always been conscious that if we don't have services that work for patients, that are easy for patients to get to, that are easy for patients to use and that respond to patients' expectations, people who use us have other places they can go, and I think that consciousness has been heightened by the formalisation of the choice policy.

(NHS provider, area B)

There were other examples where patient choice was seen to have encouraged a focus on the patient experience and convenience.

One of the reasons we're looking at outpatients is that we want to make the outpatient experience better than it is, which would then attract patients... because we've got good booking systems and everything else. The outpatients is... our 'front door'. I would say that it is much more related to choice, we're doing it for that reason, to make it a better patient experience.

(NHS provider, area B)

As a trust, we are working very hard to increase our slots availability, so that patients will choose to come to us because they can get seen here first, because, of course, that maintains our activity.

(Foundation trust provider, area B)

For the independent sector provider, choice was important from the point of view of a steady income, which was less likely to be affected by the recession as their private patient income, even though the latter was more lucrative.

NHS choice is important to us, particularly at the moment, when it's recession proof. It's the nearest thing you'll get to a totally recession-proof revenue generator across any kind of industry, and that makes it extremely important. But the reality is, the more private patients we get, the more money we get, because the margins are there. But just to put the two things into context, I'm spending a lot of time and activity 'promoting'… the NHS choice work, because it is very important to us at the moment, and it will continue to be so.

(Independent sector provider, area B)

Nevertheless, a number of interviewees commented that regardless of choice or the threat of choice in terms of lost activity and hence lost income, professionalism and a simple desire to do a good job for their patients was a significant motivator.

The patient experience that people deserve is a good-quality experience. It's not because they can choose to go elsewhere, but because that's what you'd want for yourself or anyone in your family… If you look at the quality of service that people get [and ask] would you want that for you or your family… the answer is probably no, in most instances… So that's the key thing that's driving quality, not the fact that people can choose to go somewhere else.

(Foundation trust provider, area B)

We cancel a lot of appointments and we do loads of horrible things like that to patients. And a new thing I think that we're not as good on as we could be is basic customer care...

(Foundation trust provider, area B)

For one provider, actively responding to patient choice with an explicit goal of increasing volume (and hence income) was seen as irrelevant, as they were operating at capacity and had no plans for expansion.

Local health economy C

Mission and strategy

For one of the three NHS providers in this area, mission and strategy was being dominated by the fact that it had been operating at more than 100 per cent capacity for the previous three months. Attracting more referrals was not a priority as this would put beds, staff, patient safety and the 18-week target under considerable strain. However, the trust is seeking foundation trust status and aims to be 'provider of choice' for their local population.

Another trust emphasised their mission as:

…to exceed patient expectations by delivering excellent services that are innovative and as close as possible to patients' homes.

(NHS provider, area C)

The third NHS provider also noted their need to comply with national regulations, the NHS Constitution and their commissioners, as well as the professional desire 'to do the right thing for patients'.

For the independent sector provider, business, income, profit and margins were the most important drivers of their mission to '…reach our targets… set by head office' and to be the 'preferred provider of private health care within the market place'. For this provider, it was clear that their focus was on the higher-margin private payers rather than NHS patients.

For NHS providers, the general strategy was to seek to improve the quality of care they delivered and to ensure a greater degree of service provision locally.

Specific service developments

Numerous developments were noted by all interviewees in all providers (*see* box below for selected examples). Again, as in other areas, the drivers behind service improvements were many and varied. In many cases, there was a clear understanding that a particular service was not performing well and needed to be improved. While the *prompt* to do something may have initially come from information from the Care Quality Commission (CQC), or local knowledge and professional experience, the *motivation* to change was informed by a variety of factors – professional pride, a desire to 'do the right thing', etc.

Service development examples from local health economy C

Service development	Main drivers
Infection rate reduction	Concern about patient safety
'Productive wards and theatres'	Perceived need to improve efficiency; improve patient experience
Night-time noise reduction for patients	Patient complaints
Static CT scanner	GP demand
New outpatient facilities/more day surgery at independent sector provider	Responding to private insurers cost-consciousness
Planned introduction of intensive care unit (ICU) at independent sector provider	Increase private business; enable more NHS patients
Improve décor, etc	Patient survey comments
Waiting time reduction	Need to meet national targets
Quicker patient discharge	Need to reduce length of stay; desire to improve care for patients
Improved patient safety	Desire to improve patient care
End-of-life care at home	Desire to improve quality for patients; free up beds; reduce costs
Reduced length of stay for joint surgery patients	Retain referrals (as popular with patients)
Expansion in outreach clinics (eg, dermatology)	Choice and desire to provide care closer to home

The role of choice

In area C, a number of interviewees from the three NHS trusts noted that patient choice was important as an indirect driver for performance improvement – but, as in other areas, not a direct factor (in the sense that they had experienced, say, a loss of referrals and had then investigated the reasons and then changed their services/performance). Rather, providers recognised that they needed to improve on various dimensions of care and that, in doing so, patients would be happy to be referred to them.

> *One of the main things within our business plan is to try and improve the quality of care that we give to our patients in terms of patient safety, reduction of infection, rapidity of treatment, less time in hospital, and by doing that, then we hope that patients will be able to access various websites and look at the statistics of our hospital and say 'Yes, this is a good hospital, we choose to go to that hospital'.*
>
> (NHS provider, area C)

> *[Patient experience] has a knock-on effect on patient choice… in other words, if we improve patient experience, then automatically patient choice will result in more referrals to our hospital.*
>
> (NHS provider, area C)

Interviewees expressed the view that they knew what the problems were in their hospitals – high infection rates for some, long waits in others – and that it would not take a loss of referrals through patient choice to spur them into tackling such underperformance.

> *I've been in the services 35 years. I've always tried to put a lot of pride in the hospitals I've managed. I didn't need patient choice to do that.*
>
> (NHS provider, area C)

> *…irrespective of whether we have a patient choice system, then this is what I want to do, you know… I want to drive up improvements in quality and safety, patient satisfaction, that sort of thing… But as I say, it will have a beneficial knock-on effect in terms of patient choice.*
>
> (NHS provider, area C)

While interviewees noted professional pride and motivation and the desire to do a good job as important underlying drivers, as in other areas, they also mentioned service change as a result of decisions made by commissioners, the need to meet national targets and reconfiguration plans.

Local health economy D

Mission and strategy

As with providers in local health economy B, all four NHS providers in area D emphasised a general mission to provide high-quality, safe care to their patients.

> *[The mission is] to be a hospital which is known for, and with good evidence, for being a top-quality hospital… high-quality clinical outcomes. So, clinical outcomes and the patient experience.*
>
> (Foundation trust provider, area D)

> *'Putting patients first' is our strapline.*   (Foundation trust provider, area D)

> *[The mission of the hospital is to] provide the best possible quality of patient-centred care.*
>
> (Foundation trust provider, area D)

Specific service developments

General mission statements serve to highlight what may be considered somewhat obvious aspirations for health care organisations (for example, 'Putting patients first' – as opposed to what? Putting them last?). More specific developments and initiatives (*see* box below) reveal a more complex set of factors underlying change in services.

Service development examples from local health economy D

Service development	Main drivers
Speeded up purchase of new 'kit'	Single patient choosing another hospital; equipment nearing end of life
Partnership with another hospital to offer renal services	Reduce travel time for local patients
Improved car parking	Seen as important in patients' choice of hospital
New IVF facility	Increased income, attracting patients from neighbouring areas
Reducing infection rates	Desire to improve patient safety; improve a key indicator of performance assumed to influence patient choice
Purchase of a private hospital to provide a particular model of orthopaedic service	Consultant enthusiasm for new model of care; reducing competition from another provider
Refined emergency care pathway	Negative views from a patient survey
Improvement in general customer care	Professional desire to improve patient experience
Do not attend missed appointments-reduction strategy	Improve costs; improve patient experience
GP surgery-based clinics	Darzi-inspired desire to move some services closer to patients' homes
Consultant phone contact with patients post-discharge	Improve patient experience
'Restructured' neonatal unit	Longstanding historic need to upgrade the service
Activities to reduce waiting times	National 18-week target; local SHA [Strategic Health Authority] 8-week target
MRSA reduction strategy	General aspiration to improve safety and quality; maintain market share
Expansion of cardiology services	Reduce patient travel times
New CT scanner	Patient safety – to comply with NICE [National Institute for Health and Clinical Excellence] guidance

The role of choice

As in our other study areas, many developments were primarily driven by factors other than choice. However, a number of the developments and initiatives in the box were driven, in part at least, by a perception that a hospital could suffer if patients chose alternative providers. In the case of one provider, however, a high (and increasing) number of referrals meant that the hospital was operating 'over capacity'. Coupled with the fact that only around a fifth of their work was subject to choice due to a high proportion of emergency cases, there was a feeling that choice was less important to them than it may be for other providers. Interestingly, however, the very lack of choice for many of their patients heightened a (professionally inspired) desire to improve the quality of services.

> *In a sense, that [the lack of choice] drives us to be even better, because actually, if you have no choice about coming here because you've been involved in an accident or whatever, then actually we owe it to our patients to make sure… that we're providing the highest quality and the safest standard of care.*
>
> (Foundation trust provider, area D)

Patient choice, if not the main driver for one provider, is nevertheless seen as having an impact on the hospital. Interviewees consistently indicated that they aspire to become the 'provider of choice' for the local population and beyond (as they offer specialist services such as spinal injury services). Although they talk about doing things because 'that's what we should be doing' and 'we're doing it for the right reasons', they also indicated that there is a business element in the decisions they make. Patient choice clearly influences their decision-making processes. In this sense, one interviewee stated that choice 'is focusing the mind'.

For the independent sector provider in this area, however, alongside a professional desire 'to do a good job', the main driver for service developments has been demand for additional services or changes in services from the local PCT.

Discussion

What emerges fairly clearly from all the interviews across all four areas is that patient choice has not, so far, had a particularly significant impact on either the volume or quality of services provided. Moreover, with regard both to providers' general missions and strategies and specific service improvements, there are many other factors that drive or influence change. Some of these appear common across all (particularly NHS) providers, such as nationally set maximum-wait targets and targets to reduce hospital-acquired infections. Other factors include the need to comply with legislation (the European Working Time Directive, for example) and meeting managerial, financial and general performance requirements to achieve foundation trust status.

'Professional commitment' emerged as another set of factors influencing service developments. Perhaps unsurprisingly, many interviewees said that they worked to improve the quality of care for patients out of professional or organisational pride, a desire to 'do a good job' and to provide the kind of care they would want for themselves and their families. Nevertheless, all providers to some extent gathered information about their local market area and what other providers were doing, and monitored referral patterns (again, to a greater or lesser extent).

There were also examples where choice was, if not a primary factor (in the sense that a provider instigated a change in direct response to patients choosing alternative providers, and hence causing a loss of work and income), at least related to other reasons for change.

For example, while reducing waiting times was a national requirement, it can also be seen as important locally as a main factor influencing patients' choice of hospital.

To sum up, service developments and other initiatives to improve the quality of care are a function of, or driven by, one or more of a variety of factors (*see* box below). This list includes factors identified by our interviewees but is not intended to be exhaustive. There may be other drivers such as community involvement, commissioning priorities or regional strategies that could also influence local service developments.

There appear to be some indications of variation in response across our four study areas, which we explore further in the next section.

Drivers of quality improvement initiatives

Choice

- Response to actual switching by patients
- Response to anticipated or potential switching (a manifestation of a contestable market)

Other factors

External/national

- National targets/objectives
- NICE guidance
- International directives
- Legal/statutory requirements
- Requirements of national regulators (Monitor, CQC)
- Relative performance on national indicators of quality

Internal/local

- Capacity to change
- Organisational prestige
- Professionalism/intrinsic motivation
- Commissioner/GP demands
- Historic service configuration/quality
- Patient feedback (through surveys, complaints)

While it is not possible to measure, with any certainty, the relative impact of each of these drivers, we can tentatively conclude that, for the providers we interviewed in the four areas, patient choice has played a relatively minor role in directly influencing service improvements. However, this is not to underplay the indirect impact that patient choice has had (*see* below).

In particular, there was little firm evidence that any service development had been primarily driven by an actual switch in patient referrals (and hence loss of income) to alternative providers as a result of patients exercising choice. At the time of our interviews, NHS trusts were focused on achieving the 18-week waiting-time target and the resulting high activity levels meant they were often working to capacity. It seems that for many providers, external performance management of targets was the main driver of service improvements.

In this study, we mostly focused on large-scale service changes – possibly because most provider interviewees were senior executives rather than managers and clinicians. Quality improvement can occur at many levels within an organisation. It is possible that we failed to identify some of the smaller service changes that might be going on, some of which may be driven by patient choice and changes in referral activity.

However, there is evidence from our interviews that providers are aware that patients have a choice, and this was often a contributory or indirect factor prompting changes to improve service quality. There was also an awareness that patient choice may become more effective in future as patients have access to more information on which to base their choices. Moreover, there was often a clear expression that while it would not take the loss of work (as a result of patient choice) to spur action to improve performance problems, a provider's reputation would be enhanced by taking such action, and, it was assumed, patients would be happy to choose that provider as a result.

6 Choice and competition in a local context

One of the aims of this study was to understand how choice was operating in different contexts and the extent to which this influenced the behaviour of patients and providers. We have, where relevant in the individual sections, highlighted the differences between areas. In this section, we briefly summarise the findings presented in the earlier sections by area, and then discuss the implications of these findings.

How choice works in practice: area A

This largely urban area lies on the edge of a large city, includes pockets of deprivation, and has a relatively young and ethnically diverse population. The majority of referrals from the primary care trust (PCT) go to one main provider, which is spread over four sites and was formed after a series of mergers.

The implementation of patient choice was relatively advanced in this area, which was selected as having high penetration of choice. Patients were far more likely to recall being offered a choice (*see* Figure 9, p 54, and Table 8, p 58) and were given more options (*see* Figure 11, p 60) than in other areas. This may partly be explained by the structure of the incentive payment for GPs, who were paid by the PCT to offer patients a choice of at least five hospitals; in other areas, the payments did not relate to a specific number of choices. Also, in PCT A, a centralised triage system was used to manage referrals in specialties where primary care-based alternatives to hospital treatment were available. Patients who were referred into this system and referred to hospital will have had their referral processed over the telephone, which is likely to have involved a formal offer of choice.

More patients in this area (61 per cent) were aware of their right to choose before attending the GP surgery than in other areas (39–49 per cent) (*see* Table 5, p 30 and Table 2, p 27). Also, PCT A patients were more likely to say that choice was important to them (84 per cent) than in other areas (between 72 and 75 per cent) (*see* Table 6, p 31). Higher awareness levels and importance of choice might account for why more patients in area A recalled being offered a choice. Alternatively, those with previous experience of choice may be more likely to value it and therefore say it is important.

Although there was a high potential for choice in area A, the main provider felt little threat from patients choosing alternatives; they explained this as being due to high levels of demand for services and a local population that was relatively immobile and loyal to their local hospital. Data suggests that the main provider has lost some of its share of PCT A's outpatient referrals between 2005/6 and 2008/9. However, it remains the dominant provider, with more than 80 per cent of PCT A's outpatient referrals (*see* Figure 26, p 97).

The main focus for the trust was the reconfiguration of services across its four sites. Competition appeared to be driven by commissioners, with the threat of losing community service contracts. The PCT provider arm, as well as local Integrated Clinical Assessment and Treatment (ICAT) services, were competing for outpatient activity and threatened to reduce control over where they were referred. The trust was keen to embed their staff in these centres to ensure that referral levels were maintained. The trust felt little threat from the local independent sector treatment centre (ISTC).

How choice works in practice: area B

This area is in the heart of a large city, with a relatively young and ethnically diverse population and pockets of deprivation. There are three main providers, each focusing on different types of activity: a large foundation trust, a smaller district general hospital (DGH), and a large university teaching hospital foundation trust.

Although this area was selected as having a low penetration of choice (with only 51 per cent of patients reporting they were offered a choice in the Department of Health survey), a similar proportion of respondents to our questionnaire – 45 per cent – recalled being offered a choice as in the high penetration areas D and C (*see* Figure 9, p 54). Patients were, however, given fewer options in this area, with the vast majority (74 per cent) given just two hospitals to choose between (*see* Figure 10, p 54). GPs were paid an incentive based on the percentage of referrals booked through the Choose and Book system.

Despite being the only case study area to have run a public advertising campaign that included adverts on billboards and buses and on the radio, levels of awareness of choice (before visiting the GP) were similar to the other areas, which promoted choice in GP surgeries using standard marketing material provided by the Department of Health (*see* Table 2, p 27 and Table 5, p 30).

Patients in area B had a slightly different set of factors influencing their choice than in other local health economies. They were more reliant on public transport; 'accessibility on public transport' was a far more important factor than in the other three areas. Although a number of providers were relatively close, they may not have been easily accessible to patients and so may not have represented a realistic option.

Area B was selected because of its high potential for choice. However, providers said they tended not to compete for patients due to high levels of demand, their focus on different areas of activity (one focused on tertiary patients, one on developing services in the community), a close relationship between the two large acute providers, and collaboration on PCT-led initiatives to redesign services. No threat was felt from the private sector. The large foundation trust increased its market share of outpatient referrals from PCT B and remains the dominant provider, with 79 per cent of market share. The smaller district general hospital's market share had declined (*see* Figure 27, p 98).

How choice works in practice: area C

This PCT covers a mixture of urban and rural areas, with pockets of deprivation, and has an older than average population. There are three main NHS trusts in the area, one of which is a university hospital.

The area was selected as having a high penetration of choice, but its patients were the least likely to say they were offered a choice (*see* Figure 9, p 54) and least likely to be aware of their right to choose before attending the GP surgery (*see* Table 5, p 30). The PCT had done little to promote choice locally. Some GPs in this area said they only used Choose and Book because of the incentive payment they were given, and that if that were removed, they would stop using the system. Although this may not necessarily mean they stop offering choice, it indicates a lack of enthusiasm for elements of the choice programme among GPs in area C.

Although this area was chosen as an area with high potential for choice, competition for patients was not a key driver for local providers, who spoke of competing in different markets (eg, one provider competing for tertiary patients with hospitals out of the area) and of collaboration. One local provider did, however, speak about seeking to expand their market area for elective referrals. The district general hospital lost significant market share to the university hospital, but referrals from PCT C are evenly shared, with no single provider dominating (*see* Figure 28, p 99).

How choice works in practice: area D

This is a mainly rural, coastal area with a large number of retired residents and little ethnic diversity. There are four main NHS providers (all of whom are foundation trusts) and one ISTC (although this is some distance from the PCT).

Forty-four per cent of patients in the area recalled being offered a choice, similar to the average across all areas (*see* Figure 9, p 54). With a less ethnically diverse population than other areas, GPs were more likely to say they could offer choice equally to all patients.

This area was selected as having a low potential for choice, with providers located quite a distance from each other. Although providers were located further away, patients in area D were far less concerned about the accessibility of providers. 'Being accessible on public transport' and 'being close to work or home' were rated as far less important in their choices than other areas, and patients showed a greater propensity to travel than in other areas.

Providers gave some examples of collaboration and agreements not to compete, although there was some competition for patients on the edge of catchment areas, and a number of service developments were highlighted that were based on the perception that the hospital would suffer if patients chose alternative providers. There has been little change in the local providers' market share since the introduction of choice; PCT D's referrals were split between 5 providers, with one foundation trust receiving approximately half (*see* Figure 29, p 100).

Discussion

Our selection of local health economy areas was based on a series of hypotheses about how particular market factors would influence patients' choice and providers' response.

In area B, with low penetration of choice (measured by the proportion of patients who recalled being offered a choice), we expected to see less competition and a weaker provider response. According to our findings, there was little difference between the four areas in terms of the number of patients choosing a non-local provider and in the response of providers to choice. Patients living in rural areas and small towns were more likely to choose a non-local provider than those in bigger cities, irrespective of the area in which they lived (*see* Table 10, p 64).

In one area (A) that was specifically chosen for having a high penetration of choice, there was a higher number of patients who recalled being offered a choice. There were also higher levels of awareness of choice in this area, which do not appear to be accounted for by the PCT's efforts to promote choice locally. Our data suggests that this might have more to do with the way in which the implementation of Choose and Book has been actively managed by the PCT and the structure of local incentive payments. In this area (A) where specific conditions were attached to the payment (ie, that patients should be offered five choices), this was much more likely to occur. In other areas, patients were often just given two hospitals to choose between or were not offered a choice at all.

Also in this area (A), where our patient survey data indicated that choice was being offered in a way close to that envisaged in policy (patients offered a choice, usually of more than two options), very few patients were choosing to travel beyond their local provider. Factors such as transport may have had an impact. Patients in more urban areas were more reliant on public transport, which made them less mobile and less willing to travel beyond their local provider despite the fact that they had many providers located close to them. Furthermore, in this area, there is a bilateral monopoly relationship between the PCT and the provider, which has five sites. So despite a high penetration of choice and high potential for choice, concentration of the market and patients' reliance on public transport meant that there was little real competition among providers for patients.

In areas with high potential for choice and high penetration of choice, we expected to find higher numbers of active choosers (travelling to non-local hospitals), more competition and a strong provider response. We had anticipated that the area with the referral management centre would affect choice, either increasing the number of patients experiencing choice (as this would be offered more systematically by the centre) or reducing it, with more patients diverted to the referral management centre without being offered a choice.

In fact, interviews with PCTs revealed that the PCT selected as having a referral management centre in fact had a triage system for some services, which were also available in primary care. The systems for referral management were changing in the other areas; some had centres that had now been disbanded, and in some areas, triage systems existed for specific specialties. The impact of these systems was not mentioned by GPs or providers and, therefore, we do not focus on this in the analysis. Another study is focusing specifically on the impact of referral management systems (Imison and Naylor, forthcoming).

Finally, in the one area (D) with low potential for choice but high penetration of choice, we expected to find active 'choosers' but less competition and a weaker provider response. The area with the lowest potential for choice (D) according to our selection criteria, based on the number of providers within 60 minutes' travel time, actually showed little difference in the likelihood that patients chose a non-local hospital than in the other areas. This is consistent with the finding that patients in more rural areas are more willing to travel to access care and more likely to choose to travel to a provider other than their local one. It may be that patients who already have to travel to access care are more amenable to considering non-local options when selecting a hospital. This challenges the perception that choice is only applicable to urban areas, where a large number of providers exist within close proximity.

Areas that were selected as having a high potential for choice were actually often less competitive than the area with low potential. A number of factors appear to have affected the level of competition, including patients' willingness to travel to a non-local provider, the extent to which the local market was segmented (ie, little duplication of services), and the level of collaboration between local providers.

Despite the presence of private sector providers in all areas, including ISTCs in areas A and D, there was very little threat from the independent sector. Due to high levels of demand and pressure to meet the 18-week target for waiting times, NHS providers were often working with the private sector to provide additional capacity, especially where NHS providers were full. It appears that the inclusion of the private sector within the NHS market and the extension of 'free' choice have not yet had a major impact on the level of competition between NHS and private providers.

Summary

It appears that a number of contextual factors influence the way in which patient choice operates, including how actively choice is promoted by PCTs and GPs, the way in which local incentive payments are structured and GPs respond to the incentives, access to public transport, and the rurality of the area. Those responsible for supporting implementation locally may therefore need to think about:

- how much to invest in advertising and promotion, who they are targeting with this information and why

- how best to support and encourage GPs to offer choice, and ensure that they provide information and advice to patients to help them make informed choices

- what support they have in place for transportation to hospital, what information they provide about the accessibility of local providers, and how they can ensure ease of access to alternative providers for those reliant on public transport.

Our findings give no reason to suggest that choice is only relevant in particular parts of the country. In fact, it appears that, contrary to the opinions of providers and GPs, it is more likely that people in rural areas will exercise choice. The context is therefore clearly important, not only to the way in which choice operates but also in whether choice creates competitive pressures and drives quality improvements among hospital providers.

Our findings suggest that for patient choice to create competitive pressures on providers, a number of factors need to hold: patients need to be offered choice, they must be willing and able to travel to a non-local provider, there must be at least one other provider within a reasonable travel distance who offers the same services, and there must be perceived variations in quality. If there are low levels of 'switching' and high market concentration (in other words, few providers in an area), there might still be reasonable competition if there is significant rivalry or contestability for contracts. Similarly, even if there is low market concentration (many providers in an area) and high levels of switching, there may be little competition if the market is highly segmented.

7 The future of choice and competition

Patient choice at the point of referral was introduced during a period of financial growth in the NHS, but also at a time of constrained capacity, with rising demand and requirements to meet the 18-week waiting-time target. The NHS is now entering a different period in which the pressure on public finances means funding will be significantly tighter and the focus of national policy-makers and local organisations is changing. We asked providers for their views on how things might change, and this was also the subject of a discussion at an expert seminar held to discuss the findings of our research.

Interviewees cited a number of factors that would affect the level of choice and competition in the future. Some of those we interviewed felt that choice would take time to develop and that, in some sense, the NHS and patients were not yet really ready for choice. Many of those we spoke to felt that choice would become more relevant in future, and that it was here to stay.

> *Patient choice is absolutely the right thing, it's just that England possibly is ready for it more in three to four years' time than it is now.*
>
> (Foundation trust provider, area D)

> *The competition will increase, and I think patients' awareness. I mean, I think patient choice is in its infancy, and I think in four or five years' time it will be a very different animal from the one it is now.*
>
> (NHS provider, area C)

The lack of information available to patients was seen as a barrier to choice driving quality improvement, but it was felt that this would improve in the future.

> *I think it's flawed because I think that patients don't necessarily choose on the basis of the standard of clinical services, and I think that's not to say that it's not an effective model… If we were able to get to the stage where patients perhaps had access to clinical information that was presented in a clear way that they could understand, then it would become a more effective model, and I know that is being worked on.*
>
> (Foundation trust provider, area B)

Several providers felt that patients would become more discerning and 'savvy' (more aware of quality differences) and that outcome measures would have a greater influence on choice in future. Providers also thought that as waiting times fell, quality issues would begin to take on greater importance.

> *I'm sure as information is more readily available on things like individual doctors' mortality, how often they do operations, we will still see more informed patients moving around following good results and outcomes.*
>
> (NHS provider, area C)

Increasingly, patients will ask the questions around what's their particular surgeon's, you know, mortality? What's the infection rate for this particular procedure? Not just about C difficile or MRSA but actually, more, you know, more specific around infection.

(NHS provider, area C)

One GP who was generally positive about the potential of choice felt that unless patients themselves showed a greater interest in choosing beyond their local provider, the impact of choice would remain limited.

I do believe in choice being an effective lever for giving improvements, but unfortunately, at the moment, it can't do that and doesn't do that apart from understanding of waiting times... But it's getting that customer demand for choice, and I think, at the moment, in half of the discussions, it's 'No, doc, I just want to go to my local hospital'.

(GP, area A)

Providers generally felt that these changes would not happen quickly but would develop slowly as patients increased their awareness and confidence, and more information became available.

I think that will be incremental, it won't happen with a big bang. (NHS provider, area C)

I think everybody expected choice to come in and all of a sudden it will change absolutely everything, and it won't, it will take time to develop.

(Foundation trust provider, area B)

One interviewee also felt that, as waiting times fell below 18 weeks, patients would increasingly use quality to help them choose between hospitals.

What is there to distinguish between going to [one foundation trust hospital], going to [other foundation trust hospital] or going to [third foundation trust hospital]? It should be quality and it should be the standard of care that you're going to receive.

(Foundation trust provider, area D)

The tighter financial environment for the NHS over the next few years could mean that hospitals will compete to maintain activity (and income). However, even within the same trust, opinions on this were somewhat divided. One interviewee said they will need to *'grasp whatever market we can to generate the income to keep us afloat'*. Whereas another said the hospital had no plans to expand services or take over other hospitals' work, but instead, is putting resources into improving the quality of current services.

We recognise the climate we're in, we recognise that there's a lot of very difficult financial [sic] to come over these next few years... And so we've been very, very conservative about our plans... What we are trying to do is improve our quality standards further... We don't have any plans to, sort of, like, take over hospital bills or take a chunk of work that we don't already do from somebody else.

(NHS provider, area C)

In one area (D) with a number of hospitals providing the same services, providers did not expect all hospitals to be viable in the long term. Greater collaboration or 'takeovers' might become necessary as the funding situation becomes tighter.

I can't believe that there are going to be that number of fully fledged DGHs [district general hospitals] on the map in 10 years' time. So I think there are going to have to be allowances, even if you don't say a dirty word like 'takeovers' or anything, there have to be allowances between organisations where there is some collaboration about how you are going to deliver these services.

(Foundation trust provider, area D)

One interviewee from an NHS provider in area C thought that a further reduction in waiting times within the NHS would reduce the competitive threat from the private sector in future. Indeed, this view was shared by an interviewee from an independent sector treatment centre (ISTC) in area D, which was currently meeting their contract on volume, but thought that as waiting times became less of an issue in the area, they might have to work harder to retain referrals.

Others thought that, as a consequence of lower waiting times, the impact of a new private provider would be felt harder, as the primary care trust (PCT) would not be willing to spend more and therefore it would result in a loss of activity. One private provider was clear that their NHS choice patients were 'recession proof' in contrast to privately paying patients, who are vulnerable in a recession. This suggests that private sector providers might compete more aggressively for NHS-funded patients in future.

There were some service areas where NHS providers perceived that the private sector might develop new services to compete with existing services – for example, in rehabilitation and physiotherapy. This was borne out by one of the private providers we spoke to, who was looking to expand into other niche services.

> We have contracts with three PCTs now, we actually deal with five, so we want to increase our involvement with those other PCTs outside of our area, as well as increase the number of procedures.
>
> (Independent sector provider, area B)

Depending on how practice-based commissioning (PBC) develops, this could present a competitive threat to some hospitals. Providers perceived there could be greater competition as PCT provider arms and GPs start to provide more services that directly compete with the services offered by hospitals.

> ...If and when PBC gets stronger, we could get competition from the, our own... primary care trusts, if their provider arm is strong.
>
> (Foundation trust provider, area D)

> ...I suspect that practice-based commissioning is going to mean that GPs are looking to provide more services locally... some of the minor surgery, I suspect GPs will be wanting to get into that.
>
> (Foundation trust provider, area D)

Some felt that public opposition to the role of the private sector would mean that it would be difficult to allow the closure of local services or hospitals as a result of competition. This view was further compounded by the reluctance of senior leaders within NHS organisations to destabilise other NHS providers in their area.

The mindset within the NHS not to enter into open competition was widespread, but there were signs that some providers thought that it would not be long before a provider with a more aggressive approach would 'break ranks'.

> There's still a, sort of, cosy relationship between NHS trusts, well, certainly providers don't tread on other people's toes. And at some point, I don't know who's going to be the first one to break ranks and say 'Sod that, this is about market share, this is about profit, we need it, and we think we should go and market ourselves in your areas'. Because it's still very restricted, we couldn't just wander into someone's PCT and set up an outpatient clinic and say 'Right, come on, refer to us', because the PCT are saying 'Oh, we haven't commissioned services from you'.
>
> (NHS provider, area A)

In general, the view across providers was that patient choice was here to stay, and indeed, it will become more important as people become more aware of their right to choose and more information becomes available to inform their choices. These changes, however, would not happen suddenly, but take some time to develop.

This research was carried out at a time when most providers were still operating at full capacity in order to meet the 18-week waiting-time target. As waiting times reduce across the board and the 18-week backlog is cleared, spare capacity will emerge in the system. This will heighten competition for activity volumes at a time when PCTs may be looking to manage demand more aggressively, either directly or through practice-based commissioners. Wave 1 contracts for ISTCs also come to an end. The original contracts had guaranteed volumes, but under the new contracts, ISTCs will have to compete for elective patients more proactively.

Finally, lower waiting times may result in reduced use of the established independent sector by NHS trusts for waiting list patients. Together with the reduced demand from private-pay patients due to the recession, the independent sector may become more interested in competing for NHS choice patients in future. While the market for NHS elective services may not currently appear to be very competitive, there are signs that this may change.

Implications and discussion

As new pathways of care are developed, with more outpatient activity taking place in the community, the locus of choice may change. Now, most patients are choosing where to be seen for an outpatient consultation and are not given another opportunity to choose their provider. In future, patients may be offered a choice at the point of referral for treatment *after* diagnostic tests and specialist consultations have taken place. This may mean that GPs are less involved in choice than at present. Patients will be more certain about their need for treatment and therefore may value different factors than those we identified in this study. Most of the data on quality relates to outcomes for surgery or treatment; this may become more relevant if choice is offered at a later stage of the treatment pathway.

In future, patients will be able to choose their GP and may more often be able to choose a consultant. Choice of GP, combined with the development of federations and stronger primary care-led commissioning, may change the incentives for offering choices to patients. There may be stronger incentives to keep patients within primary care, perhaps using GPs with special interest. While this might offer better value and outcomes for patients, it may also reduce competition. Choice of consultant, while likely to be valued by patients and GPs alike, is likely to affect providers differently, in practical ways (eg, managing appointments and waiting lists) and in terms of increasing patients' interest in the reputation of individual clinicians and data on their performance.

The NHS Constitution introduced a legal right to choose (Department of Health 2009b). This might shift the focus from performance management of choice and use of Choose and Book by PCTs (as described in this study), putting the onus on patients to exercise their right to choice instead. How such a right would be enforced needs to be carefully considered in order to protect those who may be less informed about their rights or capable of exercising them. It is possible that, as patients become more aware of their right to choose, they will increasingly request a choice. This may change GPs' beliefs about the importance of choice and reduce the sense that it is something they feel obliged to offer.

There are already increasing amounts of data in the public domain about the performance of hospitals. The NHS Information Centre has recently published a set of Indicators for Quality Improvement (IQIs). All trusts will be required to publish quality accounts in 2010, and the Care Quality Commission (CQC) continues to see itself having a role as an independent source of information for the public. Routine data on patient-reported outcome measures (PROMs) was published for the first time in April 2010. Among its many applications, it is intended that this data will be presented for use by patients to inform choice (Devlin and Appleby 2010).

Demands for increased transparency, particularly of public bodies, and political commitments to openness and empowering the public suggest that this trend will continue. However, the data is not yet widely used by patients. If patients become more familiar with a common set of variables with which to judge services and are supported in this by improved support to make informed decisions, we may yet see greater use of such information in future. Providers consider that the availability of information to inform choice in future will sharpen the incentives.

The ability of patients to choose any provider means commissioners' position vis-à-vis providers is relatively weak, simply requiring reimbursement of care at tariff under 'any willing provider' contracts. As funding becomes tighter, commissioners will need to extract more value from their contracts. If the tariff reforms signalled in the Operating Framework 2010/11 (Department of Health 2009c) are implemented, commissioners may be able to negotiate prices. If such contracts were in place, commissioners (be they PCTs or practice-based commissioners) would have an incentive to encourage patients to go to the most financially competitive provider, thus potentially limiting the scope of choice. According to one PCT, 'choice only works when prices are the same', suggesting that patients are already being discouraged from choosing off-tariff services if they are more expensive.

The economic context is also likely to accelerate the need to reconfigure services, including consolidating some services onto fewer sites. While some of these changes are justified on clinical grounds and are being reviewed nationally following the recommendations of the *NHS Next Stage Review* (such as paediatric cardiology, renal medicine, major trauma and stroke), there will be a perception that these are being driven by cost considerations, and this may generate local opposition. These changes will also reduce the number of choices available to patients for some specialised services.

There is a trade-off to be made between enabling greater choice and ensuring quality and safety of services, which policy-makers will need to address. Rationalisation of local services may involve discussions between providers about the most efficient way to provide services to a local population. The extent to which such agreements are deemed collusive will ultimately depend on how competition rules are applied to the NHS. Cases may rest on the extent to which commissioners are leading local planning decisions and whether the public interest has been upheld. Policy-makers will need to provide greater clarity about how co-operation and competition should co-exist.

There is also a cost to providing care at multiple locations. The policy of choice was introduced in the context of increasing investment in the NHS and a desire to drive increased activity to bring down waiting times. The period of austerity which the NHS is now entering means that the focus will be on reducing demand for and utilisation of the NHS (wherever the activity takes place). If demand management is successful, spare capacity may become available in the system. In the short term, this is likely to engender stronger competition between existing providers for patients until excess capacity is closed.

There is likely to be less scope for new entrants to the market during a period of tighter funding unless they are able to clearly demonstrate better value for money to commissioners. It is difficult to predict how demand for treatment in the private sector by NHS patients under choice will develop. If demand from private-pay patients reduces, then the private sector may seek to compete more aggressively for NHS-funded patients than it has to date.

Finally, there is increasing interest in promoting greater integration of services – both vertical integration of acute and community services and horizontal integration of primary, community and social services. While this is likely to be beneficial for patients with chronic conditions and long-term medical and social care needs, there is a risk that it will limit choice and competition. The choice policy was mainly designed to address issues such as long waiting times for patients needing non-urgent and elective procedures. The types of choice available and the factors that are important may be different for patients with chronic conditions, and therefore, require the policy to be refined. The extent of integration and its impact on local markets will, in part, be shaped by the decisions of the Co-operation & Competition Panel.

Significant changes in the NHS resulting from the tighter financial context are to be expected. These, along with other policy developments, are likely to affect how choice operates and the impact it has on providers. The choice policy will need to be adapted to fit these very different circumstances.

8 Discussion and conclusions

The aim of this research project was to establish how patients choose and how providers respond to patient choice. We have collected and reported on a significant body of empirical research, which has documented how choice of hospital at the point of referral was operating in four local health economies in England during 2008 and 2009. Using a range of data collected from patients, GPs and senior executives within provider organisations in each area, we have been able to describe how patients are experiencing choice in practice, the factors that are important to patients when choosing a hospital, and the support, advice and information available to patients to help them choose. Through interviews with senior executives, we have also been able to establish providers' perceptions of the extent to which competition is operating in each area, and the resulting impact of choice and competition on local service improvements.

In this final section, we summarise what our findings reveal about the reality of choice at the point of referral as it currently operates in England (*see* Table 13, p 150). We compare our empirical findings with the policy model, and discuss the extent to which our findings are in line with the theory reviewed in Section 1. We then conclude by discussing some of the implications of our findings for policy.

Revisiting the analytical framework

In the introduction, we set out our analytical framework and described a model of choice based on key policy assumptions (*see* Figure 3, p 17). For this model to operate effectively, the beliefs and behaviours of three key actors – patients, GPs and providers – are central. The policy model assumes the following actions on the part of each:

- patients act as informed consumers – using quality as the primary factor in choosing between hospitals, and accessing information about alternative providers to inform their choice

- GPs act as agents of choice – supporting patients to make an informed choice based on information about quality

- providers respond to market signals – monitoring changes in demand and improving quality in areas valued by patients, especially those areas where they know their standard has fallen below that of their competitors.

Table 13, overleaf, summarises the findings of our study and maps the extent to which they match the model of choice set out earlier.

Table 13 The reality of patient choice at the point of referral in England

	Model of choice assumed by policy	Reality of choice found in this study
Patient	Aware of ability to choose	Around half of patients aware of ability to choose ('How aware are patients of their ability to choose?', p 25)
	Want to choose and think choice is important	Most patients want choice (75% important or very important) ('How important is choice to patients?', p 30)
	Offered choice of providers – including NHS and independent sector	Half of patients recall being offered choice ('Are patients offered a choice?', p 47)
		Few patients recall being offered non-NHS provider options ('Are patients offered a choice?', p 30)
		Age, level of education, ethnicity and employment status not significant predictor of whether offered choice ('Who is offered a choice?', p 56)
	Quality is primary discriminator in choosing which provider to attend	Patients with previous bad experience of a local hospital are more likely to travel to a non-local hospital, as are those with higher levels of education, those who live outside of cities and large towns, and older people ('Who is exercising choice?', p 63)
		Quality is important to patients when choosing (cleanliness, quality of care and standard of facilities) ('Why are patients choosing particular providers?', p 69)
	Has access to relevant and appropriate information on quality, and ability to interpret	Patients make little use of available information, rely on personal experience and their GP ('What support, advice and information do patients receive?', p 86)
GP	Believes choice is important to patients	Most GPs interviewed supported choice in principle ('What do GPs and providers think about patient choice?', p 34)
		Have experienced frustration with Choose and Book; incentive payments are important ('Opinions of Choose and Book', p 41)
	Offers choice to all patients needing a referral	Believe that only a few patients want to make a choice beyond their local hospital, and likely to be more relevant to people in urban areas and important to younger and better educated ('How important is choice to patients?', p 30, and 'Who is offered a choice?', p 56)
	Involves patient in decision-making	Some resistance to being required to offer choice to every patient regardless of circumstance; many GPs only offer choice in a tokenistic way ('Who is offered a choice?' and 'Are patients offered choice?', p 56)
	Has access to information about the quality of providers and conveys this to patient	GPs do not trust or have access to 'reliable information' on quality, rely on their own knowledge of providers and distrust marketing information from hospitals ('What support, advice and information do patients receive?', p 86)
	Has time and resources to support patients to make an informed choice	Many GPs feel that they only have limited time to support choice, ie, by guiding patients through their options. Little additional information offered to patients to support choice ('What support, advice and information do patients receive?', p 86)
Provider	Competes for patients with other providers	Some agreements between providers, which may limit competition ('Are providers competing for patients?', p 101)
		Limited competition with the private sector for patients ('Are providers competing for patients?', p 101)
		Competition for patients at the fringes of 'catchment' areas only (where patients/practices are equidistant) ('Are providers competing for patients?', p 101)
		Competition for the market stronger than competition in the market ('Are providers competing for patients?', p 101)
	Receives clear signals as a result of patients' choices	Providers believe GPs continue to have influence on demand and focus on their 'custom' ('What are providers competing over?', p 111)
	Analyses and understands meaning of choices	Focus on patient experience of care and feedback, little information on 'potential' patients' preferences ('Collecting and using marketing information', p 118)
		Choice is one of several factors influencing provider behaviour ('Patient choice and quality improvements', p 124)
	Responds to loss of market share by improving services	Choice has an indirect impact through sharpening providers' desire to maintain reputation, loyalty of local population and be provider of choice ('Patient choice and quality improvements' p 124)
		Providers are not directly responding to patient choices and changes in market share ('Patient choice and quality improvements', p 124)
	Providers that don't respond lose money and may eventually fail and exit the market if fail to attract patients	Many providers operating at capacity; growth in demand and 18-week wait mean choice not posing threat to activity/income ('The future of choice and competition', p 143)

Patients as informed consumers?

The model of patient choice which underpins policy requires that patients are aware of their ability to choose, want to choose, and think choice is important (*see* Table 13, opposite). In our research, we found that about half of patients are aware of their ability to choose, and that older people and those with higher levels of education are more likely to be aware of choice than other groups. Most patients want a choice and think that it is important. It appears there is some intrinsic value in offering patients a choice of provider. It is likely, therefore, that regardless of whether choice has any instrumental value, the NHS will need to continue to enable patients to have some choice over the location of care.

We found that patients who were more aware of choice before visiting their GP were also more likely to be offered choice. This suggests that one way of increasing the numbers of patients who are offered a choice is to increase patients' awareness. However, it is not clear from our research that greater investment in general advertising by PCTs makes much difference to levels of awareness. Older people, who are generally in more frequent contact with the NHS, were more aware of choice before visiting their GP, as were those with higher levels of education. The shift to patient choice becoming a 'right' may give patients more confidence to ask to be referred to another hospital. However, leaving the responsibility to patients to ask for choice may increase inequities.

Policy also assumes that patients are offered a range of options (including private sector providers), that they use quality as the main factor when choosing a hospital, and have relevant and appropriate information on quality to inform their decision (*see* Table 13, opposite). In our research we found that about half of patients recalled being offered a choice. In contrast to our expectations and the opinions of providers and GPs – that choice is more relevant in urban settings where there are more providers to choose from – we found that patients living in small towns, villages and rural settings were more likely to have been offered a choice than those living in a city, large town or suburb. Age, level of education and ethnicity were not significant predictors of whether patients were offered a choice.

Very few patients recalled being offered treatment at a private sector facility. This might be due, in part, to patients' lack of awareness that some treatment centres are independently owned and run, as they often use NHS branding. Less than 20 per cent of patients were aware of the option to be treated in the private sector on the NHS. The expectation of policy-makers that choice would improve equity by extending the opportunities to those who could not previously have afforded the choice to 'go private' have not been fully realised.

Despite the extension of choice from five options to any willing provider under 'free' choice, in reality, patients are generally faced with fewer options. The vast majority of patients were offered up to five hospitals from which to choose (2 per cent were offered more than five). Evidence from decision theory research and behavioural economics suggests that narrowing the choice set reduces the cognitive burden of decision-making.

Patients (and GPs) may need help to filter those hospitals which most closely fit their preferences from the extended list of providers now available to them. Web-based information has greater potential to achieve this level of support to help patients choose. Further research is needed to explore how web-based information – for example, on NHS Choices or within Choose and Book – can be adapted to help create a tailored choice set. Currently, the design of Choose and Book means that the list of options generated by the GP or practice staff are likely to have been selected on the basis of proximity (to the patient's postcode) or the time of the next available appointment.

Our research found that most patients who are offered a choice remain with their local provider (69 per cent). Under hypothetical situations, almost one in five respondents chose the local provider in all choice sets, regardless of their attributes. We might suppose from this that the majority of patients are happy with the service provided by the local hospital. This would be consistent with surveys which show that public satisfaction with the NHS is running at an all-time high (Appleby and Phillips 2009) and that, generally, people are more satisfied with their local service.

Alternatively, it may reflect a lack of awareness or information about the quality of a hospital's services (especially if someone has had no previous experience there) and how it differs from other hospitals. The high levels of loyalty to the local provider which we observed may also arise because the patient assumes that the quality of care is the same regardless of where they are treated, because of the omnipotence of the NHS brand across providers (and despite high-profile failures elsewhere in the NHS).

There may, therefore, need to be greater flexibility for providers to differentiate their services from others using brand recognition in order to help patients to choose between services. There is already some limited use of franchised service brands by specialist providers within the NHS. Despite there being a strong propensity to choose a local provider, the hypothetical data we collected also shows that in 45 per cent of all scenarios presented, patients chose a non-local provider. This suggests that a significant number would be willing to change providers in response to differences in characteristics.

We found that in practice patients who are offered a choice are more likely to travel to a non-local provider than those who are not offered a choice, but the difference was small (29 per cent vs 21 per cent using unweighted data). Yet, empirical work from other markets suggests that only a small proportion of consumers are required to 'switch' in order to send a signal to providers and create sufficient stimulus for improvements. Indeed, theory suggests that switching is not actually needed, as long as the threat of exit exists. Our research suggests that approximately 5–14 per cent of patients may be actively 'switching' to a non-local provider.

There may be many reasons why a patient (including one who is not offered a choice) attends a non-local provider – for example, they may need specialist care not available at the local hospital. We found that, among those who were offered a choice, one of the main predictors of going to a non-local hospital was a bad experience with the local hospital. This strong relationship suggests that one of the main motivations for patients to travel further is to avoid a poor-quality local hospital. This suggests that the biggest threat to a hospital's market share is providing poor-quality care to individual patients, because they are less likely to return, more willing to go to a non-local provider, and may not recommend the hospital to friends and family.

Concerns were raised in the literature about the possible negative impact of choice on equity (Appleby *et al* 2003) due to the perceived greater ability of better-educated groups and middle-class patients to exercise choice. Others have argued that choice can increase equity (Dixon and Le Grand 2006). In this research, while there were no apparent inequities among those who were offered a choice (*see* above), there were differences in the kind of patients who attended a non-local provider; older people, those with higher levels of education, and those living outside of cities, large towns or their suburbs were more likely to travel to a non-local provider when offered a choice.

This is consistent with findings from other forthcoming research by Carol Propper that competition has increased more in areas away from the main urban centres. One reason for this might be that, as these small towns are unlikely to have their own hospital, there is no obvious 'default' hospital to attend, so patients (and GPs) may therefore perceive there to be a genuine choice. Patients with higher levels of education were more likely to choose a non-local provider under both hypothetical conditions and in practice.

While mode of transport for getting to hospital was not a significant factor in predicting whether patients were more likely to choose a non-local provider in practice (when data was weighted), those who normally do not travel to their local hospital by car were more likely to select their local trust, irrespective of performance or other attributes under hypothetical conditions. This suggests that less-educated people living in cities and without access to a car may be less likely to switch to a non-local provider. Some inequities might arise if these patients are not able to exercise choice in line with their preferences while others can choose to travel further to access a higher-quality alternative.

Our research found that patients place high value on aspects of quality, including the quality of care, cleanliness of the hospital and the standard of facilities. However, they make little use of available information on the performance of hospitals (such as that available on NHS Choices) and instead rely heavily on their own experience, that of friends and family, or the advice of their GP.

The factors rated highly by patients as important when choosing the hospital were consistent with the patients' revealed preferences, which showed that patients chose to attend hospitals that had lower *C difficile* infection rates, higher CQC ratings for quality of service, and higher patient ratings of the hospital environment. In hypothetical choice sets, patients similarly placed a high value on infection rates, outcomes and good hospital environment. Patients may need more help if they are to choose on the basis of quality dimensions such as infection rates or clinical outcomes, which are not easily directly observed by patients, and where available measures may be difficult to understand.

Given that patients place a high value on the quality of care and other related dimensions of quality and safety, systems that provide information to patients about the quality of hospital services may need to be designed to make it easier for patients to search and compare on these dimensions. Currently, Choose and Book displays and sorts options by distance and waiting times, but does not allow sorting by any quality dimension. Designs which 'nudge' patients towards higher-quality providers could also be tested.

Nationally, there is a significant investment going into the publication of performance information to support choice – for example, through NHS Choices. Our research found that only 4 per cent of patients consulted NHS Choices when making their decision. This is in line with previous research, which found that patients make relatively little use of public reports of hospital performance (Shekelle *et al* 2008).

Consumers in other markets are capable of making seemingly rational decisions about complex purchases, *if they are sufficiently comfortable with the variables*. Hence, without a background in engineering or IT, consumers are making decisions about which car or laptop to buy because they can assimilate information about things like fuel consumption, emissions, service intervals, available memory, RAM, and so on. However, to be able to do this, there needs to have been a period of time where the product variables have become the common, *hard* currency. It is not perhaps surprising, therefore, that patients are making little use of comparative hospital information when the indicators of quality are frequently changing, are difficult to interpret and are often very general (relating to the organisation's performance as a whole rather than to a specific site, service or consultant).

Continual revisions to the set of indicators used to measure quality and changes in the way this information is calculated and presented are likely to confuse patients. Recent debates about the method and meaning of standardised mortality rates produced and published by Dr Foster (Hawkes 2009) suggest that more work is needed to establish a set of standardised variables for acute hospital care, with which patients can become more familiar over time. In future, patient experience data at the level of service lines and PROMs data will be available. These offer an opportunity to present more specific data of relevance to patients when making a choice in future.

In the absence of price, brand or information to differentiate services and products, consumers use other available clues or information to make decisions. We found that patients use their own personal experience (41 per cent), that of friends and family (8 per cent), and the GP's recommendation (36 per cent) to inform their choices rather than using objective information. Recent investments to expand NHS Choices to include a feedback section will enable patients to access more 'soft' knowledge. Research is needed to understand how patients use such feedback when presented alongside objective measures of quality.

Overall, our findings suggest that patients who are offered a choice are, to some extent, acting as informed consumers, avoiding a local hospital if they have had a bad experience there. However, despite rating quality as important in making a choice, they do not make use of 'hard' information on the performance of hospitals but instead rely on 'soft' knowledge and the recommendation of their GP. It is to the role of GPs as agents of choice that we now turn.

GPs as agents of choice

The choice policy was designed to give patients a choice of provider at the point of referral (usually by a GP) to a specialist (usually in hospital outpatient clinics). This creates an important role for the GP in supporting and implementing patient choice.

The design of Choose and Book allows patients to make a choice themselves and book an appointment at the chosen hospital online or through a telephone booking adviser. However, it was envisaged that GPs (or practice staff) would frequently be involved in the choice and booking process. For most patients in our study, choice was offered by the GP (60 per cent). From GP interviews, it seems that a number of practices delegate responsibility for booking appointments to other practice staff, although the number of patients reporting being offered a choice or booking an appointment with other practice staff was small (4 per cent).

Our research also found a significant number of patients make their choice when speaking to telephone booking advisers (20 per cent) or after receiving written correspondence (21 per cent). In areas with high use of Choose and Book, some patients received a booking letter with a number of options; they then booked an appointment via telephone even though they had not had a discussion about choice with the GP or had 'decided' on a hospital during the consultation. It is important that policy-makers consider the way in which options are presented in booking letters, and what information and advice is available to patients over the phone.

In order for the policy of patient choice to operate in the way that it was envisaged, GPs need to believe that choice is important to patients, then offer choice to all patients who need a referral, and involve them in the decision (*see* Table 13, p 150).

GPs we spoke to were generally supportive of choice in principle but felt that it was nothing new. They were, on the whole, supportive of involving patients in decisions about where to refer, if patients wanted this. Some GPs felt that a more collaborative discussion with the patient about the decision to refer and the available treatments was important, but that the specific decision about where to go could be left to the patient (or practice staff). This is, in part, explained by the fact that GPs saw choice of provider as being largely an issue of timing and convenience rather than differences in the quality of care provided.

Practice staff are more able to assist with booking an appointment than they would be if choice was primarily about clinical quality issues. The policy, some felt, had focused minds on what matters to patients. While GPs were able to identify a number of benefits for their patients such as convenient appointments, any benefits in terms of improved efficiency, quality or equity were clearly not apparent to them, whereas the time and resources needed within the practice to offer choice were very apparent.

GPs tend to conflate patient choice with Choose and Book, and this colours their views of the choice policy to some extent. The system was seen to be unreliable, containing inaccurate and inconsistent information, increasing consultation times, and lacking functionality to fit with how clinical referrals are made (in particular, the ability to refer to named consultants). A few GPs saw some benefits in giving patients greater control and certainty.

Financial incentives appeared to be important, with some GPs indicating that they would stop using Choose and Book if the incentive payments stopped. However, these payments reinforced the feeling that this is something they should do rather than want to do. While GPs acknowledge that the system has improved and some of the initial technical problems have been fixed, there remains reluctance among GPs to use it themselves during the consultation. Such negative attitudes among GPs about Choose and Book may have acted as a barrier to the successful implementation of the choice policy. Information for GPs about choice may need to emphasise involving patients in decision-making and focus less on the use of the Choose and Book system.

We found little evidence that access to choice is inequitable. Indeed, there were no differences by age, education or ethnicity in terms of whether patients recalled being offered a choice. The perception of GPs about the type of patients who value choice (younger people and middle-class patients) is not borne out by the data.

The GPs we interviewed also felt that choice was more relevant in urban areas where there were more local providers from which to choose. In fact, patients in small towns were significantly more likely to be offered a choice than those living in a city, large town or suburbs. We were not able to evaluate the impact of language. Some GPs working in areas of greater ethnic diversity felt that non-English speakers were disenfranchised by the choice process. This group of patients may not be getting equal opportunity to choose. The lack of congruence between GPs' views about which patients value choice and the data from patients suggests that there is a risk of inequity. Furthermore, GPs' preconceptions could lead them to offer choice selectively.

There was some resistance, even among our sample of 'enthusiastic' GPs, to offering choice to every patient regardless of their circumstances. GPs appeared to be more willing to let patients choose when the referral was fairly routine but are more directive when more specialist treatment is required – in part, because they have more knowledge of specialist centres. Our data suggests, for example, that GPs are more likely to offer choice to patients who anticipated needing an operation or inpatient stay at the time of referral; but those whose referral was 'urgent' or whose self-rated health was lower were less likely to be offered choice.

This raises a question as to whether the requirement that every patient in need of a referral is systematically offered a range of providers from which to choose is appropriate. However, there is a risk that if GPs do not feel obliged to offer choice routinely to all patients, or are not financially rewarded to do so, then inequities might increase. Changes in the demographics of patients who recall being offered a choice should be routinely monitored in order to assess whether any changes in the incentives are having an impact. In addition, it may be worth communicating to GPs the diversity of patients who think choice is important.

In terms of how choice is working locally, we found that GPs are sometimes offering choice in a mechanistic or tokenistic manner. Some GPs offer choice in such a way as to fulfil requirements of the incentive payments, but without much meaningful discussion of the options unless the patient requests it. Most GPs believe the patient will usually want to go to a local hospital. The requirement to generate up to five choices therefore is seen as tokenistic (and is usually limited to a set of local options anyway), as both parties are already agreed on what the choice will be.

Only a few GPs thought that Choose and Book provided an opportunity to discuss choice with patients in a meaningful way – apart from cases where a more specialist referral was required. If GPs are to be more engaged with offering patients choice, they need to see this as part of involving patients in decision-making and not simply as a 'tick box' exercise to be completed in order to get an incentive payment. This suggests a need to make a clear distinction between the role of GPs in offering choice and use of Choose and Book as a system for booking appointments.

For many patients, the decision about *where* to be referred is tied up with the decision to refer and is made by the GP. For an increasing number of patients, there is a separation between the decision to refer (taken by or with the GP in the consultation) and the choice of where to be referred. The design of Choose and Book has created the possibility that these decisions are separated. The GP or someone in the practice can generate a booking reference, which a patient can use to book an appointment with a chosen provider directly over the telephone or online. Among our sample, about half of the patients who were offered a choice took control of this decision and booked the appointment themselves on the phone. When patients were not offered a choice, about half had the GP book the appointment. This system, while giving patients greater control over the time and location of an appointment, also puts the onus on patients to ensure they actually book an appointment. There is a greater risk that patients get lost in the system, or simply do not follow through on the referral. Clearer responsibility needs to be given to practices to ensure that referred patients actually book in and are seen by the clinic.

In order to support choice effectively, policy assumes that GPs (or their equivalents) would have access to information about the quality of providers, and convey this to patients. It also depends on GPs having the time and resources to support patients to make an informed choice.

Our data suggests that, for patients, the GP's recommendation is important in deciding where to go. A perfect principal–agent relationship is one where the choice that is made by the agent is the one that the principal would have made if they were themselves fully informed. In order for an agent to make this decision, they must, in turn, be fully informed about the principal's preferences and have incentives to take account of them.

Our data also suggests that patients value quality, cleanliness, and standard of facilities when choosing. In the hypothetical choices, our analysis shows that low infection rates, health outcomes and friendly staff, together with proximity and low waiting times, are all important to patients. These may not be the attributes that are important to GPs, who might instead value timely discharge information, for example. If GPs presume to choose a hospital for their patients or a reduced set of hospitals, they may reduce the likelihood that the optimal option is in the choice set. Our research found that most patients in the NHS who are offered a choice are able to attend the hospital they wanted. Among those not offered a choice, very few patients were not able to attend the hospital they wanted. This suggests that the choice made on their behalf (usually by the GP) was in line with their preferences (whether articulated or not).

If GPs wished to discuss aspects of quality with patients when making a referral, they would have to go to NHS Choices to access this information (the main Choose and Book screen presents information on waiting times and travel distances but not on quality). However, GPs in our study, in line with previous research (Rosen *et al* 2007), were sceptical about the use of objective information, and relied instead on soft knowledge such as relationships with consultants and feedback on the experiences of patients who they have previously referred. They are also distrustful of information provided by local hospitals (eg, marketing information).

This may mean that GPs are reluctant to offer options to patients with which they themselves are not familiar. Furthermore, GPs are likely to have little or no information on which to base a referral outside of the local area. If GPs are to make greater use of 'hard' information, sources such as NHS Choices need to be promoted to GPs in order to convince them of the validity and reliability of such data. Many of the issues discussed above in relation to usability of information by patients would apply equally to GPs – that is, ensuring the information was clearly presented and easy to interpret.

Most GPs we interviewed did not feel they have enough time for an in-depth discussion about different options in a standard 10-minute consultation. At the moment, a GP is only likely to encounter a few patients per week that need a referral, and it may be appropriate therefore to facilitate extended consultation times in these cases. In future, if there is more direct access to diagnostics and consultant advice, GPs may be referring fewer patients to hospital and may be more likely to be referring for treatment when they do so. This could also change the nature of the referral consultation, and make it more likely that GPs will be willing and able to engage patients in a decision about *where* to refer.

Providers' response to choice

In our analytical framework, choice was assumed to stimulate competition between providers for individual patients; hospitals and other providers would attract patients by improving the quality of services relative to their competitors. If quality falls relative to other providers, they will not attract patients, will lose income, and may eventually fail and exit the market. In order to understand the reasons why patients choose to be treated at the hospital or elsewhere, providers need to analyse patient demand. Finally, providers must be in a position to change their services in response to patients' preferences.

In our research, providers did not feel they were actively competing, either with other NHS providers or with the private sector. Indeed, there were many examples where NHS hospitals were collaborating with other providers. Agreements between NHS providers were justified on the basis of reducing duplication, managing workforce shortages, and enabling strategic reconfigurations. At least some of these activities may either intentionally or inadvertently be limiting the impact of choice and competition. Policy-makers will need to be clear about how acceptable such arrangements are, and whether some of these activities are collusive. In the tighter financial climate that the NHS is now operating in, it is likely that provider-initiated plans to better manage services across local health economies are likely to become more common.

One potential source of competition for NHS providers as a result of the choice policy was from private hospitals and ISTCs. Our findings suggest that the private sector, on the whole, was not viewed as a significant competitor, in part, because of the small volumes treated. The established independent hospitals were attracting few 'choice' patients and continued to provide extra capacity to help NHS providers meet waiting-time targets. There were isolated examples where the NHS had actively sought to repatriate patients from the private sector, responding to competition by expanding their own facilities.

At the time of our research, it appeared that the private sector was seen as a collaborator, bringing extra capacity into the system at a time when waiting times were having to be reduced. However, providers were clear that this was likely to change in future – in particular, in a context where more care is delivered out of hospital, there is less funding available, and there is spare capacity in the system as waiting times reduce. If demand from private-paying patients falls, the private sector may be keen to attract more 'choice' patients and compete more actively with the NHS. The extent of competition from ISTCs in future will largely depend on their ability to develop a more positive reputation and to market their services to GPs and patients successfully.

The main competitive threat was felt where PCTs were actively tendering community services and new outpatient services, particularly by small and medium-sized trusts. Competition *for* the market as a consequence of PCTs tendering for services was perceived to pose a greater threat than competition *in* the market driven by patient choice. However, NHS providers were looking to build partnerships with new private sector entrants, particularly those providing diagnostic and outpatient services. Policy-makers will need to ensure that such agreements are in the best interests of patients and taxpayers. While competitive tendering of services may provide an initial competitive threat, policy may need to ensure that competition for patients is encouraged once these services are awarded.

The motivation for providers to attract patients (and the associated income) appears to have been dulled by a number of contextual factors. In our study, providers understood the link between increased activity and income through Payment by Results and saw this as a potential benefit of attracting new patients. However, many providers were not interested in attracting more patients, as they were already faced with rising demand and operating at or near capacity in order to meet the 18-week waiting-time target. The emphasis across the majority of providers was on retaining patients rather than expanding into new markets. It seems that spare capacity or lower demand within the system would be a necessary prerequisite for providers to compete more actively for patients in future. For others, even small shifts in elective activity could be enough to bring about change given the implications for income. However, there was no evidence that any of the providers we interviewed were concerned about the financial impact of choice.

For some providers, the proportion of income at risk from choice was small, due to their case mix of activity (dominated by emergency admissions or tertiary referrals). Specialist or tertiary providers were not competing for patients in the local area, but seeking to attract patients from across a much wider regional area. The focus of such providers was on building collaborative relationships with feeder hospitals on which they rely for consultant-to-consultant referrals. Networks of providers are likely to be the basis of these relationships in future, with franchising arrangements (whereby renowned specialist centres run local services under their own brand) becoming more common.

Where there was competition for patients, it was in areas which were equidistant from at least two providers. This is consistent with our findings that patients in rural areas were more likely to exercise choice to attend a non-local hospital. Few providers were undertaking market research to understand the preferences of 'potential' patients when choosing a hospital, but instead were focused on the experience of 'current' patients (that is, feedback and complaints) and the interests of GPs. Many providers were using patient experience and feedback to drive quality improvement.

Providers were quite sceptical about the extent to which patients were acting as informed consumers. Their perception was that GPs remained significant in the decision of where to refer a patient. The focus was, therefore, on the GPs as referrers rather than on patients. Where providers were doing market analysis, the focus was on the market share from GP practices and not on individual patient demand.

Any observed changes in referral patterns were largely understood as being a result of GP decisions rather than the preferences of individual patients. Consequently, activities to promote the services on offer were focused on GPs. Some providers were keen to ensure that GPs, as referrers, were 'satisfied customers', focusing on issues such as ease of booking and prompt discharge letters.

If the objective of choice is to make providers focus on patients and the quality of services, it appears that providers are, at least in theory, signed up to this. However, their focus on patients and the quality of care is motivated by a complex set of factors, of which choice is but one. A whole range of internal and external factors appeared to influence the priorities of organisations and the service changes they were implementing. At the time of our research, other factors such as targets appeared to be more important than choice.

Many organisations emphasised a focus on patients as part of their 'mission' to provide a good service to the local population. Many of those we spoke to saw it as their job to be aware of what problems the hospital had (eg, high infection rates) and to resolve them. They did not wait for 'signals' as a result of choice to highlight the weaknesses or problems with the services. More research is needed to understand what motivates individuals within organisations to improve quality.

The presence of choice, however, did appear to provide a motivation to maintain reputation in order to ensure that patients returned or, through word of mouth, spoke highly of their experience. Choice provided an edge through the threat of losing patients (ie, contestability) rather than because of the active choices of patients. Providers talked about wanting to be the local provider of choice. This suggests they are interested in maintaining the loyalty of their local population, in particular, where they provide general hospital services. Taken together with our finding that patients base their choices on personal experience or 'soft' knowledge, the emphasis placed on delivering a positive patient experience is not surprising.

In health care, the reputation of a hospital is highly dependent on those who deliver the service (that is, doctors, nurses and cleaners) and who exercise the most control over the 'moment of truth' – when patients experience the service. Given that clinical outcomes are often intangible or not fully experienced until after the patient is discharged, the way the service is delivered (ie, the patient experience) becomes more important to reputation. The implications of this are that engaged staff who understand the impact of their behaviour on their patients are likely to be key to whether patients recommend or return to a particular provider. Our research suggests that reputation and loyalty, combined with patients' ability to choose not to return to a hospital, create pressure on providers to deliver a high-quality service.

The main policy interest in patient choice has been its instrumental value in creating competition for NHS-funded patients and thereby increasing efficiency and improving quality. Our research suggests that, from the perspective of providers, the policy is bringing only limited direct pressure to improve quality, especially when compared to pressures from other factors such as waiting-time targets. However, providers believe this might change in the future, as choice beds in, more information becomes available and financial pressures mean activity growth levels off. There do appear to be indirect effects resulting from choice, such as concerns about reputation and the desire to be the provider of choice for the local population.

There may be a number of reasons why choice seems to be having only a limited impact on provider behaviour. First, it could be that the policy has not had sufficient time to have a greater impact. However, the bulk of the data collection took place three years after the introduction of choice at the point of referral, and a year after it was extended to choice of any willing provider.

Second, it may be because choice has not been fully implemented. While our research suggests that about half of patients recall being offered a choice, this has been the case for some time, according to time series data collected by the Department of Health. This should, according to theory, provide sufficient potential for switching to exert pressure on providers.

Third, it may be because patients, even when offered a choice, are very loyal to local providers. This is the perception of providers we interviewed. The results of the stated preference analysis also suggest a proportion of patients are loyal: 25 per cent of respondents chose the local provider regardless of other attributes in all hypothetical cases, and across all respondents, the local provider was chosen in 61 per cent of scenarios.

Fourth, there may be other more powerful influences on provider behaviour. In our study, the growth in emergency activity, combined with requirements to meet the 18-week wait target, appears to have cancelled out any interest in attracting patients.

Finally, the effects of patient choice on providers may, in part, be limited because of the activities of providers themselves to dampen the effects of choice and competition through agreements and collusive behaviour. There was evidence of this in our study.

Addressing the key policy questions

Our study relied on the perception and views of those working in provider organisations to establish the impact of choice. We are, therefore, able to report on the impact of choice on provider behaviour rather than the impact of choice per se. Other forthcoming research commissioned by the Department of Health Policy Research Programme from Carol Propper has used quantitative data to assess the impact of choice and competition on patient outcomes.

It was difficult to disentangle the impact of patient choice from the wide range of other factors influencing the way organisations operate. For example, an interviewee might say that an organisation implemented a particular service change in order to provide a good service for patients, but might not have been specific as to whether this was motivated by a desire to attract patients and the money that comes with them, professional pride, or a customer service ethos. It was also not possible from our interview data to understand the relative importance of different factors influencing these decisions. Further research is needed to understand the motivations of organisations and individuals for service improvement and how different factors influence these.

Most policy evaluation studies find that it is difficult to isolate the impact of a single policy change when there are other policies being implemented simultaneously. This was particularly true of patient choice, which was implemented alongside other reforms such as Payment by Results, the introduction of ISTCs and the creation of foundation trusts (to name but a few). Data collection took place in a period just before the deadline for trusts to meet the 18-week referral to treatment target, and this was therefore a major focus for many providers.

Although the fieldwork for this research took place at a time when patients had been entitled to a limited choice at point of referral for nearly three years, 'free choice' of any eligible provider had only been operating for six months. Our findings on providers' response to patient choice are, therefore, likely to reflect the impact of local choice (of at least four providers) rather than the wider choice policy, the impacts of which may take some time to emerge.

While it is not possible to generalise completely from the four local health economies we studied (due to some of the limitations set out in Appendix A), the findings do provide some insights which we hope will be useful for policy-makers as they consider the role of choice and competition in driving quality and efficiency in the NHS and for those locally who are responsible for working out how best to operationalise choice and support patients in making choices.

Having made some specific policy recommendations in relation to aspects of choice policy and how it is working in practice, we turn now to some of the high-level questions that policy-makers are grappling with. What are the overall implications of our findings for patient choice policy?

First, should the NHS continue to promote patient choice? If patient choice is seen as an end in itself, our work suggests that choice is valued by patients and enables more patients to be treated at the hospital they choose. It seems to be particularly important to enable those who have had a bad experience of a local hospital to exercise choice to go elsewhere. Regardless of its effectiveness as a driver for quality improvement, we therefore conclude that, given its intrinsic value, the NHS should continue to offer patients a choice of hospital. Even if few patients use their ability to choose to go to a non-local provider, the ability to exit appears to be important to the majority of patients. Currently, the focus of policy has been on choice at the point of referral. There may be other decision points in the patient pathway where patients would wish to exercise choice, and policy needs to be clear about how willing it is to support and enable patients to make such choices.

Second, how is patient choice affecting providers? If the policy is seen as instrumental – that is, as a means to drive quality competition and improvements in services – then our research suggests that choice is an important factor, but it is only one of many. Providers identified only a few examples where patient choice had directly resulted in a service change, but it was clear that the desire to be the 'provider of choice locally' was important in driving some service improvements. In that sense, reputation matters.

The factors which motivate leaders of health care organisations are complex and varied, and it was not possible in this research to establish their relative importance. However, our research does suggest that policy-makers need to recognise that other factors (for example, national targets) may crowd out the impact of choice locally on providers. Providers themselves understood the theory behind the incentive effects of choice, but most were clear that their commitment to providing a high-quality service was driven by their organisation's mission or professional altruism rather than the threat of losing patients and income. It is important that the rhetoric on choice and competition does not obscure the ultimate objective of choice – that is, to improve quality of services.

Choice appears to affect quality indirectly, by creating a threat to providers that they might potentially lose patients. This suggests that choice can have an effect even if few (or any) patients actively choose to attend a different hospital. It is important that observed changes in market share are not taken as markers of the extent of competition or choice in a particular market – patients may be choosing to stick with a local provider. Because patients rely on their own or others' experience to inform their choice, providers must deliver a high-quality experience in order to retain the loyalty of patients. Patient feedback is therefore likely to remain a significant driver of quality improvement in the future. Because patients do not use objective measures of quality, it is hard for those with no experience to differentiate services. Brand and customer loyalty may become increasingly important for providers, and they may need to be given more scope to differentiate themselves from other providers.

Third, is patient choice working everywhere and for everyone? Our research was limited to four local health economy areas in England. However, despite differences between those areas, choice and competition were operating to some extent in each of them. We found that providers were competing most actively for patients (or GP referrals) on the geographical fringes of their catchment areas, and that patients in rural areas and small towns were more likely to be offered choice and attend a non-local hospital. This suggests that the effects of choice may be greater on hospitals serving rural areas and small towns. It also challenges the belief (widely held among those we interviewed) that choice is only relevant in urban areas. Choice may, therefore, have increased competition in areas that had not previously seen much competition, a finding that appears to be supported by other recent empirical research (Cooper *et al* 2009a) and by Carol Propper's forthcoming research.

There were no significant differences between different population groups (by age, gender, ethnicity or education) in whether patients were offered a choice, suggesting that the opportunity to choose is reasonably equitable at present. However, older people, those with higher levels of education, and those living outside of large cities and towns were more likely to travel to a non-local provider when offered a choice. Under hypothetical conditions, less-educated people living in cities and without access to a car were more likely to choose their local trust, irrespective of performance or other attributes.

It is important to understand why these differences between actual and hypothetical choices exist. But there is at least a potential risk, which policy-makers need to be aware of, that where a trust is failing to maintain quality standards and large numbers of people exercise choice to be seen or treated elsewhere, that local patients without access to transport could get 'left behind'. It underlines the need to ensure, through regulation, that all providers meet minimum standards, in order to protect patients.

Fourth, is choice cost-effective? This is a more difficult question to answer, and was not something that our study sought to answer. However, through the data collection process, we became aware of a variety of costs, nationally and locally. Some GPs and providers we spoke to shared the view that the costs of implementation may outweigh the benefits. While the exact costs of patient choice are not available, according to the regulatory impact assessment that accompanied the introduction of free choice, the additional costs of implementing a free choice of provider from April 2008, over and above the cost associated with a choice of four providers, ranged from £4.9 million to £43.1 million (Audit Commission and Healthcare Commission 2008). There is a need for policy-makers to quantify more clearly the costs and benefits of choice in order to convince GPs and providers of its value.

There has also been considerable investment in NHS Choices (£60 million over three years) (*Hansard* 2009–10). PCTs have funded marketing and advertising campaigns to raise patients' awareness of choice, but awareness levels remain low. Few patients had heard or seen an advert for NHS Choices (10 per cent) or choice (16 per cent). Awareness appears to be greatest among older people, who are in more frequent contact with the NHS. It may be that, over time, awareness will gradually increase as people experience it for themselves.

Incentive payments for GPs in the 2006/7 GMS contract were equivalent to about 50p per patient for offering choice, and a further 50p for booking that choice. The removal of incentives for GPs, while saving money, may have the unintended effect of reducing equity if GPs become more selective about which patients they offer a choice, or rely on patients asking for a choice. Providers also faced costs in implementing Choose and Book, which required changes to appointments systems and marketing to GPs. Policy-makers need to consider carefully how best to invest resources to support patient choice. It is unlikely that promoting choice will be a priority locally as PCT funding becomes tighter.

Finally, has choice been implemented effectively? Both GPs and providers had complaints about the way in which Choose and Book operates. While some of the technical problems have been solved, there remains a perception that the functionality does not support referral practices (Dixon *et al* 2010). Continued improvements in the system and training in the functionality of new versions of Choose and Book are needed if usage is to be maintained beyond the enthusiasts, especially if local incentives are dropped. If Choose and Book is intended to be a referral system, then it needs to be adapted to support a high-quality referral process. Alternatively, it should be simply regarded as a booking system and focus on increasing its usability for patients and those supporting patients to book an appointment at a convenient time.

There also remains some resistance among GPs to offering choice routinely to all patients, regardless of their circumstances. Presenting choice of provider as part of a wider agenda to engage patients in shared decisions about treatment and care may help to overcome some of this cultural resistance, as would a greater understanding among GPs of the value of choice to a diversity of patients. There may be limits to the extent to which the implementation of choice can be improved and, indeed, to GPs' willingness to offer choice systematically in all circumstances.

In conclusion, the policy of offering patients a choice of provider is valued by patients, and is operating to some extent within the NHS but is not necessarily operating in exactly the way envisaged by policy. While the implementation of choice has not been perfect, it still represents a threat to providers that keeps them focused on what is important to patients.

Appendix A: Methodology

Within each local health economy, a variety of research methods were used:

- patient interviews
- survey of patient views
- GP interviews
- provider interviews
- primary care trust (PCT) interviews
- analysis of Hospital Episode Statistics.

Before outlining the methodologies used for data collection and analysis, we outline our approach to site selection.

Site selection

The research took place in four local health economies in England. PCTs were initially identified across two dimensions: high and low potential for choice, measured according to the number of NHS trusts within 60 minutes' travel time (Damiani *et al* 2005);[1] and high and low recollection of choice by patients, measured using the Department of Health-commissioned MORI patient survey from November 2007 (Department of Health 2008b).[2] There is some debate about the validity of using travel time to calculate measures of provider competition (Cooper *et al* 2009a). However, the purpose of our measure was to capture, from a patient perspective, the number of options within a reasonable travel time.

The characteristics of the PCTs selected are outlined in the box opposite. Since our study sought to explore patient, GP and provider experiences of choice, and we anticipated that contestability (proximity of multiple, potentially competing providers) would influence the way in which choice operates, we did not select any sites which had both low recollection of choice and low potential for choice. Instead, we selected two PCTs from the 'high–high' category, which enabled us to select one PCT with a referral management centre (RMC) and one without.

[1] The distribution of PCTs according to the number of providers within 60 minutes' travel time was cut into quartiles, and PCTs with an average number of hospitals above the median (> = 4 hospitals within 60 minutes' travel on average) were classified as 'high potential for choice'. PCTs with an average number of hospitals below the median were classified as 'low potential for choice'.

[2] The distribution of PCTs according to the percentage of patients who recalled being offered a choice in the Department of Health's November 2007 monitoring survey was cut into percentiles, and PCTs whose score fell above the 70th percentile (> = 52 per cent) were classified as high penetration of choice; those whose score fell below the 70th percentile were classified as low penetration of choice.

Characteristics of case study PCTs

	Potential for choice (No of providers within 60 minutes' travel time)		Penetration of choice (% offered choice)	
A	HIGH [+ RMC]	(6)	HIGH	(70)
B	HIGH	(11)	LOW	(51)
C	HIGH	(4)	HIGH	(57)
D	LOW	(2)	HIGH	(61)

All PCTs in England that met the selection criteria were considered for the study, except for the following.

- PCTs with low take-up of Choose and Book, since this is the intended mechanism through which choice referrals are processed.

- London PCTs, since London is atypical in terms of its demographic and geographic characteristics, and evaluations of early choice pilots were conducted in London.

- PCTs bordering Wales or Scotland, since the choice policy is not in operation in those countries.

- Reconfigured PCTs, since complex mapping would be required to calculate referral volumes.

- PCTs involved in other projects funded by the Department of Health or being run by The King's Fund, in order to avoid research burden and contamination.

Trusts receiving 5 per cent or more of their outpatient referrals from the selected PCTs[3] were asked to take part in the study. Not all of the trusts approached were located within the case study PCTs, but together they formed the local health economy that would be expected to compete for patients residing in the PCTs. All of the trusts approached in the selected areas agreed to take part, except for one specialist children's hospital, which received 7 per cent of referrals from PCT A. It was decided to include this local health economy despite this trust's non-participation, as the majority of referrals from the PCT went to a participating trust, which is spread across five sites.

One independent sector provider was also approached to take part in each local health economy, based on recommendations from the PCTs. Although these providers only completed a relatively small number of procedures for NHS patients, we expected their staff and the patients using them to have particular, distinct experiences of choice that we wished to capture.

Across the four local health economies, five NHS trusts, six NHS foundation trusts, two ISTCs and two independent sector hospitals took part in the study.

By selecting four local health economies as case study areas, we were able to look in more depth at how patient choice is operating at the point of referral. However, it does mean that the findings may not be representative of England as a whole. While we chose a diversity of areas, by excluding London we may under-represent the particular experience

[3] Calculated using 2004/5 outpatient Hospital Episode Statistics.

of patients there, although two of the local health economies were in or around large metropolitan areas.

One local health economy (area A) was specifically selected because it had a referral management centre, based on a list of centres provided by the Department of Health. Referral management centres were expected to affect the referral process and the patient's pathway to hospital, and hence their experience of choice. After the research began, it became clear that a variety of referral management systems were in place across the four areas, and that a formal referral management centre was not in place within PCT A (although there were triage systems for particular specialties where primary care alternatives were available).

The impact of the various referral management systems on the operation of choice in each area was not captured in this report. The King's Fund is, however, completing a separate piece of research on the operation of referral management centres in four PCTs in England. The report of that work (Imison and Naylor forthcoming) will address this gap in our evidence by considering how these centres affect choice at the point of referral.

Patient questionnaire

To understand how patients experience choice, and how patients choose between providers in hypothetical situations, we designed a survey that was sent to patients who had recently been referred for a first outpatient appointment at providers in our four local health economies.

Patient scoping interviews

The King's Fund conducted interviews with patients who were attending for a first outpatient appointment. The interviews were designed to ensure that the questions included in the survey reflected the reality of patients' perceptions of the GP consultation at which they were referred, and their experience of choice. A further aim of these interviews was to identify relevant 'soft' knowledge about local health care providers.

Interviews were conducted by researchers at one of the selected NHS providers within each of the four local health economies and also at one independent sector treatment centre (ISTC). Patients were recruited from a variety of outpatient clinics selected on the basis that referrals to these clinics were eligible for choice, and that there was a high volume of appointments, in order to maximise the pool of potential participants. Clinics in which patients are more likely to be distressed or vulnerable, such as cancer and psychiatric clinics, were excluded. Patients were given a £15 gift voucher to thank them for participating in the research.

A total of 18 patients were interviewed in August and September 2008. The interviews were semi-structured and based on the following broad themes:

- a description of their recent referral

- experience of choosing a hospital, including any support they were given

- knowledge about local providers.

The interviews were conducted in a private room within each hospital and lasted between 15 and 30 minutes. All interviews were audio recorded and transcribed. Transcripts were analysed by theme, and a summary of findings was published (Henderson *et al* 2009). The information gathered was used in development of the survey questions, the design of which is discussed in more detail below.

Questionnaire design

The patient questionnaire included 45 questions split into three main sections (*see* Appendix B).

1. Patients' recent experience of referral: patient scoping interview findings were used to develop a set of questions which asked patients about their experience of:

■ referral

■ appointment booking

■ the support, advice and information they received to help them choose

■ the factors important to them when choosing between providers

■ how they rated the provider they attended

■ their awareness of choice.

Some questions from the Department of Health's national patient choice monitoring survey (Department of Health 2008b) were repeated to allow comparison.

2. Hypothetical choice sets: to understand how patients make trade-offs between different factors when choosing a hospital, a second section of the questionnaire presented respondents with a series of hypothetical choices, as shown in Appendix B on page 185, in which the respondent could choose one of three hospitals, including one which was labelled 'local hospital'.

These choice experiments were included to provide additional insights into the factors that are important to patients when choosing between providers. Within these choice experiments, patients were asked to weigh up a number of different pieces of information about three different hospitals and then indicate which they would choose. The experiments are constructed such that it is not necessarily possible for patients to choose a provider that has high performance across all of the factors that could influence patients' choices. Data from the choices made within these carefully constructed scenarios provides a way of analysing and quantifying the trade-offs that underlie the choices patients say they would make.

The design of the choice experiments builds on the team's experience of running similar experiments in previous research studies, and followed a structure similar to that used when Choose and Book was being developed (Burge *et al* 2006). The attributes included sought to cover five key types of information that a patient may be expected to consider when choosing a hospital (*see* Table A1, opposite). The first two relate to information available to the GP through the Choose and Book system – that is, how far the patient would have to travel and how long they would have to wait. The decision was taken on the basis of cognitive interviews undertaken in a previous study (Burge *et al* 2004) to use travel time rather than distance as the measure of proximity, because patients find this easier to conceptualise.

The next two sets of attributes provided information on provider performance ratings and the views of other patients as reported through survey results. Information on these aspects of provider performance are available to patients through leaflets printed by PCTs and through the NHS Choices website. In practice, patients are able to access a range of information about hospital characteristics and provider performance. However, it was necessary to restrict these to a manageable number. Such information is not currently available for all providers, so we included a 'data not available' category for these attributes.

The final set of attributes related to previous experience and the opinion of others. These were included to cover the influence brought to bear by the patient's own experience and the 'softer' information on reputation that patients gain through talking to their GP, friends and family, or through the local media. In past research (Burge *et al* 2006), GP advice was found to be an important determinant of choice, so we sought to expand on this and investigate how opinions from other sources could influence the decisions patients made when traded off against official performance data.

We decided to restrict the choice experiments to a choice between three hospitals rather than a format with five hospitals, which had been used in previous research on the basis that these choice tasks were to be incorporated within a self-completion paper questionnaire rather than as part of an interview. It was therefore necessary to ensure that the task was both approachable and comprehensible, while working within the practical constraints of what can be presented within a printed questionnaire. Given these concerns, the choice experiments were tested through a series of cognitive interviews (*see* pp 164–5). The descriptions of the attributes and presentational format of the choices were reviewed and revised on the basis of feedback from patient respondents. The final list of attributes and levels is presented in Table A1 below.

In order to explain the choice task, the questionnaire included a short introduction.

The respondent was then asked to consider six different choice scenarios, an example of which is shown in Appendix B on page 185. In these choice scenarios, the levels at which the various attributes were presented were varied (using a statistically designed fractional factorial experimental design).[4] Twelve versions of the questionnaire were produced and the characteristics of hospitals in each choice set were varied across the questionnaires.

3. Demographic questions: respondents were asked a series of demographic questions, including their personal characteristics, health status (using the EQ5D measure) and use of the health service, the area in which they lived, and their household composition, occupation and income.

Table A1 Attributes and levels included in the discrete choice experiment

Attribute	Levels			
	1	2	3	4
Travel times				
Travel time to hospital	30 mins	1 hr	1 hr 30 mins	2 hrs
Waiting times				
Current waiting time for outpatient appointment	1 week	3 weeks	5 weeks	8 weeks
Performance ratings				
Number of cancelled operations	High	Average	Low	Data not available
Hospital infection rates	High	Average	Low	Data not available
Improvement in patient's health	Good	Average	Poor	Data not available
Patients' views from surveys				
Friendly staff, good communications with patients	Good	Average	Poor	Data not available
Clean hospital, good facilities	Good	Average	Poor	Data not available
Other opinions and experience				
Own previous experience	Good experience	Bad experience	No past experience	No past experience
GP's opinion of hospital	Recommended	-	-	-
Recommendation of family and friends	Recommended	-	-	-
Coverage in the local press over the past year	Positive coverage	Negative coverage	Mixed coverage	-

[4] A main-effects orthogonal fractional factorial design was developed for 11 attributes each at 4 levels, which was then adapted to a choice-based experimental design using the 'mix and match' approach described in Louviere (1988). This design was then blocked in to subsets of six choices to present to respondents in each version of the questionnaire, with an optimisation routine used to minimise the correlation between each of the attributes and the block (ie, to avoid any version having a given attribute being presented consistently at similar levels across the choices offered).

Cognitive testing

To ensure that the questionnaire was easily understandable and that patients interpreted questions in the way that was intended, the survey was cognitively tested by The Picker Institute in November and December 2008. Participants were recruited through advertisements in the local press and local libraries.

The questionnaire was initially tested on 15 people who were asked to complete the survey in the presence of a researcher and discuss their interpretation of the questions. Interviewees ranged in age from 49 to 81; seven were male and eight were female. All had recently been referred for an outpatient appointment by their GP.

During the interviews, a number of issues were identified relating to the wording of questions and response categories, and the instructions included in the questionnaire. The questionnaire was amended in line with these and then tested on a further seven people before being finalised (total n = 23).

Questionnaire distribution

The Picker Institute oversaw sampling and questionnaire distribution. Our original research design was to sample patients 'outbound' based on referrals from GP practice data. However, patients were sampled 'inbound' from hospital-held patient lists because PCTs did not hold consolidated lists of 'outbound' referrals. This means our data do not fully capture the views of patients resident in each PCT. Views were only captured from patients attending the providers who had at least 5 per cent of the PCTs' referrals. Within the analysis by resident PCT, the data is likely to underestimate the views and experiences of those patients who travelled to non-local providers.

A proportion of the respondents to the questionnaire did not live in the PCT, although they mostly lived in the nearby areas (*see* Table A2, p 167). These patients from outside the local health economy area may have had different experiences of choice due to different approaches to the implementation of the policy. Ideally, future area-based research of patient experience of choice would use 'outbound' sampling based on PCT or GP records.

The questionnaire was posted to patients who had recently been referred for an outpatient appointment at each of the providers involved in the study, with the exception of the two independent sector hospitals, who saw too few NHS patients to make distribution to a meaningfully sized sample of patients practically possible.

A total of 5,997 questionnaires were sent out between March and June 2009 to a systematic random sample of patients who booked their first outpatient appointment at participating organisations during January 2009. Providers were asked to exclude the following patients from their lists to ensure that the questionnaire was only sent to adults whose referral was eligible for 'free choice' of provider.

- Children under 16 at the date of their referral.
- Two-week-wait cancer patients.
- Referrals to rapid access chest pain clinics.
- Maternity and mental health referrals.
- Appointments concerning termination of pregnancy.
- Appointments to psychiatric outpatient clinics.

- Appointments to maternity outpatient clinics (but do not exclude all gynaecology outpatients).

- Patients attending genito-urinary medicine (GUM) or sexually transmitted disease (STI) clinics.

Sample sizes per provider were proportional to the overall volume of referrals seen at each, with a minimum of 200 per provider. As ISTCs see a small proportion of the total outpatient activity in each area, they were over-sampled at the minimum level of 200. To compensate for the over-sampling of patients who attended ISTCs, within each area a weight was applied to the data to reflect the relative volume of first outpatient referrals received by each provider during the first two quarters of 2008/9. Given that ISTCs treat a less complex case mix of patients and offer a more limited range of specialties, it is likely that these patients may differ systematically from those attending NHS trusts. This must be borne in mind when interpreting the comparisons of ISTC and NHS trust data, as no further adjustment has been made in the analysis.

The sample sizes per trust are shown in Table A2 opposite. An initial mailing was followed up with two reminders. The overall response rate from the sample was 36 per cent, which compares favourably to the 35 per cent response rate to the Department of Health's far shorter patient choice monitoring survey. The average response rate from ISTCs was higher than from NHS organisations (46 vs 36 per cent).

Table A3 opposite shows the characteristics of the survey respondents. They ranged in age from 16 to 99, 43 per cent were male and 90 per cent had a white background. One-third of respondents (31 per cent) had no formal qualifications, and one-third (34 per cent) were in paid work. Respondents were attending outpatient clinics in more than 40 specialties, although over 50 per cent of respondents were accounted for by the five main specialties: trauma and orthopaedics, general surgery, ophthalmology, ear, nose and throat (ENT), and dermatology. The majority of referrals (88 per cent) were routine, with 12 per cent classified as urgent. Respondents came from a mix of rural and urban areas, and 65 per cent had access to the internet.

Compared to the sample population as a whole, respondents had a similar gender split, but their age distribution differed significantly,[5] with more respondents aged between 51 and 80. Respondents also differed significantly in age and gender to Health Episode Statistics on all first outpatient attendances in England in January 2009 in specialties eligible for choice. There were fewer respondents aged 16–35 (10.5 per cent vs 26.3 per cent) and more male respondents (42.8 per cent vs 37.3 per cent).

When compared with population data from the main PCTs, three of the four had more white respondents[5] (differences significant at 1 per cent level), although respondents' ethnicity was similar in distribution to national Census figures for England and Wales (National Statistics 2009).

Translation services were made available to questionnaire respondents via a helpline. However, those with difficulty understanding English were likely to have been under-represented in the sample. We would expect non-English speakers to be less likely to be offered a choice, and some of the equity issues relating to this (such as these patients missing opportunities to access better-quality care) may be understated in the findings.

In this study, we relied on patients recalling accurately the consultation with the GP where the referral was made. In order to reduce recall bias, hospitals were asked to

---

[5] Differences are significant at 1 per cent level.

Table A2 Provider sample size and response rates

PCT	Provider	N	Number (%) of respondents	Respondents (%) from main PCT
A	A1 NHS	1,300	441 (34)	138 (31)
	A2 ISTC	202	87 (43)	9 (10)
	Case study total	1,502	528 (35)	147 (28)
B	B1 NHS FT	686	231 (34)	112 (48)
	B2 NHS	490	122 (25)	21 (17)
	B3 NHS FT	325	114 (35)	5 (4)
	Case study total	1,501	467 (31)	138 (30)
C	C2 NHS	285	109 (38)	96 (88)
	C3 NHS	344	126 (37)	125 (99)
	C4 NHS	870	321 (37)	119 (37)
	Case study total	1,499	556 (37)	340 (61)
D	D1 NHS FT	250	112 (45)	108 (96)
	D2 NHS FT	415	166 (40)	59 (36)
	D3 NHS FT	285	110 (39)	43 (39)
	D4 NHS FT	345	144 (42)	29 (20)
	D5 ISTC	200	98 (49)	9 (9)
	Case study total	1,495	630 (42)	248 (39)
Total		5,997	2,181 (36)	873 (40)

Table A3 Description of the sample

Characteristic	Categories	Number	%
Gender	Male	934	42.8
	Female	1,247	57.2
	Total	2,181	100
Age group	16–35	228	10.5
	36–50	473	21.7
	51–65	712	32.6
	66–80	608	27.9
	81 and over	160	7.3
	Total	2,181	100
Ethnicity	White	1,958	89.8
	Mixed background	11	0.5
	Asian	101	4.6
	Black	42	2.0
	Chinese	2	0.1
	Other	14	0.6
	Missing	53	2.4
	Total	2,181	100
Employment status	In paid work	746	34.2
	Unemployed	76	3.5
	Retired from paid work	833	38.2
	Unable to work because of disability/ill health	194	8.9
	Looking after my family, home or dependants	89	4.1
	In full-time education including government training programmes	20	0.9
	Other	34	1.6
	Missing	189	8.7
	Total	2,181	100
Level of education	No formal qualifications	683	31.3
	GCSE/O level/A level or equivalent	604	27.7
	Professional qualification below degree level	211	9.7
	Degree-level qualification or higher or equivalent	311	14.3
	Other	32	1.5
	Missing	340	15.6
	Total	2,181	100

draw a sample of patients who booked their appointment in January 2009. This meant patients were added to the sample as soon as they were referred to the hospital, rather than by appointment date, which may be up to six weeks after referral. However, the questionnaires were not distributed until March 2009, meaning there was a time lag and therefore a greater possibility that patients would not recall the offer of choice accurately.

Questionnaire data analysis

Survey data were analysed as follows.

Direct responses

Patient responses to direct questions about their recent referral and what influenced their choice of provider (survey questions 1–24, see Appendix B) were analysed by researchers at The King's Fund using SPSS statistical software. Descriptive statistics, cross tabs and stepwise binary logistic regression analyses were completed on the dataset. Analyses were conducted on unweighted and weighted data (to compensate for the oversampling of ISTCs). Unweighted results are presented, and where the weighted results differ significantly from the unweighted analysis, this has been noted in the text.

Revealed preferences

RAND Europe conducted this part of the questionnaire analysis using Alogit 4.2.[6] Using information about the hospital to which each patient was referred and their home postcode, it is possible to identify the attributes of the choices that patients are actually making. This information can be used to form the basis of a model of what is driving the decision to stay with the local provider or move to an alternative hospital.

The first step is the specification of a choice set, that is, a set of hospitals from which patients may have chosen. The data was used to identify the hospitals which respondents chose to attend and the name of the hospital which they identified as their 'local hospital' for those that chose to attend a 'non-local' hospital. In addition, we identified a series of other hospitals that patients may have considered due to their geographic proximity. The postcode of each hospital was used to calculate the crow-fly distance from the approximate location of each respondent's home postcode to each hospital,[7] providing a measure of travel distance.

Data was then added into the model to capture the hospitals that are included within the choice set. The first step was to incorporate publicly available information published on NHS Choices (see Table A4 opposite).

Further information on hospital sites was included from a database of hospital attributes compiled by researchers at the University of York, including the number of beds, number of doctors, and number of nurses.

The data on distance, hospital characteristics and performance was then utilised alongside information on the individual characteristics of each patient to estimate a model of the choices being made under choice at the point of referral.

In analysing this data, it is important to recognise that the sample frame of patients was drawn from those joining waiting lists at a subset of hospitals, so we have less variation in the characteristics of those hospitals that were actually chosen than we would have obtained had we been able to sample 'outbound' rather than 'inbound' respondents. However, due to practical constraints, outbound sampling from GP surgeries was not

[6] ALOGIT (2007) ALOGIT, ALOGIT Software & Analysis Ltd, www.alogit.com, London.
[7] Calculated as crow-fly distances from postcodes at sector level.

Table A4 Revealed preference model: information on provider performance

Category	Scale
Waiting times - referral to treatment	% of patients treated within 18 weeks
Overall quality of service	Weak, fair, good, excellent
Mortality ratios	(Actual deaths / expected deaths) x 100
Overall care for inpatients	0-10 (10 = best)
Dignity and respect for inpatients treated	0-10
Involvement in decisions about treatment	0-10
Cleanliness of wards	0-10
Availability of same-sex accommodation	0-10
MRSA blood infection rates	Blood infections for every 10,000 bed days for people having a planned operation
C difficile infection rates	C difficile for every 1,000 bed days for people aged 65 and over staying 3 or more days
Quality of hospital environment	Acceptable, good, excellent
Quality of food provided	Acceptable, good, excellent
Number of car parking spaces	Number of car parking spaces provided
Number of disabled car parking spaces	Number of disabled car parking spaces provided
Average hourly cost of car parking	In pounds per hour

It should be noted that in some cases, information for some of these factors was not available for a given hospital through NHS Choices, in which case they were coded as missing.

feasible, and the information collected from patients from this subset of hospitals still provides some valuable data from which we can analyse the choice that patients decided to exercise.

Using this data, we estimated a series of discrete choice models. These models provide insights into the preferences of patients when considering choices of hospital and the trade-offs they are observed to make when exercising choice. The analysis uses data only from respondents who said they were offered a choice of provider. The steps involved in the estimation and development of the discrete choice models are discussed in detail within the RAND Europe Technical Report (TR-807-DOH).

There are, of course, some caveats. First, the GP may also be influencing this choice, either directly or indirectly, through giving advice or interpreting initial preferences as a fully rationalised choice. Second, patients may not know the attributes of the provider they choose – for example, they may not be aware that a particular hospital has a low MRSA rate, and this may not have been an important factor in their decision to go there. However, the hypothesis would be that factors that are found to be significant within the choice model are those that together inform patients' perceptions of what is a good (or poor) hospital, either directly, through looking up published performance data, or more likely through the awareness that patients develop from their own prior experience and the reports of others that they consult.

Stated preferences

In the scoping of this study, there were a number of reasons why it was considered useful to collect stated preference data from patients regarding their choice of hospital under a range of different scenarios. First, the extent to which revealed preference data on the hospital choices exercised by respondents would be capable of supporting the estimation of a choice model was unclear. There are many potential sources of complication in such data, including co-linearity or lack of variation in variables, which can hinder the identification of the role of these variables upon the choices being made.

Second, stated preference data has the distinct advantage that the analyst has full control over specifying the variables which the respondent is being asked to consider in making their choice. As such, they have full knowledge of both the choice set being considered and the attributes that are being weighed up within a given choice scenario. This allows the analyst to specify scenarios that will allow the identification of the weight placed on a range of factors of interest.

Third, it is of interest for policy analysis to understand how patients may respond in scenarios beyond those that they may currently experience – for example, how would patients respond if they were offered options with longer waiting times, or experienced situations where the GP's advice appeared to contradict that of the published data, or the published data contained additional information that is not currently provided, such as information on health outcomes. The patient survey therefore included a section that presented patients with six different hypothetical choices. For each one, they were given information on three hypothetical hospitals and asked to select where they would wish to be treated.

Patients' direct responses to questions about their referral (as collected through survey questions 1–24, *see* Appendix B) provide valuable insights into their perceptions, but also suffer from the potential issue that patients often state that everything is important to them in principle. Stated preference data from the discrete choice experiment complements that information, and provides us with insights into how patients exercise choice when their options are constrained and they need to make trade-offs – that is, when they cannot have the best of all worlds.

Stated preference data from patient responses to six hypothetical choice sets (survey questions 24–29, *see* Appendix B for the full questionnaire) was used for the discrete choice experiment. This data also comes with the caveat that it represents what patients *say* they would do, rather than what patients have been *observed* to do.

A full description of the modelling process is given in the RAND Technical Report (TR-807-DOH). In summary, a series of multinomial and nested logit models were developed to explain the choices that respondents made in the discrete choice experiment and the weight that they placed on the different factors presented when making these hypothetical choices. These models were then developed to explore the extent to which the observed preferences for different factors varied according to any personal characteristics of the patients, for example, whether the value placed on information on improvements in health varied by age, gender, whether in paid work, current health status, and so on. These model developments were informed by a series of tests where the fit of the model to the stated choices was examined across a broad range of patient characteristics to identify potential areas of under-specification.

Within the choice experiment, one of the alternatives offered was labelled as being the 'local hospital'. A series of model tests were therefore undertaken to identify whether some groups of patients were more likely to choose to stay with the local provider than others. The final model is strongly estimated and identifies a range of intuitive and statistically significant coefficients that explain the factors influencing the choices being made within the questionnaire.

Finally, the logit model being estimated is based on the assumption that the observations within the model are independent, which we know not to be the case in this situation, as each respondent responded to six choice scenarios. As a result, this data may contain correlation in the responses of patients to these scenarios. A non-parametric re-sampling procedure was therefore run to correct for this correlation and other potential areas of model mis-specification.

The discrete choice models estimated from the stated preference and revealed preference data represent our best understanding of the factors that could influence the choices being made by patients. However, the two sources of data used to inform these models have different strengths and weaknesses.

In the case of the stated preference model, as analysts, we have a great deal of control over the stimulus within the experiment, as we specify the alternatives available to the respondents and tell them what we wish them to consider in making their choices. However, the responses are hypothetical – that is, they are based on what patients state they may do in these situations, and this may not perfectly translate into real world behaviour.

In the case of the revealed preference model, there is less uncertainty in the choice being exercised (these are real patients making real choices), but the choice set from which they are choosing is less clear and needs to be inferred, and the hospital attributes which may be driving their choices are also less clear. Therefore, when interpreting the revealed preference data, it is important to remember that although patients were referred to providers with particular characteristics, or who have a particular performance rating, patients may not have chosen these providers based on those attributes. We can observe the types of providers that patients tended to choose but cannot conclude that patients chose the provider based on perfect information on their attributes.

Patient follow-up interviews

Patient follow-up interviews were conducted by The King's Fund with a small subset of questionnaire respondents (n = 19) in August and September 2009 to validate and enrich the data provided in the questionnaires. A slip was included with the questionnaires which asked respondents to indicate if they were happy to be interviewed about their responses. Participants were given £30 in vouchers to thank them for taking part in the interviews.

A total of 614 respondents indicated that they were willing to be interviewed. Participants were selected based on their responses to particular survey questions, specifically, whether they had:

■ a high level of activation (aware of choice before visiting their GP, degree-level education, said choice was important to them, internet access)

■ a low level of activation (no internet access, no qualifications)

■ experienced 'textbook' choice (ie, offered choice by their GP, received advice from the GP, and went to the hospital they wanted)

■ had no choice (not offered a choice).

Nineteen respondents were interviewed over the telephone, and the box overleaf shows the number of respondents interviewed in each of the above categories. It was not possible to interview an equal number of patients in each category, but the sample did provide data from patients with different experiences of choice and different levels of activation.

Interviews were semi-structured and lasted between 10 and 30 minutes. They were audio recorded and transcribed and then analysed and used to supplement findings from the survey dataset.

Follow-up interviewees

	High activation	Low activation
Textbook choice	6	3
No choice	6	4

Provider interviews

Information on how patients experienced referral and choice was complemented by interview data on how the hospitals they chose responded to their choices. This part of the project was completed by The King's Fund.

A semi-structured interview schedule was drafted and the broad themes sent to chief executives at each of the participating providers. They were invited to interview and asked to suggest others within their organisation who would provide insight into their response to patient choice policy. The interview schedule covered the following areas:

- context and background
- strategy of the organisation and drivers behind this
- major service improvements within the organisation and the drivers behind these
- understanding of the local market
- how patient choice is operating locally.

Interviews were conducted with 49 senior staff in participating NHS and independent sector organisations between November 2008 and April 2009. Between one and six people were interviewed at each provider, and in some cases, a snowball sampling strategy was used where interviewees suggested further staff with relevant knowledge to be interviewed. In total, six chief executives, twenty-six directors, eight senior managers and nine managers were interviewed. Table A5, below, provides a breakdown of the number of interviewees at each provider. Only a minority of those interviewed were clinicians (usually the medical director). Although those we spoke to had highly relevant knowledge of the organisation's overall strategy and large-scale service improvements, our research failed to fully capture a clinical perspective on choice, quality and service improvements.

Table A5 Number of provider interviewees

Provider	No of interviewees
A1 NHS	6
A2 ISTC	1
B1 NHS FT	4
B2 NHS	3
B3 NHS FT	3
B4 Independent sector	2
C1 Independent sector	4
C2 NHS	3
C3 NHS	3
C4 NHS	4
D1 NHS FT	4
D2 NHS FT	4
D3 NHS FT	3
D4 NHS FT	3
D5 ISTC	2
Total	**49**

The interviews lasted for approximately one hour and were mainly conducted in person, although some were conducted over the telephone. Interviews were audio recorded and transcribed.

Researchers developed a qualitative analysis framework and transcripts were analysed thematically. Themes included provider perception of choice policy, the operation of patient choice locally, and the impact of patient choice on provider behaviour; these have been used as the basic structure for this report. Summaries for each theme were produced for each provider and each local health economy. Initially, a set of transcripts from one area was analysed by four researchers and summary analyses were compared to calibrate analysis techniques. The remaining transcripts were then analysed by individual researchers.

The advantage of this methodological approach was that the data collected from each interviewee was treated as a whole during the first stage of the analysis. Preliminary exploration of the interview data indicated that interviewees frequently gave multiple and conflicting opinions on the impact of patient choice at different points during the interview. For example, a respondent who said choice had no impact on their action might later list some instances which did appear to show a response to choice. Similarly, negative attitudes to choice might later be balanced with a more positive slant on actions or outcomes from the policy. If an analytic approach based on the coding of transcripts had been used, there is a danger that by fragmenting the data, such subtleties would have been lost, and subsequent interpretation could have been inaccurate as a result.

When presenting analysis from the provider interviews, we have not attempted to quantify the strength of particular findings, and the quotes included in the report are designed to be illustrative.

GP interviews

The Picker Institute collected and analysed interview data from GPs practising within the PCTs in each area.

Recruitment

Telephone interviews were conducted with 25 GPs from the four local health economy areas (*see* Table A6, overleaf). Participants were recruited with the assistance of the Choose and Book leads within each of the relevant PCTs. They drew up shortlists of practices that are broadly representative of those in the area in terms of size and utilisation of Choose and Book. Letters of invitation were then sent to GPs via their practice managers. If this failed to produce the required number of volunteers, a blanket approach was adopted, and all practices in the PCT were contacted. Engaging GPs as research participants was challenging, and we had to provide a financial incentive (not originally planned) in order to reach the size of our sample. An incentive of £100 was offered to each participant, which they could donate to charity if they chose to do so.

To ensure that the study heard views from a cross-section of GPs, PCTs were asked to suggest practices with a range of Choose and Book usage levels to take part in the study. However, although a good cross-section of GPs was recruited in terms of practice size and population served, it proved impossible to recruit GPs from practices who were not high users of Choose and Book. Although a GP who uses Choose and Book does not necessarily offer patients a choice, the GP views reported here come from a self-selected group of volunteers who may be more likely to have offered patients a choice than the GP population as a whole. That these GPs are likely to have been choice 'enthusiasts' makes our findings on the way they offered choice even more interesting.

Table A6 Characteristics of GP participants

GP	Practice
A/1	Six GPs; mixed rural/urban
A/2	Six GPs; urban
A/3	Five GPs; semi-rural
A/4	Two GPs; urban
A/5	Five GPs; urban
A/6	Four GPs; urban
A/7	Five GPs; small town
B/1	Two GPs; suburban
B/2	Eight GPs; urban
B/3	Eight GPs; urban
B/4	Six GPs; urban
B/5	Four GPs; urban
B/6	Two GPs; urban
B/7	Seven GPs; suburban
C/1	Single handed; urban
C/2	Six GPs; suburban
C/3	Three GPs; PMS practice; urban
C/4	Three GPs; PMS practice; urban
C/5	Five GPs; suburban
C/6	Two GPs; semi-rural
D/1	Four GPs; suburban
D/2	Thirteen GPs; urban
D/3	Five GPs; rural
D/4	Two GPs; rural
D/5	Three GPs; rural

PMS: Personal Medical Service

Data collection and analysis

A topic guide was developed for the telephone interviews covering GPs' general attitudes to choice, their experience of offering choice, the information they use when doing so, and how referral decisions are made. The average length of the interviews was 45 minutes, and with the consent of the GPs involved, all were recorded. Interviews were then fully transcribed and thematically analysed following standard qualitative research methods facilitated by NVIVO (v7) software.

PCT interviews

The original research proposal for this study did not include interviews with PCTs. However, during the course of our research, a number of issues arose that required clarification from the PCTs in the four local health economies we studied. Choose and Book leads within each PCT were contacted over the telephone and asked to describe how the referral process worked in their area, whether referral management initiatives were in place, GP usage of the Choose and Book system, and the incentives payments and support in place to encourage GPs to offer choice. These informal interviews aided interpretation of the data collected in other parts of the study. Some information about the local context and the way in which each PCT implemented choice may therefore have been missed.

Analysis of Hospital Episode Statistics data

Outpatient Hospital Episode Statistics (HES) data was used to calculate each NHS provider's share of referral activity from each PCT between 2005/6 and 2008/9. Outpatient HES is a record-level dataset reporting all outpatient attendances within a financial year. A referral was defined as a first attendance (FIRSTATT=1) whose referral source was a GP (REFSOURCE=3). A referral was assigned to a PCT using the *PCT of residence* of the patient. From 2006/7 onwards, RESPCT06 (indicating PCT boundaries post-October 2006) was used. For the financial year 2005/6, referrals were mapped to the new PCT of residence boundaries using the Output Area codes (OACODE). The analysis was conducted using STATA/MP 11 and Excel.

Providers with at least 1 per cent share of a PCT referral activity in 2005/6 were retained and their share was plotted over time using area charts. Trends in total volume of referrals from the PCT were also calculated.

Expert seminar on project findings

The data collected in each local health economy provided a picture of the operation and impact of patient choice policy within the four areas under study. To understand whether these findings resonated with the experience of others involved in implementing choice across England, a seminar was held to test their validity and discuss their implications.

Around 30 experts attended the event, held at The King's Fund on 18 November 2009. Participants included researchers as well as senior managers from other NHS organisations, independent sector providers, patient representatives, and those working in relevant areas of academia, research, policy and government.

picker
INSTITUTE
making patients' views count

TheKingsFund>

PATIENT CHOICE QUESTIONNAIRE

What is the survey about?

This survey is about the **most recent time** your GP referred you to the hospital or treatment centre named in the letter enclosed with this questionnaire

Who should complete the questionnaire?

The questions should be answered by the person named on the front of the envelope. If that person needs help to complete the questionnaire, the answers should be given from his/her point of view – not the point of view of the person who is helping.

Completing the questionnaire

For each question please tick ☑ clearly inside one box using a black or blue pen.

Sometimes you will find the box you have ticked has an instruction to go to another question. By following the instructions carefully you will miss out questions that do not apply to you.

Don't worry if you make a mistake; simply cross out the mistake and put a tick in the correct box.

Please do not write your name or address anywhere on the questionnaire.

Questions or help?

For more information about this questionnaire see the enclosed information sheet. You can also call the Picker Institute Europe FREEPHONE helpline number: **0800 783 2896.**

Taking part in this survey is voluntary. **Your answers will be treated in confidence.**

FINAL Choice Questionnaire_P1279_v1   Picker Institute Europe   1

Think about the most recent time your GP referred you to a hospital/treatment centre when answering questions in this survey

<u>Your referral</u>

1. Did you discuss which hospital you might go to with any of the following people?

	Yes	No	Don't know/can't remember
a). GP	☐1	☐2	☐3
b). GP Receptionist	☐1	☐2	☐3
c). Someone else in the GP surgery	☐1	☐2	☐3
d). Family /friends	☐1	☐2	☐3
e). Telephone booking line advisor	☐1	☐2	☐3
f). PALS / patient advisor	☐1	☐2	☐3
g). Other (please write in box)	☐1	☐2	☐3

2. Were you able to go to the hospital that you wanted to go to?

Yes........ ☐1   No........ ☐2   I didn't have a preference........... ☐3

3. Were you offered a choice of hospital?

Yes................. ☐1   → Go to 4

No.................. ☐2   → Go to 11

Don't know........ ☐3   → Go to 11

4. Who offered you that choice? *(tick as many as apply)*

GP	☐1	Telephone booking line advisor...... ☐5
GP receptionist....	☐2	In a letter received after GP consultation........ ☐6
Someone else in the GP surgery....	☐3	Other *(please write in box)*...... ☐7
PALS / patient advisor....	☐4	

FINAL Choice Questionnaire_P1279_v1   Picker Institute Europe   2

5. How many choices of hospital were you offered?

2 ... [1]   3 – 5 ... [2]   More than 5 ... [3]

6. Were any of those hospitals from the private sector?

Yes ... [1]   Don't know/can't remember ... [3]

No ... [2]

Support with making your choice

7. Did any of the following people give you advice on which hospital you should go to?

	Yes	No	Don't know/can't remember
a). GP	[1]	[2]	[3]
b). GP Receptionist	[1]	[2]	[3]
c). Someone else in the GP surgery	[1]	[2]	[3]
d). Family / friends	[1]	[2]	[3]
e). Telephone booking line advisor	[1]	[2]	[3]
f). PALS / patient advisor	[1]	[2]	[3]
g). Other (please write in box)			

8. Which, if any, of the following sources of information did you use to choose the hospital?
(tick as many as apply)

GP [1]

A booklet or leaflet about my choices [2]

NHS Choices website [3]

Hospital/treatment centre website [4]

Other internet site [5]

Friends/family members [6]

Own experience [7]

Someone else at GP surgery [8]

Local patient organisation [9]

Staff at clinical assessment or referral centre [10]

Telephone booking line advisor [11]

None of these [12]

Other (please write in box) [13]

9. Were you given the right amount of information to help you choose a hospital?

Yes - about right [1]

No - I would have liked more [2]

No - I was given too much information [3]

I didn't want any information [4]

Don't know/can't remember [5]

The hospital you chose

10. How important were each of the factors below in influencing which hospital you chose?

	Essential	Very Important	Somewhat important	Not Important
a). Cleanliness	[1]	[2]	[3]	[4]
b). Car parking	[1]	[2]	[3]	[4]
c). Close to your home or work	[1]	[2]	[3]	[4]
d). Accessible on public transport	[1]	[2]	[3]	[4]
e). Travel costs	[1]	[2]	[3]	[4]
f). Convenience of appointment time	[1]	[2]	[3]	[4]
g). Waiting time for appointment	[1]	[2]	[3]	[4]
h). Personal experience of the hospital	[1]	[2]	[3]	[4]
i). Experience of friends or family members	[1]	[2]	[3]	[4]
j). Reputation of the hospital	[1]	[2]	[3]	[4]
k). Friendliness of staff	[1]	[2]	[3]	[4]
l). How well organised the clinic is	[1]	[2]	[3]	[4]
m). Quality of food	[1]	[2]	[3]	[4]
n). Quality of care	[1]	[2]	[3]	[4]
o). Standard of facilities	[1]	[2]	[3]	[4]
p). Waiting time in waiting room	[1]	[2]	[3]	[4]
q). Ability to see consultant of your choice	[1]	[2]	[3]	[4]
r). Other (please write in box)	[1]	[2]	[3]	[4]

Hospital Performance

16. How would you rate the hospital you are attending for the following factors?

	Very good	Good	Fair	Poor	Very poor	Don't know
a). Cleanliness	☐₁	☐₂	☐₃	☐₄	☐₅	☐₆
b). Car parking	☐₁	☐₂	☐₃	☐₄	☐₅	☐₆
c). Close to your home or work	☐₁	☐₂	☐₃	☐₄	☐₅	☐₆
d). Accessible on public transport	☐₁	☐₂	☐₃	☐₄	☐₅	☐₆
e). Travel costs	☐₁	☐₂	☐₃	☐₄	☐₅	☐₆
f). Convenience of appointment time	☐₁	☐₂	☐₃	☐₄	☐₅	☐₆
g). Waiting time for appointment	☐₁	☐₂	☐₃	☐₄	☐₅	☐₆
h). Personal experience of the hospital	☐₁	☐₂	☐₃	☐₄	☐₅	☐₆
i). Experience of friends or family members	☐₁	☐₂	☐₃	☐₄	☐₅	☐₆
j). Reputation of hospital	☐₁	☐₂	☐₃	☐₄	☐₅	☐₆
k). Friendliness of staff	☐₁	☐₂	☐₃	☐₄	☐₅	☐₆
l). How well organised the clinic is	☐₁	☐₂	☐₃	☐₄	☐₅	☐₆
m). Quality of food	☐₁	☐₂	☐₃	☐₄	☐₅	☐₆
n). Quality of care	☐₁	☐₂	☐₃	☐₄	☐₅	☐₆
o). Standard of facilities	☐₁	☐₂	☐₃	☐₄	☐₅	☐₆
p). Waiting time in waiting room	☐₁	☐₂	☐₃	☐₄	☐₅	☐₆
q). Ability to see a consultant of your choice	☐₁	☐₂	☐₃	☐₄	☐₅	☐₆
r). Other (please write in box)	☐₁	☐₂	☐₃	☐₄	☐₅	☐₆

Booking your appointment

11. Who booked your hospital appointment?

Me - on the telephone.... ☐₁   GP receptionist............ ☐₄   Don't know/can't remember........ ☐₇

Me - on the internet....... ☐₂   Another person in the GP surgery.......... ☐₅   Other (please write in box)............ ☐₈

GP................... ☐₃   PALS / patient advisor.... ☐₆   [   ]

Choice general

12. Before you visited your GP, did you know that you now have a choice of hospitals that you can go to for your first hospital appointment?

Yes.................. ☐₁   No.................. ☐₂

13. Before you visited your GP, did you know you now can choose to have NHS treatment in a private sector hospital?

Yes.................. ☐₁   No.................. ☐₂

14. At the time you were referred for your outpatient appointment, did you think you would need to have an operation or stay in hospital for treatment?

Yes.................. ☐₁   No.................. ☐₂   Don't know........ ☐₃

15. How important to you is being offered a choice of hospital?

Very important .... ☐₁   Of little importance............ ☐₄

Important.................. ☐₂   Unimportant............ ☐₅

Somewhat important.............. ☐₃

17. **Have you heard about the performance of hospitals in your area from any of the following sources?** *(tick as many as apply)*

Personal experience ...1
Experience of friends and family ...2
Local media ...3
Grapevine/gossip ...4
GP ...5
Internet ...6
Official performance reports ...7
Newspaper ...8
Other *(please write in box)* ...9

Marketing

18. **Have you ever seen/heard an advert for any of the following?**

	Yes	No	Don't know/can't remember
a). The hospital you are attending	1	2	3
b). Other NHS hospitals in your area	1	2	3
c). Other private sector hospitals in your area	1	2	3
d). Patient choice	1	2	3
e). Choose and book	1	2	3
f). NHS Choices website	1	2	3

Your local hospital

19. **Do you think of the hospital/treatment centre you are attending as your 'local' hospital?**

Yes ...1 → **Go to 21**
No ...2 → **Go to 20**
Not sure ...3 → **Go to 20**

20. **What is the name of what you think of as your local hospital?**
(Please write in box below)

---

21. **What is your past experience of your local hospital?**

Generally good ...1   Mixed ...3
Generally bad ...2   No previous experience ...4

22. **How would you normally travel to your local hospital?**

Walk ...1   Taxi ...4
Car ...2   Other ...5
Public transport ...3

23. **About how long does it take you to travel to your local hospital?**
Write the approximate number of minutes journey time in the box.

24. **How would you normally travel to hospitals further away?**

Car ...1   Taxi ...3
Public transport ...2   Other ...4

Which hospital would you choose?

PLEASE READ CAREFULLY

Imagine that you are in the situation where your GP needed to refer you for your most recent outpatient appointment and you are offered a **choice** of which hospital you would like to go to.

Each question in this section asks you to choose between three different hospitals using **only** the information provided.

The information about each hospital may change from question to question. Sometimes the information may be missing altogether.

One of the hospitals is called **Your Local Hospital**. Imagine that this is the hospital you think of as your local hospital. We will present you with some situations where the service provided by this hospital might also be better or worse than now.

Remember, use the information provided for each hospital to make your choice, and tick **one** box only in each question.

There are no right or wrong answers to these choices; we are only interested in your views.

25.
Choice 1

If you had been offered these choices when your GP referred you to the hospital, which hospital would you have chosen?

Hospital details	Your Local Hospital	Hospital 2	Hospital 3
Travel times			
Travel time to hospital	Current travel time	1 hour	2 hours
Waiting times			
Current waiting time for outpatient appointment	1 week	1 week	8 weeks
Performance ratings			
Number of cancelled operations	Low	High	Low
Hospital infection rates	High	High	Average
Improvement in patient's health	Data not available	Average	Good
Patients' views from surveys			
Friendly staff, good communications with patients	Good	Average	Good
Clean hospital, good facilities	Average	Good	Data not available
Other opinions and experience			
Own previous experience	Good experience	Good experience	Good experience
GP's opinion of hospital	-	-	-
Recommendation of family and friends	-	Recommended	-
Coverage in the local press over the past year	Mixed coverage	Positive coverage	Negative coverage
Please select ONE of the following options	[1]	[2]	[3]

26.
Choice 2

If you had been offered these choices when your GP referred you to the hospital, which hospital would you have chosen?

Hospital details	Your Local Hospital	Hospital 2	Hospital 3
Travel times			
Travel time to hospital	Current travel time	1 hour	1 hour
Waiting times			
Current waiting time for outpatient appointment	8 weeks	8 weeks	5 weeks
Performance ratings			
Number of cancelled operations	Data not available	Low	High
Hospital infection rates	High	Average	High
Improvement in patient's health	Good	Poor	Average
Patients' views from surveys			
Friendly staff, good communications with patients	Data not available	Data not available	Good
Clean hospital, good facilities	Poor	Good	Good
Other opinions and experience			
Own previous experience	No past experience	No past experience	Bad experience
GP's opinion of hospital	-	-	-
Recommendation of family and friends	-	-	-
Coverage in the local press over the past year	Mixed coverage		
Please select ONE of the following options	[1]	[2]	[3]

27.
Choice 3

If you had been offered these choices when your GP referred you to the hospital, which hospital would you have chosen?

Hospital details	Your Local Hospital	Hospital 2	Hospital 3
Travel times			
Travel time to hospital	Current travel time	2 hours	1 hour
Waiting times			
Current waiting time for outpatient appointment	3 weeks	1 week	1 week
Performance ratings			
Number of cancelled operations	Low	Data not available	High
Hospital infection rates	Average	Data not available	Data not available
Improvement in patient's health	Average	Data not available	Poor
Patients' views from surveys			
Friendly staff, good communications with patients	Good	Poor	Average
Clean hospital, good facilities	Data not available	Data not available	Average
Other opinions and experience			
Own previous experience	Bad experience	No past experience	Bad experience
GP's opinion of hospital	-	-	-
Recommendation of family and friends	-	-	-
Coverage in the local press over the past year	Mixed coverage	Negative coverage	Negative coverage
Please select ONE of the following options	[1]	[2]	[3]

28.
Choice 4

If you had been offered these choices when your GP referred you to the hospital, which hospital would you have chosen?

Hospital details	Your Local Hospital	Hospital 2	Hospital 3
Travel times			
Travel time to hospital	Current travel time	30 mins	1 hour 30 mins
Waiting times			
Current waiting time for outpatient appointment	8 weeks	1 week	1 week
Performance ratings			
Number of cancelled operations	Low	Data not available	Low
Hospital infection rates	Data not available	High	Average
Improvement in patient's health	Poor	Data not available	Average
Patients' views from surveys			
Friendly staff, good communications with patients	Good	Average	Data not available
Clean hospital, good facilities	Good	Average	Data not available
Other opinions and experience			
Own previous experience	No past experience	Good experience	No past experience
GP's opinion of hospital	-	-	-
Recommendation of family and friends	-	-	-
Coverage in the local press over the past year	Mixed coverage		Positive coverage
Please select ONE of the following options	[1]	[2]	[3]

Health and healthcare

31. How many times have you visited your GP in the last 12 months?

Once [1]
2-5 times [2]
6-10 times [3]
More than 10 [4]

32. By placing a tick in one box in each group below, please indicate which statements best describe your own health state today.

a). Mobility
I have no problems in walking about [1]
I have some problems in walking about [2]
I am confined to bed [3]

b). Self-Care
I have no problems with self-care [1]
I have some problems washing or dressing myself [2]
I am unable to wash or dress myself [3]

c). Usual Activities (*e.g. work, study, housework, family or leisure activities*)
I have no problems with performing my usual activities [1]
I have some problems with performing my usual activities [2]
I am unable to perform my usual activities [3]

d). Pain/Discomfort
I have no pain or discomfort [1]
I have moderate pain or discomfort [2]
I have extreme pain or discomfort [3]

e). Anxiety/Depression
I am not anxious or depressed [1]
I am moderately anxious or depressed [2]
I am extremely anxious or depressed [3]

29.
Choice 5   **If you had been offered these choices when your GP referred you to the hospital, which hospital would you have chosen?**

Hospital details	Your Local Hospital	Hospital 2	Hospital 3
Travel times			
Travel time to hospital	Current travel time	1 hour 30 mins	1 hour 30 mins
Waiting times			
Current waiting time for outpatient appointment	8 weeks	3 weeks	3 weeks
Performance ratings			
Number of cancelled operations	Low	Low	Data not available
Hospital infection rates	Low	Data not available	High
Improvement in patient's health	Poor	Data not available	Average
Patients' views from surveys			
Friendly staff, good communications with patients	Average	Data not available	Data not available
Clean hospital, good facilities	Poor	Average	Poor
Other opinions and experience			
Own previous experience	Bad experience	Good experience	No past experience
GP's opinion of hospital	Recommended	Recommended	-
Recommendation of family and friends	-	-	Recommended
Coverage in the local press over the past year	Positive coverage	-	Negative coverage
Please select ONE of the following options	[1]	[2]	[3]

30.
Choice 6   **If you had been offered these choices when your GP referred you to the hospital, which hospital would you have chosen?**

Hospital details	Your Local Hospital	Hospital 2	Hospital 3
Travel times			
Travel time to hospital	Current travel time	30 mins	1 hour
Waiting times			
Current waiting time for outpatient appointment	1 week	8 weeks	8 weeks
Performance ratings			
Number of cancelled operations	Data not available	Data not available	Average
Hospital infection rates	Low	Low	Average
Improvement in patient's health	Average	Average	Average
Patients' views from surveys			
Friendly staff, good communications with patients	Poor	Good	Good
Clean hospital, good facilities	Average	Good	Average
Other opinions and experience			
Own previous experience	No past experience	Good experience	Good experience
GP's opinion of hospital	-	Recommended	-
Recommendation of family and friends	-	-	Recommended
Coverage in the local press over the past year	Positive coverage	Positive coverage	Mixed coverage
Please select ONE of the following options	[1]	[2]	[3]

Where you live

34. How would you describe the area where you live?

City / large town ☐ 1   Small town ☐ 3

Suburbs of a city/large town ☐ 2   Village / rural area ☐ 4

Occupation and household income

35. What is your education level?

No formal qualifications ☐ 1   Degree level qualification or equivalent ☐ 5

GCSE / O level or equivalent ☐ 2   Higher degree ☐ 6

'A' levels or equivalent ☐ 3   Other (please write in box) ☐ 7

Professional qualification below degree level ☐ 4

36. Which of these best describes your current situation?

In paid work ☐ 1   Looking after my family, home or dependants ☐ 5

Unemployed ☐ 2   In full time education (including government training programmes) ☐ 6

Retired from paid work ☐ 3   Other (please write in box) ☐ 7

Unable to work because of disability or ill health ☐ 4

37. Which of the following describes your annual household income, before tax and national insurance?
(Please take pensions, benefits and any extra earnings into account)

Less than £5,000 ☐ 1   £30,000 to £39,999 ☐ 6

£5,000 to £9,999 ☐ 2   £40,000 to £49,999 ☐ 7

£10,000 to £14,999 ☐ 3   £50,000 to £74,999 ☐ 8

£15,000 to £19,999 ☐ 4   £75,000 or more ☐ 9

£20,000 to £29,999 ☐ 5   Don't know ☐ 10

33.

To help people say how good or bad a health state is, we have drawn a scale (rather like a thermometer) on which the best state you can imagine is marked 100 and the worst state you can imagine is marked 0.

We would like you to indicate on this scale how good or bad your own health is today, in your opinion. Please do this by drawing a line from the box below to whichever point on the scale indicates how good or bad your health state is today.

Best imaginable health state

100

Worst imaginable health state

Your own health state today

41. Do you have access to the internet?

Yes ☐₁   No ☐₂

About you

42. Are you male or female?

Male ☐₁
Female ☐₂

43. What was your year of birth? *(please write in below)*   e.g. 1934

☐☐☐☐

44. What is your postcode?
(please write in below)

☐☐☐☐ ☐☐☐

45. To which of these ethnic groups do you belong?
(Tick one only)

White: British ☐₁
White: Irish ☐₂
Any other White background ☐₃
Mixed: White and Black Caribbean ☐₄
Mixed: White and Black African ☐₅
Mixed: White and Asian ☐₆
Any other Mixed background ☐₇
Asian or Asian British: Indian ☐₈
Asian or Asian British: Pakistan ☐₉
Asian or Asian British: Bangladeshi ☐₁₀
Any other Asian background ☐₁₁
Black or Black British: Caribbean ☐₁₂
Black or Black British: African ☐₁₃
Any other Black background ☐₁₄
Chinese ☐₁₅
Other ethnic group (please write in box) ☐₁₆

Thank you very much for your help

Please post this questionnaire back in the FREEPOST envelope provided
No stamp is needed

---

38. Please tick one box to show which best describes the sort of work you do.
(If you are not working now, please tick a box to show what you did in your **last** job).

Please tick one box only

Modern professional occupations ☐₁
Such as: *teacher - nurse - physiotherapist - social worker - welfare officer – artist - musician - police officer (sergeant or above) - software designer*

Clerical and intermediate occupations ☐₂
Such as: *secretary - personal assistant - clerical worker - office clerk - call centre agent - nursing auxiliary - nursery nurse*

Senior managers or administrators ☐₃
(Usually responsible for planning, organising and co-ordinating work and for finance)
Such as: *finance manager - chief executive*

Technical and craft occupations ☐₄
Such as: *motor mechanic - fitter - inspector - plumber - printer - tool maker - electrician - gardener - train driver*

Semi-routine manual and service occupations ☐₅
Such as: *postal worker - machine operative - security guard - caretaker - farm worker - catering assistant - receptionist - sales assistant*

Routine manual and service occupations ☐₆
Such as: *HGV driver - van driver - cleaner - porter - packer - sewing machinist - messenger - labourer - waiter / waitress - bar staff*

Middle or junior managers ☐₇
Such as: *office manager - retail manager - bank manager - restaurant manager - warehouse manager - publican*

Traditional professional occupations ☐₈
Such as: *accountant - solicitor - medical practitioner - scientist -civil /mechanical engineer*

Household composition

39. Do you live alone (single person household)?

Yes ☐₁   No ☐₂

40. Are you the parent or guardian of anyone under 18 who lives with you?

Yes ☐₁   No ☐₂

References

Appleby J, Phillips M (2009). 'The NHS: satisfied now?' in Park A, Curtice J, Thomson K, Phillips M, Clery E (eds), *British Social Attitudes: The 25th report*. National Centre for Social Research, pp 25–54. London: Sage Publications.

Appleby J, Harrison A, Devlin N (2003). *What is the Real Cost of More Patient Choice?* London: The King's Fund. Available at: www.kingsfund.org.uk/publications/what_is_the_real.html (accessed on 19 March 2010).

Arrow KJ (1963). 'Uncertainty and the welfare economics of health care'. *American Economic Review*, vol 53, no 5, pp 941–73.

Audit Commission and Healthcare Commission (2008). *Is the Treatment Working? Progress with the NHS system reform programme*. London: Audit Commission.

Bandura A (1997). *Self-Efficacy: The exercise of control*. New York: Freeman.

Bandura A (1977). 'Self-efficacy: toward a unifying theory of behavioral change'. *Psychological Review*, vol 84, no 2, pp 191–215.

Barber S, Gordon-Dseagu V (2003). *Equity Issues Relating to Elective Care and Patient Choice*. London: Council of Ethnic Minority Voluntary Sector Organisations. Available at: www.cemvo.org.uk/downloads/publications/Equity_Issues_Relating_to_Elective_Care_and_Patient_%20Choice.pdf (accessed on 21 December 2009).

Barnett J, Ogden J, Daniells E (2008). 'The value of choice: a qualitative study'. *British Journal of General Practice*, vol 58, pp 609–13.

Batley R (2007). 'On ordinal utility, cardinal utility, and random utility'. *Theory and Decision*. Institute for Transport Studies, University of Leeds. Available at: http://eprints.whiterose.ac.uk/2544/1/ITS2094-On_ordinal_utility_uploadable.pdf (accessed on 19 March 2010).

Bentham J (1789). *The Principles and Morals of Legislation*. English translation published by Clarendon, Oxford in 1907.

Berwick DM, James B, Coye MJ (2003). 'Connections between quality measurement and improvement'. *Medical Care*, vol 41, no 1, suppl, ppI-30-I-38.

Bettman J, Luce M, Payne J (2006). 'Constructive consumer choice processes' in Lichtenstein S, Slovic P (eds), *The Construction of Preference*, Chapter 17. Cambridge: Cambridge University Press.

Bloom N, Propper C, Seiler S, Van Reenen J (2009). 'Management practices in the NHS'. *CentrePiece*, winter 2009/10. Available at: http://cep.lse.ac.uk/pubs/download/cp305.pdf (accessed on 19 March 2010).

Boadway R, Bruce N (1984). *Welfare Economics*. Oxford: Basil Blackwell.

British Medical Association (2009). *Factors Capable of Influencing an Increase in GP Referral Rates to Secondary Care*. British Medical Association Health Policy and Economic Research Unit. Available at: http://www.bma.org.uk/images/refrates_tcm41-186413.pdf (accessed on 9 April 2010).

Burge P, Devlin A, Appleby J, Gallo F, Nason E (2006). *Understanding Patients' Choices at the Point of Referral*. RAND Technical Report 359. Available at: www.rand.org/pubs/technical_reports/TR359/ (accessed on 19 March 2010).

Burge P, Devlin N, Appleby J, Rohr C, Grant J (2005). *London Patient Choice Project Evaluation: A model of patients' choices of hospital from stated and revealed preference choice data*. Cambridge: RAND Europe.

Burge P, Devlin N, Appleby J, Rohr C, Grant J (2004). 'Do patients always prefer quicker treatment? A discrete choice analysis of patients' stated preferences in the London Patient Choice Project'. *Applied Health Economics and Health Policy*, vol 3, no 4, pp 183–94.

Calem P, Rizzo JA (1995). 'Competition and specialisation in the hospital industry: an application of Hotelling's location model'. *Southern Economic Journal*, vol 61, pp 1182–98.

Callahan D (2008). 'Consumer-directed health care: promise or puffery?' *Health Economics, Policy and Law*, vol 3, pp 301–11.

Conservatives (2010). *Conservatives Draft Manifesto 2010*. London: The Conservative Party.

Cooper ZN, Gibbons S, Jones S, McGuire A (2009a). *Does Hospital Competition Save Lives? Evidence from the recent English NHS choice reforms*. London: LSE. Available at: http://personal.lse.ac.uk/gibbons/Papers/Does%20Hospital%20Competition%20Save %20Lives%20Dec%2009.pdf (accessed on 22 March 2010).

Cooper ZN, McGuire A, Jones S, Le Grand J (2009b). 'Equity, waiting times and NHS reforms: retrospective study'. *British Medical Journal*, vol 339, b3264.

Coulter A, Le Maistre N, Henderson L (2005). *Patients' Experience of Choosing Where to Undergo Surgical Treatment: Evaluation of London Patient Choice Scheme*. Oxford: Picker Institute Europe.

Coulter A, Noone A, Goldacre M (1989). 'General practitioners' referrals to specialist outpatient clinics. I. Why general practitioners refer patients to specialist outpatient clinics'. *British Medical Journal*, vol 299, no 6694, pp 304–6.

Damiani M, Propper C, Dixon J (2005). 'Mapping choice in the NHS: cross sectional study of routinely collected data'. *British Medical Journal*, vol 330, no 7486, p 284.

Dawson D, Gravelle H, Jacobs R, Stephen Martin S and Smith P (2007). 'The effects of expanding patient choice of provider on waiting times: evidence from a policy experiment'. *Health Economics*, vol 16, no 2, pp 113–28.

Dawson D, Jacobs R, Martin S, Smith P (2004). *Evaluation of the London Patient Choice Project: System wide impacts. Final report*. York: University of York.

de Chernatony L, McDonald M (2003). *Creating Powerful Brands*, 3rd ed. Oxford: Elsevier, Butterworth/Heinemann.

Department of Health (2009a). *Report on the National Patient Choice Survey – March 2009 England* [online]. Available at: www.dh.gov.uk/prod_consum_dh/groups/dh_ digitalassets/documents/digitalasset/dh_103681.pdf (accessed on 22 March 2010).

Department of Health (2009b). *The National Health Service Constitution*. London: HMSO.

Department of Health (2009c). *The NHS Operating Framework for England for 2010/11*. London: The Stationery Office.

Department of Health (2009d). *The Primary Care Trusts (Choice of Secondary Care Provider) Directions 2009*. Available at: http://www.dh.gov.uk/en/Publicationsandstatistics/Publications/PublicationsLegislation/DH_093004 (accessed on 9 April 2010).

Department of Health (2008a). *High Quality Care for All: NHS next stage review final report*. Cm 7432. London: Department of Health. Available at: www.dh.gov.uk/en/publicationsandstatistics/publications/publicationspolicyandguidance/DH_085825 (accessed on 22 March 2010).

Department of Health (2008b). *Report on the National Patient Choice Survey – November 2007 England* [online]. Available at: www.dh.gov.uk/en/Publicationsandstatistics/Publications/PublicationsStatistics/DH_083974 (accessed on 22 March 2010).

Department of Health (2006). *Report on the Results of the Patient Choice Survey, England – May/June 2006 and Headline Figures for July 2006* [online]. Available at: www.dh.gov.uk/en/Publicationsandstatistics/Publications/PublicationsStatistics/DH_062972 (accessed on 22 March 2010).

Department of Health (2004). *The NHS Improvement Plan: Putting people at the heart of public services*. London: Department of Health.

Department of Health (2000). *The NHS Plan: A plan for investment, a plan for reform*. Cm 4818-I. London: The Stationery Office.

Department of Health (1989). *Working for Patients: The health services: Caring for the 1990s*. Cm 555. London: HMSO.

Devlin N, Appleby J (2010). *Getting the most out of PROMs: putting health outcomes at the heart of NHS decision-making*. London: The King's Fund.

Devlin N, Maynard A, Mays N (2001). 'New Zealand's new health sector reforms: back to the future?' *British Medical Journal*, vol 322, no 7295, pp 1171–4. Available at: http://eprints.whiterose.ac.uk/56/1/maynarda2.pdf (accessed on 3 April 2010).

Dixon A, Le Grand J (2006). 'Is greater patient choice consistent with equity? The case of the English NHS'. *Journal of Health Services Research & Policy*, vol 11, no 3, pp 162–6.

Dixon A, Robertson R, Baal R (2010). 'The experience of implementing choice at point of referral: a comparison of the Netherlands and England'. *Health Economics, Policy and Law*.

Enthoven A, Kronick R (1989). 'A consumer-choice health plan for the 1990s. Universal health insurance in a system designed to promote quality and economy (1)'. *The New England Journal of Medicine*, vol 320, no 1, pp 29–37.

Enthoven AC, van de Ven WPMM (2007). 'Going Dutch: managed-competition health insurance in the Netherlands'. *The New England Journal of Medicine*, vol 357, no 24, pp 2421–3.

Escarce JJ, Kapur K (2009). *Do Patients Bypass Rural Hospitals? Determinants of Inpatient Hospital Choice in Rural California*. Dublin: UCD School of Economics University College Dublin. WP09/02. Available at: www.ucd.ie/t4cms/wp09%2002.pdf (accessed on 13 April 2010).

Fabri D, Robone S (2009). *The Geography of Hospital Admission in a National Health Service with Patient Choice: Evidence from Italy*. University of York HEDG Working Paper 08/29. Available at: www.york.ac.uk/res/herc/documents/wp/08_29.pdf (accessed on 13 April 2010).

Ferlie E, Freeman G, McDonnell J, Petsoulas C, Rundle-Smith S (2005). *NHS London Patient Choice Project: Evaluation Organisational Process Strand Final Report*. London: Royal Holloway, University of London and Imperial College London.

Fotaki M, Boyd A, Smith L, McDonald R, Roland M, Sheaff R, Edwards A, Elwyn G (2005). 'Access to healthcare patient choice and the organisation and delivery of health services: scoping review'. Manchester: National Institute for Health Research Service Delivery and Organisation programme, R&D (NIHRSDO). Available at: www.sdo.nihr.ac.uk/projdetails.php?ref=08-1410-080 (accessed on13 April 2010).

Frank R, Lamiraud K (2009). 'Choice, price competition and complexity in markets for health insurance'. *Journal of Economic Behaviour & Organization*, vol 71, no 2, pp 550–62.

Frank RG, Zeckhauser RJ (2009). 'Health Insurance Exchanges — Making the Markets Work'. *New England Journal of Medicine* (22 July, 2009).

Fung C, Lim Y-W, Mattke S, Damberg C, Shekelle PG (2008). 'Systematic review: the evidence that publishing patient care performance data improves quality of care'. *Annals of Internal Medicine*, vol 148, pp 111–23.

Gaynor M (2006). 'What do we know about competition and quality in health care markets?' CMPO (Centre for Market and Public Organisation) working paper 06/515, University of Bristol.

Gauthier B, Wane W (2008). *Bypassing Health Providers: The quest for better price and quality of health care in Chad*. The World Bank: Policy Research Working Paper Series No. 4462.

Gowrisankaran G (2008). 'Competition, information provision and hospital quality' in Sloan F, Kasper H (eds), *Incentives and Choice in Health Care*, Chapter 12. Cambridge, MA: MIT Press.

Gravelle H, Masiero G (2002). 'Quality incentives under a capitation regime: the role of patient expectations' in Lindgren B (ed), *Individual Decisions for Health*. London: Routledge.

Hansard (House of Commons Debates) (2009–10) 6 April 2010 col 1316W. Available at: www.publications.parliament.uk/pa/cm200910/cmhansrd/chan67.pdf (accessed 14 April 2010).

Hanson K, Yip W, and Hsiao W (2004). 'The impact of quality on the demand for outpatient services in Cyprus'. *Health Economics*, 13 pp 1167–80.

Harrison A, Appleby J (2009). 'English lessons: waiting times reduction'. *Journal of Health Services Research & Policy*, vol 14, no 3, pp 168–73.

Hawkes H (2009). 'The mysterious Dr Foster'. *British Medical Journal*, vol 339, p 1336.

Henderson S, Robertson R, Dixon A (2009). 'Are patients choosing?' *British Journal of Healthcare Management*, vol 15, no 2, pp 105–8. Available at: www.bjhcm.co.uk/cgi-bin/go.pl/library/contents.html?uid=2488%3Bjournal_uid=22 (accessed on 3 April 2010).

Hibbard J, Stockard J, Tusler M (2003). 'Does publicizing hospital performance stimulate quality improvement efforts?' *Health Affairs*, vol 22, no 2, pp 84–94.

Hicks, JR (1939). *Value and Capital: An inquiry into some fundamental principles of economic theory*, 2nd ed. Oxford: Clarendon.

Hirschman AO (1970). *Exit, Voice and Loyalty*. Cambridge MA: Harvard University Press.

HM Government (2009). *Building Britain's Future*. Cm 7654. London: The Stationery Office.

Hood C, Bevan G (2005). 'Governance by targets and terror: synecdoche, gaming and audit'. *Westminster Economics Forum*, Issue 15.

Hotelling HH (1929). 'Stability in competition'. *Economic Journal*, vol 39, pp 41–57.

Hurley J (2000). 'An overview of the normative economics of the health sector' in Culyer AJ, Newhouse JP (eds), *Handbook of Health Economics*, Chapter 2 pp 55–118. Oxford: Elsevier, edition 1, volume 1.

Imerman M, Eathington L, Jintanakul K, and Otto D (2006). *Preliminary Investigations of Hospital Geography and Patient Choice in Iowa*. Iowa State University: Economics Working Paper 06023. Available at: www.econ.iastate.edu/sites/default/files/publications/papers/p3854-2006-05-22.pdf (last accessed 13 April 2010).

Imison C, Naylor C (2010 forthcoming). *Referral Management: A means to manage demand and improve quality*. London: The King's Fund.

Iyengar S, Lepper M (2006). 'When choice is demotivating: can one desire too much of a good thing?' in Lichtenstein S, Slovic P (eds), *The Construction of Preference*, Chapter 16. Cambridge: Cambridge University Press.

Jacobs A (1998). 'Seeing difference: market reform in Europe'. *Journal of Health Politics, Policy and Law*, vol 23, no 1, pp 1–33.

Kahneman D (2006). 'New challenges to the rationality assumption' in Lichtenstein S, Slovic P (eds), *The Construction of Preference*, Chapter 27. Cambridge: Cambridge University Press.

Le Grand J (2009). 'Choice and competition in publicly funded health care'. *Health Economics, Policy and Law*, vol 4, pp 479–88.

Le Grand J, Bartlett W (1993). *Quasi-Markets and Social Policy*. London: Palgrave Macmillan.

Le Maistre N, Reeves R, Coulter A (2003). *Patients' Experience of CHD Choice*, Oxford: Picker Institute Europe.

Leonard K, Mliga G, Mariam D (2002). 'Bypassing Health Centres in Tanzania: Revealed Preferences for Quality'. *Journal of African Economies*. 11: 441–71.

Lim JNW, Edlin R (2009). 'Preferences of older patients and choice of treatment location in the UK: a binary choice experiment'. *Health Policy*, vol 91, no 3, pp 252–7.

Lipsky M (1983). *Street-Level Bureaucracy : Dilemmas of the individual in public services*. New York: Russell Sage.

Louviere JJ (1988). 'Analyzing decision making: metric conjoint analysis'. Sage University Paper Series on Quantitative Applications in the Social Sciences, 07–67. Beverly Hills: Sage.

Marschak J (1960). 'Binary choice constraints and random utility indicators' in Marschak J (1974), *Economic Information, Decision and Prediction: Selected essays (Volume 1)*. Dordrecht: D. Reidel.

Marshall M, Shekelle PG, Leatherman S (2000). 'The public release of performance data: what do we expect to gain? A review of the evidence'. *Journal of the American Medical Association*, vol 283, no 14, pp 1866–74.

McFadden D (1975). 'The revealed preferences of a government bureaucracy: theory'. *The Bell Journal of Economics and management science*, vol 6, no 2, pp 401–16.

Mill JS (1863). *Utilitarianism*. London: Parker, Son and Bourne.

Montefiori M (2003). 'Hotelling competition on quality in the health care market'. Discussion paper, Department of Public Finance, University of Genoa.

Morris S, Devlin N, Parkin D (2007). *Economic Analysis in Health Care*. Chichester: Wiley.

Norwood F, Bailey J, Lusk B, Henneberry S (2009). 'An empirical investigation into the excessive-choice effect'. *American Journal of Agricultural Economics*, vol 91, no 3, pp 810–25.

Pareto V (1906). *Manual of Political Economic*. English translation, New York in 1971: Augustus M. Kelley.

Propper C, Burgess S, Gossage D (2008). 'Competition and quality: evidence from the NHS internal market 1991–9'. *The Economic Journal*, vol 118, no 525, pp 138–70.

Propper C, Burgess S, Green K (2004). 'Does competition between hospitals improve the quality of care? Hospital death rates and the NHS internal market'. *Journal of Public Economics*, vol 88, nos 7–8, pp 1247–72.

Propper C, Wilson D, Burgess S (2006). 'Extending choice in English health care: the implications of the economic evidence'. *Journal of Social Policy*, vol 35, no 4, pp 537–57.

Rosen R, Florin D and Hutt R (2007). *An Anatomy of GP Referral Decisions: A qualitative study of GPs' views on their role in supporting patient choice*. London: The King's Fund.

Ryan M, McIntosh E, Dean T and Old P (2000). 'Trade-offs between location and waiting times in the provision of health care: the case of elective surgery on the Isle of Wight'. *Journal of Public Health Medicine*, vol 22, pp 202–10.

Salop SC (1979). 'Monopolistic competition with outside goods'. *Bell Journal of Economics*, vol 10, no 1, pp 141–56.

Samuelson W, Zeckhauser R (1988). 'Status quo bias in decision making'. *Journal of Risk and Uncertainty*, vol 1, no 1, pp 7–59.

Satterthwaite M (1979). 'Consumer information, equilibrium industry price and the number of sellers'. *Bell Journal of Economics*, vol 10, no 2, pp 483–502.

Schwartz B (2005). *The Paradox of Choice: Why more is less*. New York: Harper Perennial.

Schwartz B (2000). 'Self-determination: the tyranny of freedom'. *American Psychologist*, vol 55, no 1, pp 79–88.

Shekelle PG, Lim Y-W, Mattke S, Damberg C (2008). *Does Public Release of Performance Results Improve Quality of Care? A systematic review*. London: The Health Foundation.

Siciliani L, Martin S (2007). 'An empirical analysis of the impact of choice on waiting times'. *Health Economics*, vol 16, no 8, pp 763–79.

Simon H (1978). 'Rationality as process and as product of thought'. *American Economic Review*, vol 68, no 2, pp 1–16.

Stevens S (2004). 'Reform strategies for the English NHS'. *Health Affairs*, vol 23, no 3, pp 41–4.

Tay A (2003). 'Assessing competition in Hospital Care Markets: The importance of accounting for quality differentiation.' *RAND Journal of Economics*, vol 34, no 4, pp 786–814.

Taylor R, Pringle M, Coupland C (2004). *Implications of Offering 'Patient Choice' for Routine Adult Surgical Referrals*. Project final report submitted to Department of Health, March 2004, London: Dr Foster and the University of Nottingham.

Thomson S, Dixon A (2006). 'Choices in health care: the European experience'. *Journal of Health Services Research & Policy*, vol 11, no 3, pp 167–71.

Trucano M, Kaldenberg DO (2007). 'The relationship between patient perceptions of hospital practices and facility infection rates: evidence from Pennsylvania hospitals'. *Patient Safety and Quality Healthcare* [Online]. Available at: www.psqh.com/enews/0807feature.html (accessed on 26 March 2010).

Tversky A (2004). 'Elimination of aspects: a theory of choice' in Tversky A, Shafir E (eds), *Preference, Belief, and Similarity: Selected writings of Amos Tversky*. Chapter 20. Cambridge, MA: MIT Press.

Tversky A (1972). 'Elimination by aspects: a theory of choice'. *Psychological Review*, vol 79, pp 281–99.

Varkisser M, van der Geest S, Schiut F. (2010). 'Assessing hospital competition when prices don't matter to patients: the use of time elasticities'. *International Journal of Health Care Finance and Economics*, vol 10, no 1, pp 43–60.

Varkevisser M, van der Geest SA (2007). 'Why do patients bypass the nearest hospital? An empirical analysis for orthopaedic care and neurosurgery in the Netherlands'. *The European Journal of Health Economics*, vol 8, no 3, pp 287–95.

von Neumann J and Morgenstern O (1944). *Theory of Games and Economic Behavior*. New Jersey: Princeton University Press.

Wanless D (2002). *Securing Our Future Health: Taking a long-term view*. London: HM Treasury.

Zeithaml V, Bitner MJ (1996). *Services Marketing*. London: McGraw-Hill.